Uneasy Balance

PUBLISHING FOR THE WORLD
125 Years
THE JOHNS HOPKINS UNIVERSITY PRESS

Uneasy Balance

Civil-Military Relations in Peacetime
America since 1783

Thomas S. Langston

The Johns Hopkins University Press
Baltimore and London

*To the memory of Sergeant Thomas Robert Harmon
(1898–1933), a pilot in the U.S. Army Air Corps, who
gave his life in peacetime service to his country*

© 2003 The Johns Hopkins University Press
All rights reserved. Published 2003
Printed in the United States of America on acid-free paper
9 8 7 6 5 4 3 2 1

The Johns Hopkins University Press
2715 North Charles Street
Baltimore, Maryland 21218-4363
www.press.jhu.edu

Library of Congress Cataloging-in-Publication Data

Langston, Thomas S.
Uneasy balance: civil-military relations in peacetime America since
1783 / Thomas S. Langston.
  p. cm.
Includes bibliographical references and index.
  ISBN 0-8018-7421-1 (alk. paper)
  1. Civil-military relations–United States–History. I. Title.
JK330.L36 2003
322'.5'0973—dc21

                              2002156772

A catalog record for this book is available from the British Library.

Contents

Acknowledgments

I am grateful to a number of specialists in civil-military relations and security studies. Thomas Berger at Boston University and Peter Feaver at Duke University provided detailed responses to two separate early drafts of the manuscript. Aaron Friedberg at Princeton University, Andrew Bacevich at Boston University, and my former Tulane colleague, Peter Liberman, now at the City University of New York, Queen's College, commented on papers that presented aspects of my research and argument. The readers for Johns Hopkins University Press gave the author valuable criticism and advice. One reader in particular, who wishes to retain anonymity, provided exhaustive substantive and organizational suggestions that greatly improved the work.

I also wish to thank the civilian and military defense personnel in Washington, D.C., and elsewhere who consented to be interviewed for this work and those who visited my seminar on the military in American politics over several years at Tulane University. The interaction of enlisted and commissioned men and women from different branches of the armed forces with the mostly full-time civilian students in my classroom was instructive, I like to think, to all participants. I know I learned from these encounters. I am especially grateful to Major General Thomas Wilkerson, USMC (ret.); Major Oliver Spencer, USMC; Lt. Col. John Carey, USMC; Rear Admiral Tom Rivard, USN (ret.); Captain Warren Hudson, USN (ret.); and Colonel Pat Garrison, USAF (ret.) for their assistance in this seminar and for sharing with me their perspectives on civil-military relations.

The librarians and archivists at the Military History Institute at the U.S. Army War College, Carlisle Barracks, Pennsylvania, and in the manuscripts division at the Library of Congress provided professional assistance to the author on research trips to these facilities. Several students at Tulane University provided research assistance. I am especially grateful to

Eliyahu Petel and J. Clegg Ivey III, for their diligent and creative work at different stages of this project. Tulane University's Graduate Council provided two timely grants that contributed to the completion of this book.

It is a pleasure once again to be able to thank Henry Y. K. Tom, executive editor at the Johns Hopkins University Press, for his editorial acumen and his willingness to entertain a civil-military relations manuscript from a "presidency person." Finally, I express my gratitude to my family for their own indispensable contributions.

Uneasy Balance

The Civil-Military Bargain

Now that the Cold War is history, what should the United States ask of its military? This became the basic problem of American military policy when the Berlin Wall fell in 1989. When an unprecedented terrorist attack more than a decade later brought down the Twin Towers of the World Trade Center, the question had still not been answered. Even a year later, following the military defeat of the terrorist-harboring Taliban regime in Afghanistan and the president's repeated assertion that the United States was "at war," the question remained. Indeed, conflict over how best to answer the question of the U.S. military's role in the post–Cold War world has been so unending that it has begun to seem routine. This is unfortunate because prolonged conflict over military policy has divided civilian and military officials and made civil-military relations unusually tense.

Bill Clinton was the first U.S. president elected after the Cold War ended and the first nonveteran in the White House since Franklin Roosevelt. Shortly after he came to office, there were numerous signs of civil-military discord. In one often repeated story, a White House staffer snubbed Lieutenant General Barry McCaffrey on the walkway leading to the West Wing. "We don't talk to the military," was the alleged response to the general's casual greeting.[1] The president moved quickly to smooth over the situation, but it was an indication of the difficulty ahead. His effort in his second week in office to repeal the ban on gays in the military turned into a political debacle for the White House and a headache for the armed forces, burdened with a "Don't Ask, Don't Tell" compromise that left no one pleased.

By the end of the Clinton administration, the return of budget surpluses had helped to erase some of the hard feelings, but problems remained. Should women be admitted into the all-male preserves of ground combat and special forces? The British decision in 2000 to study the performance of women in combat units was met in the United States with both applause and loathing as the issue divided the military establishment from civilian policymakers animated by a desire to use the armed forces as a sort of "social laboratory."[2] President Clinton's behavior with a young female intern, which resulted in his impeachment but not his removal from office, infuriated critics within the military, who saw a double standard at work.[3]

In Clinton-era military missions overseas, there were likewise moments of success and years of frustration. Over and above the question of how well the military and its civilian commander performed in Somalia, Bosnia, Kosovo, or Haiti, the question lingered: Should the U.S. military have been sent to such places in the first place?[4] A major survey of U.S. military personnel at the close of the 1990s concluded that "conditions within the armed forces are far less favorable than they were a decade ago" and that the culture of the military was undergoing serious strain "with attending damage to future operational effectiveness." A fundamental source of difficulty, the survey found, was the pace of non-war-fighting deployments, which increased more than 300 percent from 1989 to 1999.[5] At the same time that deployments increased so dramatically, military forces were cut by roughly a third, and weapons systems were permitted to decay. Neither party in Congress made fixing these problems a priority, though Republicans gave rhetorical support to defense modernization in their Contract with America in the 1994 elections.[6]

On the surface, the civil-military controversies of the 1990s had much to do with the particularities of President Clinton as commander in chief. But military officers who pinned their hopes for a sudden improvement in relations on a Republican victory in the 2000 presidential elections witnessed little change in the first two years of the new administration. In 2001 and 2002 few if any stories circulated about disrespect from the military toward the new commander in chief, and cultural transformation of the armed forces was not on his agenda for military policy. But aside from renaming peacekeeping operations "stability operations," the new administration did nothing to alter the practice or slow the pace of such missions. The missions are draining the forces, acknowledged Joseph Collins, the civilian head of the Pentagon's Office of Stability Operations: "The water's not coming out in a great torrent, like a fire hose, but over time the amount of water that you are losing is tremendous."[7] Similarly, the president's team in the Pentagon was not empowered by the change of administrations to take on such controversial policies as "Don't Ask, Don't Tell" or the integration of women into an ever-greater array of military occupational specialties.

President Bush entered office, moreover, with an aggressive plan for military "transformation" that met with resistance within the Pentagon. Congressional defenders of obsolete military bases and strategically suspect weapons platforms joined in 2001 with leaders of the armed services who were wary of the doctrinal implications of transformation in blocking Secretary of Defense Donald Rumsfeld. In August 2001, *New York Times* columnist Maureen Dowd chastised Rumsfeld for his lack of influence, suggesting that his many years of experience as a Cold War defense specialist had not prepared him for the challenges of peacetime leadership. "Rip Van Rummy" was out of touch, wrote Dowd.[8]

The respected defense journalist Thomas E. Ricks observed in the same month that Bush's military reforms were "fighting for life." Ricks quoted retired Marine General Anthony Zinni, moreover, as commenting that even with the change in civilian leadership, "there's a strong sense of alienation between the uniformed leadership and the civilians."[9]

The government's aggressive military response after September 11, 2001, changed this situation only slightly. The secretary of defense suddenly became popular with the media and the public, and the country took renewed pride in its military and confidence in its government.[10] But neither the terrorist attack nor the rapid success of Operation Enduring Freedom, as the initial military response to the attack was named, resolved deep-seated problems of military policy. In fact, the transition in Afghanistan from limited war fighting to an open-ended commitment to preserve the peace presaged a replay in a harsh environment of by-now-familiar debates over post–Cold War military policy. And indeed, by 2003, 8,000 U.S. soldiers in Afghanistan "kept the peace" by searching for Al Qaeda members; warding off assassination attempts against the American-approved head of state, Hamid Karzai; training a new, ethnically diverse national army; building and operating coeducational schools;

assisting nongovernmental organizations in the distribution of health care and humanitarian assistance; and otherwise attempting to do what President Bush, Secretary of Defense Donald Rumsfeld, and chairman of the Joint Chiefs of Staff General Richard Myers had all agreed they did not want to do—"nation building" in Afghanistan.[11]

The "war" against terrorism did give the president leverage to propose significant new military spending across the board. The proposed increases for 2003 and beyond marked an overdue end to the "procurement holiday" of the 1990s. Ironically, though, the promise of $400 billion annual defense budgets, with $100 billion for procurement, might set back the transformation of the services by relaxing pressure on defense officials to make difficult choices about priorities.[12] The military's place in the struggle against terror, moreover, remains a considerable source of uncertainty.

The uniformed leaders of the armed forces are divided over what priority to assign to anti-terror operations overseas. In the conduct of covert missions against Al Qaeda, many military leaders are content to let the Central Intelligence Agency (CIA) take the lead. Others support the ongoing overhaul of U.S. Special Forces and join the secretary of defense in disparaging the contribution to be made by the CIA's paramilitary operatives.[13] In fighting terror at home, military officials are united in not wanting the services to take on a leadership role. They could, however, find themselves with a larger role than they would prefer because of their unique capabilities and the ever-present military temptation to volunteer.[14]

On September 17, 2002, President Bush sought to resolve some of this confusion. On that day his administration issued its first "National Security Strategy of the United States of America."[15] The president's strategic document provided a criterion for military effectiveness: success in wars against the "axis of evil" and other emerging threats, including terrorist assaults on the homeland and abroad. Most provocatively, the strategy called for the occasional use of U.S. forces to wage wars of "preemption" against enemy states such as Iraq. This dramatic turn in the nation's security strategy might presage the end of peacetime divisions and uncertainties over military policy. Then again, President George W. Bush's national security strategy might foreshadow something far less encompassing of the nation's energy and attention than a return to wartime status, something more like the first Gulf War than like either the Vietnam War or the Cold War. If so, then the Bush administration's ambitious strategic pronouncements would likely make the future direction of U.S. military policy more murky than it already is.

At the midway point of President Bush's first term, the only thing that had been made clear about the transition from the Cold War was that it was still ongoing. The president was intent on giving U.S. military forces new wartime responsibilities but was unwilling to edit the forces' lengthy list of peacetime duties. This "all of everything" approach to military policy struck some objective observers as reckless in the extreme. As John Lewis Gaddis wrote in an appraisal of Bush's strategic thinking: "There's no evidence that the Bush administration is planning the kind of military commitments the United States made in either of the two world wars, or even in Korea and Vietnam. This strategy relies on getting cheered, not shot at."[16] The same thing, it bears recalling, could have been said of the Kennedy administration's plan to liberate Cuba at the Bay of Pigs.

The Importance of Balance in Adjusting to Peace

The problems of the post–Cold War presidents and the tensions those problems reveal should not come as a surprise. Just because the United States has never witnessed a military coup does not mean that it has escaped the inherent difficulties of civilian control of the military. The professional military has to be kept under the control of its civilian commanders, but it needs sufficient autonomy to be a professional military, which requires, among other things, preparing for a return to major war.[17] The issue is one of balance. In the aftermath of war, there is an inevitable sorting-out period when a new balance, encompassing both civilian and military conceptions of the usefulness of the armed forces, has to be negotiated.

The return to peace poses problems for the militaries of all nations. These problems are exacerbated by features of American culture and history. Historically, for many Americans the "state" with its power to compel has been little more than an abstraction until the nation goes to war. The United States, a famously anti-authoritarian, liberal nation, has proven willing, in almost all of its wars, to do what was necessary to prevail. But classical liberals don't make sacrifices for the state easily. The consequence has been a rush back toward the prewar social contract, to an easier way of life, and to a restoration of economic and social liberties sometimes surrendered in war.

But the return to war is not simply the swinging of a pendulum. Wars change states and nations alike. The legacies of war in the United States include the independence and unity of the nation itself as well as the modern regulatory state. In the return to peace, it has never been easy for Americans to decide what to do with the military. To some critics of the military's way of doing things, the best solution has been to civilianize military forces, so that they pose no threat to the mores of a nation at peace. In reaction to such pressures, some military professionals have sought in peacetime to focus exclusively on preparing for future war, wanting as little to do as possible in the meantime with civilian society and its problems.

The proponents of what might be termed the "Fatal Embrace" and the "Leave Us Alone" approaches to military-society relations face off against one another today. To the military professionals who seek to maximize their autonomy, the civilizers are "agenda pushers" without regard for the armed forces' true purpose. From the other side, the military's leadership seems riddled with "extremists" in need of not merely civilianizing, but "civilizing."[18]

My purpose in this book is to demonstrate that there is a middle ground in this conflict. The inevitable conflicts of civil-military relations after war are best resolved when neither the civilianizers nor their opponents win a complete victory. The postwar period is a time for both preparing for future wars and advancing (other) civilian objectives. At the time that they have been required to perform such tasks, building roads, conducting "gunboat diplomacy" (and its modern parallel, "cruise missile diplomacy"), and policing imperial acquisitions have seemed to many military professionals unworthy distractions. By contrast, I will argue that they were contributions to the core mission of the nation at particular stages in its development. Taking on these and other civilian-like chores has required a short-term sacrifice of readiness for war, but in return, a skeptical civilian public has permitted military leaders to make necessary plans and reforms for the unavoidable return to combat. In a more perfect world, this compromise would deserve to be critiqued as an impossible "squaring of the circle." But in the practice of U.S. military-society relations, it appears a good enough arrangement, a civil-military "bargain" that satisfies the interests of all parties. It is my contention that the United States was still in a postwar period at the midpoint of the first term of President George W. Bush and that this episode in its public life can profitably be compared with previous periods of transition after wars.

Looking to the Past

What problems of military policy did the nation face after its previous wars, and how were these problems resolved? Tables 1 and 2 summarize important features of nine U.S. postwar transitions. In the nineteenth century, a tangle of ideological and material issues brought civilian and military spheres into contention (see Table 1). In the readjustments of that century, the drive for postwar economy was a constant and provided leverage to those who wished for a rapid and thorough demobilization. The nineteenth century also featured lengthy conflicts along ideological dimensions, as the military fought to professionalize amid lingering civilian suspicion of standing armies.

Another factor to observe is the duration of postwar readjustments. Setting a precise chronological border around a period in history is difficult, but the effort should be made. The post–Revolutionary War period can be said to have come to an end when President Thomas Jefferson accepted the necessity of a professional military and founded the United States Military Academy at West Point. The War of 1812 ended with a significant victory at New Orleans but otherwise left the nation with a new appreciation for the necessity of military preparations. The postwar realignment was a tug-of-war between the desire to improve military readiness for a return to war and an equal desire to make immediate use of the army in settling the West. This realignment came to an end with Congress's actions in 1833 to permit the army to make some much-needed reforms while maintaining its role in peacetime operations. The post–Mexican War period, touched on only briefly in this book, was brought to a shattering end with the onset of the Civil War, while the realignment after the Civil War terminated in 1882. The average duration of nineteenth-century postwar transitions was just under fifteen years.

In terms of their resolutions and consequences, the postwar readjustments of the nineteenth century offer a wide range of precedents. In the most successful, after the American Revolution and after the War of 1812, the military emerged from the transition to peace not only with sufficient strength but also with enhanced capabilities to aid the nation in peace. Civilian society prospered after these wars thanks, in part, to the contributions that peacetime services made to civilian projects. The period after the Civil War offers the worst precedent. Not only were the armed forces

Table 1. *Postwar Realignments, 1783–1882*

Era	Issues	Duration	Resolution	Consequences
Post–Revolutionary War	Fear of military vs. need for security	1783–1802	Small Professional army proves its usefulness at home, is supported by political consensus	Promotion of westward settlement and military competence
Post–War of 1812	Rationalization of the military establishment	1815–1833	Professional military is built up, broadens usefulness at home while preparing for future war	Promotion of national sentiment, democratic rule, and westward expansion; promotion of military competence
Post–Mexican War	Military needed out West; military preparedness feared in context of North/South divide	1848–1860	Professional military stays busy on frontier	Promotion of expansion; competence threatened because military preparedness is politicized
Post–Civil War	Military Reconstruction; how much service is too much?	1865–1882	Reconstruction fails for lack of public will; professionals turn inwards	Military failure in peace missions in the South; military reforms come late; military becomes entangled in partisan conflict

reduced to a bare sufficiency, but half-hearted efforts to redirect the services toward new purposes in peacetime embroiled the military in partisan politics before being abandoned for want of public support.

In the case of twentieth-century wars, there is again a record of mixed conflict over material and ideological issues, and sometimes lengthy periods of readjustment (see Table 2). Because of the rise of professionalism in the military (and other institutions) in the past century, the debates of the 1900s took place within a narrowed range of opinion. Isolationists succeeded in pushing the army and navy to the sidelines of national affairs after World War I, for instance, but no one seriously imagined any longer that we could simply do without a professional military force. After World War II, moreover, large standing forces were accepted in peacetime for the first time in the nation's history.

In terms of duration, the realignments of the past century ranged from five years after World War II, abruptly ended by the beginning of another

Table 2. Postwar Civil-Military Realignments, 1898-Present

Era	Issues	Duration	Resolution	Consequences
Post–War of 1898	Military reform vs. bureaucratic interests of traditional officer corps, imperial service for the military	1898–1913	Military professionalism increases; military supports US empire abroad	Military usefulness extended as nation develops new external interests
Post–WWI	Military preparations and "citizenship" initiatives vs. the "return to normalcy"	1919–1940	Rejection of war retards war preparedness	Military penetrates public consciousness, studies the requirements of future war, but lacks resources for war preparedness

(*continued*)

Table 2.   (continued)

Era	Issues	Duration	Resolution	Consequences
Post–WWII	Duties of a world power vs. desire for a return to peaceable prosperity	1945–1950	Tensions over military policy resolved only in rush back to war	Beginning of postwar international order and U.S. world leadership, but a near disaster in Korea
Post–Vietnam War	Can the military be used? Can it fight? Who decides when and where?	1973–1984	All Volunteer, Force at home; Vietnam Syndrome abroad; military elite develops an elitist military doctrine	U.S. military weakness challenged around the world; military professionals take charge of military policy
Post–Cold War	Unrivalled military power, for what purpose?	1989-Present	In process	?

war, to twenty-one years after World War I, which came to an end with the passage of the nation's first peacetime draft in 1940. The period of transition following the Spanish-American War reached an equilibrium in 1913 when the Democratic president, Woodrow Wilson, accepted much of the progress in military reform made by his Republican predecessors. The post-Vietnam realignment was a roller coaster of military implosion and renaissance, coming to a troubling halt with the articulation of the Weinberger-Powell Doctrine in 1984. The average duration of these realignments was about thirteen years.

In terms of their results, the realignments of the 1900s ranged from effective to nearly disastrous. The War of 1898, like the War of 1812, was entered into rashly. The military results were positive, but as in the earlier war, combat revealed such stupendous difficulties that military reform in favor of enhanced professionalism was given a boost after the war. Moreover, after the War of 1898, voters gave their resounding approval in the elections of 1900 to the imperial uses to which the army and navy were put. Whatever one makes of the birth of the United States as an imperial power, the military was critical to the effort. After World War I, military policy did not permit the forces to achieve adequate strength, but educational and organizational advances were nevertheless made. In the 1930s the under-strength army was put to work battling the Great Depression in the Civilian Conservation Corps (CCC) and other New Deal agencies.

Among the more recent periods, the post–World War II readjustment overlapped with the beginning of the Cold War, but for the five years from victory in Japan to war in Korea, the direction and scope of U.S. military efforts were up for grabs. Moving to the 1970s and 80s, the debacle in Vietnam was part of the larger Cold War but had an independent effect on the military. It left the professional military in a state of crisis and civilian society deeply divided over the relevance of force to the pursuit of national interests abroad. The consequence was a challenging new conception of the military's "right" not to be sent into possible defeat as it was in Vietnam.

As for the issues of military policy that divide Americans today, it is possible, but far from certain, that September 11, 2001, will be remembered as the end of the post–Cold War period. President George W. Bush, in his public statements of late 2001, suggested that the heightened fight against terror that began on that day would be like the Cold War—a long, multi-layered struggle in which the public and Congress looked naturally to the president for leadership. Just as "the struggles against Nazism and communism helped to define the 20th century," the president remarked on one occasion, so "the war on terror will be the defining conflict of the 21st century."[19] In 2001 and 2002, Secretary of Defense Donald Rumsfeld joined the president in underlining what he saw as the historic nature of the terrorist assault. In a typical statement, the secretary asserted to the press that "the cold, hard fact is that the United States lives in a very different security environment today in this 21st century than we did prior to September 11th."[20]

It is understandable that the president and his secretary of defense were quick to make these arguments, but in truth the fight against terrorism might come to bear a closer resemblance to the "war" on drugs than to the Cold War. President Bush suggested as much in remarks to homeland security workers in July of 2002: "These are shadowy killers," he said, "and we're treating them just as they are—as international crooks, international criminals."[21] In a "war" against crooks and criminals, the military is often useful and sometimes necessary. But the anti-drug war, and perhaps the anti-terror war as well, are essentially police operations. Neither, significantly, targets an enemy, but something different: an illegal commodity in one case; a weapon of unconventional warfare in the other. If Korea was a war masquerading as a police action, the fight against terror is quite possibly a police action in the rhetorical clothing of war.

To put the ongoing debate on military policy in the context of earlier episodes requires that we examine what the United States has done right and what it has gotten wrong in these previous postwar periods. That is, we want to know what a balance of reform and service looks like in practice and what specific policies have made for a good postwar realignment. We also want to know what factors favor the achievement of a balanced realignment.

The Plan of This Book

A mixture of empirical and evaluative concerns dictates the plan of this book. In Chapter 1, I develop my perspective on the postwar episode as an important moment in civil-military relations. I review various theoretical perspectives on the transition to peace and the postwar era, and set forth a criterion for the evaluation of the success of postwar realignment. This criterion is an elaboration of the civil-military "bargain" introduced above.

In successful realignments, military policy is balanced between reform and service. Reform in areas such as education, training, and promotion orients the services toward the requirements of future war. The military thereby retains professional identity and expertise. In the most successful realignments, however, profession-enhancing reform is complemented by more immediate service to civilians. In promoting the national interest through missions other than war, the armed forces help to maintain public support.

This, I will argue in Chapter 2, was the pattern of events after the Revolutionary War, the War of 1812, and the Spanish-American War. The less-successful realignments, ranging from fair (post–World Wars I and II, post–Mexican War) to worse (post–Civil War and post–Vietnam War), are considered in Chapters 3 and 4. The two worst-case scenarios show what happens when balance is neglected. After the Civil War, the military was reoriented toward civilian tasks without adequate support and without compensatory autonomy to prepare for war. All service and no reform make for an unbalanced, unsatisfactory adjustment to peace. After the Vietnam War, the military met the challenges of an All Volunteer Force, but in doing so, developed an elitist doctrine that motivated senior officers to resist legitimate civilian desires to orient the forces toward non-war-fighting missions after the end of the Cold War. All reform and no service also makes for an unbalanced, unsatisfactory adjustment to peace.

In Chapter 5, I examine the decade of the 1990s as a case study in the adjustment to peace. As in the prior cases, its beginning and possible end points are identified, along with key events in military policy. Military reform is assessed by reference to its influence on military professionalism. Finally, the orientation of the military to peacetime civilian purposes is considered. During this period, I will argue, U.S. military policy got off to a shaky start at readjustment.

The analysis of the previous chapters proves helpful here, not only in highlighting the importance of both reform and service but also in revealing the conditions (the "independent variables") that have historically made it possible for balance to be achieved between them. Those conditions, civil-military cooperation and political consensus in support of a new military policy, were lacking at the opening of the twenty-first century.

In Chapter 6, I bring the narrative of the present adjustment to peace up to date by highlighting key events in the first two years of the George W. Bush administration. Next, I examine the barriers to a more successful resolution of present civil-military tensions. One of the key problems to address is the prevalence of utopian ideas about war's demise. I argue in this chapter that, even though future wars involving the United States may be different from those of the past, we must permit the military to plan for a variety of war scenarios, including prolonged war against conventionally armed forces, as in Vietnam. At the same time that we should insist that civilian planners take war seriously, however, we should also insist that military professionals take such nonwar missions as they may be assigned seriously. Military inflexibility has been as much a barrier to a successful realignment as civilian utopianism.

In the final chapter, Chapter 7, I set forth a historically informed perspective on the resolution of current issues in civil-military relations. This resolution will require balance and restraint in the more civilian-minded tasks assigned to the services. It will also, I think, require a little finesse—separating in organization and personnel some of the most civilizing tasks that the armed services have been called on to perform since the 1990s.

CHAPTER ONE

Postwar Realignment and the Perils of Peace

The period after a war is fraught with tension for military policy and danger for the military. This is the theme of what defense strategist Eliot Cohen has described as the "doctrine of the 'Cycle.'" The Cycle, "a stylized view of American military history," Cohen observes, has become the common wisdom of "politicians and pundits, as well as historians and soldiers."[1] According to proponents of the Cycle, Americans in peacetime persuade themselves of their immunity to international violence, discover in time that they are not immune after all, belatedly rush to arms at the last minute, win (typically) in the field through "enormous and unnecessary sacrifice of life and treasure," and immediately thereafter dissolve the armed forces in a headlong rush.[2]

The Ideological Foundations of Civil-Military Tensions after War

The Cycle may be interpreted as a popularization of classic works in American military history and social science, including those by the late-nineteenth-century army reformer Emory Upton and the contemporary social scientist Samuel P. Huntington. Huntington argued in 1957 in *The Soldier and the State* that in the United States there is a constant ideological tension between an inherently conservative military profession and a decidedly liberal political culture.[3] During war, a liberal civilian society tolerates the buildup of military power. After war, there is a predictable rush to restore the nation to its liberal roots. As Huntington notes, the United States was founded, after all, in a revolutionary war that targeted a strong state as its enemy and was sparked by taxes imposed by that state as a consequence of a prior war. Consequently, it is no surprise that in the United States, the onset of peace is routinely accompanied by a campaign for achieving new economies, relaxing wartime taxes, and overturning wartime policies that impinge on individual freedom.

To relieve the perceived threat that the military poses to civilian society and values, the military may be "extirpated," Huntington writes. But since extirpation has always been an "ideal" and has thus never been fully achieved, the military must also expect after war to face pressures of "transmutation." The civilian proponents of transmutation seek to make the military conform more closely to civilian values, to become more democratic in organization and tone. Transmutation may also involve pressure placed on the military to perform civilian-like tasks. If they cannot be disbanded, that is, the forces might at least be made "useful."

Recent analyses of different aspects of American military policy suggest that the ideological foundations of tension in postwar American civil-military relations have not been erased. Fareed Zakaria's work on U.S. national security over time demonstrates that even after the United States assumed an imperial role in world affairs, national leaders remained skeptical of the utility of military forces and wary of the military's alleged threat to civilian values.[4]

Before the 1880s, Zakaria demonstrates, presidents and senators routinely articulated the antagonism of liberal society toward the military. This antagonism was so strong that even when threats to the state from abroad existed, national leaders often chose to ignore them rather than to acknowledge the nation's dependence upon its military. During this time, moreover, opportunities to use military power to advance the interests of the nation outside of major war were routinely passed over. In the 1880s and 1890s, state capacity was matched with a new sense of state ambition, and the utility of the military was seized upon by a succession of presidents and congresses. But the imperial turn in U.S. history did not change civil-military relations once and for all. If the Spanish-American War of 1898 demonstrated the meshing of state capacity and state will, the resurgence of isolationism after World War I showed that the United States could still turn its back on the military, even in the face of mounting external threats.

Aaron Friedberg's analysis of Cold War state policy suggests that even during the Cold War the basic antagonism between a liberal civilian society and a conservative military institution persisted.[5] The Cold War was in many ways a grand departure from tradition. For the first time in U.S. history, no serious political leader campaigned against a standing army in peacetime. The difference that the Cold War made is most clearly seen in the acceptance of a decades-long draft. As Friedberg notes, generations of Americans from 1940 through the 1960s gave voice to the theory that all able-bodied American males have a duty to participate in military service.

In practice, however, "the exercise of compulsion has been avoided whenever possible, and reliance has been placed instead on voluntarism."[6] Thus, the United States relied for manpower during the Cold War on what was in fact only a moderately coercive form of draft (Selective Service) and abolished even that before the Soviet threat imploded. Friedberg identifies a similar pattern of reluctant mobilization across a number of fields of state endeavor, including government spending, industrial planning, the development of new technologies for war, and the procurement of weapons. Even in the Cold War, then, military strength was constrained by a national consensus on an anti-statist ideology and by the fragmented constitutional system that is that ideology's concrete expression.

Finally, in the 1990s a "third wave" of studies of civil-military relations emerged that underscored the continuing and perhaps widening "gap" between civilian and military America.[7] In the analysis of Peter Feaver and Richard Kohn, the work of Huntington that we have just reviewed represented the beginnings of the "first wave" of research on the civilian and military divide. In the first wave, the political scientist, Huntington, and the sociologist, Morris Janowitz, engaged in a classic debate.

Huntington argued that, given the very real threat to the nation posed by its enemies in the Cold War, it would be best if the "constant" of ideological tension were resolved by an alteration in *civilian* culture. Janowitz agreed with some portions of Huntington's analysis, but disagreed with the implications of ideological tension and the most appropriate response to that tension. In his 1960 book *The Professional Soldier*, Janowitz argued that the chasm that once separated a conservative and aloof military establishment from civilian Americans was narrowing as the military adjusted to the professional dictates of the modern defense apparatus.[8] Civilian values, meanwhile, were themselves in transition in the early Cold War as a result of the diffusion throughout society of bureaucratic organization and technological skill requirements.

Distinctive features of the Cold War were also responsible for a narrowing of the gap. Weapons of mass destruction, Janowitz noted, were "socializing danger to the point of equalizing the risks of warfare between soldier and civilian" (32). The increased size of the military in the United States, moreover, yielded a "constant flow of civilians into and out of the ranks of the military," and this flow exerted "a powerful influence against military traditionalism and authoritarian forms" (32). At the same time as these congeries of forces worked to close the gap, Janowitz observed, the military was nevertheless compelled by its need to engage in "dangerous and irksome tasks" to maintain an ideal of "heroic leadership" (33, 34).

Janowitz believed that the dilemmas created by a constant, if closing, gap between civilian and military values could best be overcome, not by a conservative transformation of civilian values, but by "self-imposed professional standards and meaningful integration [of the military] with civilian values" (420). As Feaver and Kohn observe, "many who agreed with Janowitz's analysis also argued that the civilian government would be unlikely or unable to trust the advice and reporting of a military whose value system" remained stubbornly different from the civilian mainstream.

In the second wave of scholarship, analysts turned their attention to the implications for civil-military relations of the termination of the draft and the American defeat in Vietnam.

The end of the Cold War brought on the third wave, and a return to the Huntington/Janowitz debate.

The neo-Janowitzians see a military leadership that has rejected or ignored Janowitz's fusionist argument. They describe a post–Cold War military that is partisan, hostile to popular culture, and defiant of civilian leadership. As a consequence, it is reportedly in danger of losing the respect and support of its civilian masters.

The neo-Huntingtonians agree on the data underlying some of these points but view them from a different perspective. They agree, for example, that military officers are partisan in voting, and they observe, moreover, that resentment against liberal elites is widespread within the services. It is the civilian elite, not the military, from this perspective, that is out of step with mainstream American values. To preserve its institutional integrity, the military might need to become even less deferential to civilian elites in military policymaking.

The third wave of scholarship on civil-military relations demonstrates, then, that the ideological tension of civil-military relations in the United

States is still present and may in fact have deepened with the onset of a new postwar era. The conclusion Feaver and Kohn drew from an intensive and collective study of the gap in the late 1990s supports this. "At present," they reported, "there are problems [posed by the gap] that, if left unaddressed, will undermine civil-military cooperation and hamper military effectiveness" (11).

The Structural Foundations of Civil-Military Tension after War

Almost all scholars of civil-military relations are attentive to the influence of the threat environment on their subject. Few, however, have addressed the issue explicitly and at length as Michael Desch does in *Civilian Control of the Military*. In that 1999 work, Desch hypothesizes that two independent variables determine the level of civil-military conflict in a nation at any given time: the level of external threat, and the level of internal threat.

A state facing high external threat and low internal threat should have the strongest civilian control of the military. This is because a challenging external threat is likely to bring to power civilian leaders experienced in, and knowledgeable about, military affairs. It will also tend to unify potential and actual military factions, orienting them outward. An externally oriented military will have less inclination to participate in domestic politics. Civilians in such a setting are more likely, finally, to provide the professionals in the armed forces the autonomy they require to prepare for and fight the wars of the state. In contrast, a state facing low external but high internal threats should experience the lowest level of civilian control. Direct military intervention in domestic politics and factionalism among civilian elites are likely in such a case to frustrate efforts at civilian control.

In the other two threat configurations, Desch's model is less determinate. When a state faces both serious internal and external threats, the model cannot say whether there will be good civilian control because the external threat has oriented the military outward, or bad (meaning weak) civilian control because internal threats have unified the armed forces toward action at home. When both threats are low, the model cannot say whether there will be good civilian control because the military will be divided (and thus easier to control), or bad civilian control because, without threats from abroad, the military's orientation may be uncertain, and civilian leadership may lack knowledge, expertise, and interest in military affairs. In this last setting, tension within the military and between military and civilian institutions may emerge. As a consequence, civilian policymakers may invade the autonomy of the armed forces and seek to make it conform to civilian ideas and values.[9] Table 3 shows the preponderance of U.S. postwar moments in the indeterminate zone of low external and low internal threats.

Because we have won almost all our wars and because almost all of them have been fought outside our borders, there has been considerable similarity in the structural context of our postwar realignments. The importance of Desch's model to the work of this book is that his structural theory suggests that the United States has entered into peacetime in a structural environment that invites civil-military conflict but that also leaves open the possibility of significant variation in how amicably that conflict is resolved. In the indeterminate setting of low threats, both external and internal, tension between civilians and military professionals is virtually guaranteed, even if the "winner" and "loser" in civil-military disputes is not.

Differentiating Among Postwar Eras in the United States

For reasons of both national ideology and the structural context of postwar periods, then, postwar episodes in the United States stand out as

Table 3.   The Structural Environment of Postwar Civil-Military Relations Applying Michael Desch's Model

	External Threats	
	High	Low
Internal Threats		
High	**Indeterminate:** Post–Revolutionary War ↓	**Worst:** Post–Civil War ↓
Low	**Best:** Post–Vietnam War	**Indeterminate:** Post–War of 1812 Post–Mexican War, to 1852 Post–Spanish-American War ←— Post–World War I ←——————— Post–World War II Post–Cold War

Note: Arrows indicate movement over time.

periods deserving sustained analysis. Studying such periods can provide insight into the ideological and structural tensions of civil-military relations and how these tensions have been made manifest over the course of American history. This can be thought of as a contribution to the fuller description of factors identified by the theories of others as being important in civil-military relations. The effort in this book to *compare* postwar periods is premised on the hypothesis that not all such periods have been alike in the ways in which inevitable tensions have or have not been resolved. While existing theories of civil-military relations point to constancy among postwar periods, this study attempts to identify differences in outcomes.

Certainly, all postwar transitions have been conflictual, but not all have been equally bad for either the military profession or the nation. Even Emory Upton thought so. From Upton's perspective, the American postwar pattern was irrational and harmful to the nation's defense, but sometimes sound minds prevailed, as after the War of 1812. After that war, as Upton detailed in *The Military Policy of the United States*, Congress and the executive undertook substantial improvements in military organization.

How can this be, if military leaders and civilian elites are by nature antagonistic in the United States, and especially so after war? In much of the literature of civil-military conflict, the relationship between the two "sides" is considered to be a zero-sum game. Whatever one side wins, the other loses. In Desch's work, this is particularly the case, as he defines "good" civil-military relations as the victory of civilian leaders when they come into conflict with military officers over matters of military policy. In Huntington's classic work, a similar assumption is at work. "Objective" control of the military is, for Huntington, the ideal and involves civilian elites' granting to the military the autonomy to pursue its professional interests and prepare for a return to war. "Subjective" control, conceptually related to transmutation, is bad and involves the invasion of military autonomy by civilian elites. It is my contention that civil-military relations during postwar periods can, in fact, be "positive-sum," wherein both sides gain, and that this state of affairs is superior to either a military or civilian "victory."

The choices for the military are not as stark as Huntington portrayed them. "Conform or die" was how Huntington expressed the civilian message to professionals at arms.[10] In truth, a trade-off between "extirpation" and "transmutation" may exist after war. That this is so is suggested, first, by the simple fact that after major wars there has typically been a ratcheting upward of the peacetime military (see Table 4 and Figure 1). At the same time, many postwar episodes, such as those after the Revolutionary War and the war in Vietnam, have been characterized by at least partial success in civilian assaults on the strictness of military culture. Well-known facts about the historical record suggest, then, the plausibility of a positive-sum outcome to civil-military tensions. By permitting partial change in the direction of civilian values, the military may dampen the pressures of extirpation after war.

Another reason to hypothesize a positive-sum solution to civil-military conflict is that the military is not monolithic. Because of this, it is at least logically possible that in response to civilian pressures from the outside and professional pressures from within, the military leadership might in essence sacrifice a portion of its institution to the civilians in order to preserve control over other elements of the armed forces. To appropriate the terminology of the military sociologist Charles Moskos, organizational specialization can preserve pockets of *institutional* professionalism even while other parts of the armed forces are allowed to conform more closely to the *occupational* expectations and attitudes that permeate the civilian workforce.[11] The pluralism of military organizations, then, likewise suggests a trade-off between "objective" and "subjective" control, and between the outcomes of extirpation and transmutation.

Finally, we have a detailed account of just such a balance being struck in one highly specialized yet important area of military policy. Peter Feaver, in his analysis of Cold War control of nuclear weapons, demonstrates that in the instance of the civilian control of nuclear weapons, Huntingtonian theory offers an overly stark account of policy options.[12] In reality, Feaver argues, civilian control was neither objective nor subjective, but "assertive." Civilians were involved in military affairs, but military involvement in civilian affairs was low. Under this condition of civil-military relations, there can nonetheless be considerable conflict between civilian and military officials as they continually renegotiate their division of labor.[13]

Given the theoretical and empirical plausibility of a balancing of civilian and military values and priorities, why should achieving such a balance yield a superior outcome in (and from) civil-military relations? To begin with, a balance addresses the central problematic of civil-military relations in a democracy: the military must be strong enough to fight and

Table 4.	Govt Spending on Security after Three Major Wars		
Year	Security Spending (in billions of dollars)	USG Spending (%)	Active Duty Personnel
1860	0.028	44	27,958
1861	0.035	52	217,112
1862	0.437	92	673,124
1863	0.663	93	960,061
1864	0.777	90	1,031,724
1865	1.154	89	1,062,848
1866	0.328	63	76,749
1867	0.126	35	74,786
1868	0.149	40	66,412
1869	0.099	31	51,632
1870	0.079	25	50,348
1915	0.302	40	174,112
1916	0.311	44	179,376
1917	1.493	76	643,833
1918	11.858	94	2,897,167
1919	17.048	92	1,172,602
1920	4.432	70	342,303
1921	2.664	52	386,542
1922	0.939	28	270,207
1923	0.694	22	247,011
1924	0.662	23	231,189
1925	0.606	21	251,756
1940	1.556	16	458,365
1941	6.208	44	1,801,101
1942	25.811	75	3,858,791
1943	66.532	84	9,044,745
1944	80.516	86	11,451,719
1945	84.897	89	12,123,455
1946	47.470	77	3,030,088
1947	17.611	48	1,582,999
1948	17.666	48	1,445,910
1949	19.218	47	1,315,360
1950	17.894	41	1,460,261

Source: Historical Statistics of the United States, 1789–1970, Series Y 457–71. 472–87, and 904–16.

Note: For the years 1860–1925, "security spending" represents total outlays for the Departments of the Army and the Navy; for the years from 1940 on, it comprises national defense outlays in addition to outlays for international affairs and finance. "USG spending" is the amount of security spending as a percentage of U.S. federal expenditures. "Active duty personnel" figures are for army, navy, marines, and, from 1948 to 1950, air force.

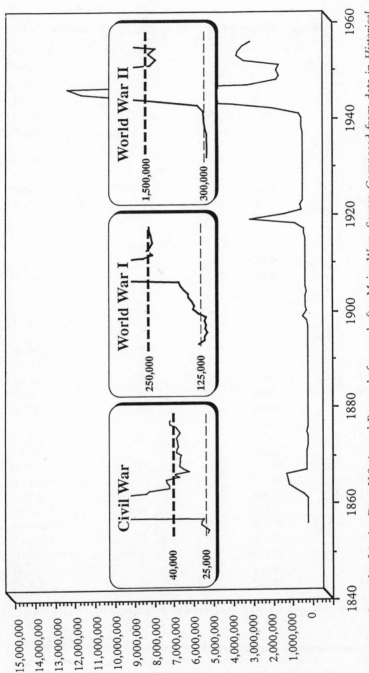

Figure 1.1 Strength of Active-Duty U.S. Armed Forces, before and after Major Wars. *Source:* Composed from data in *Historical Statistics of the United States, 1789–1970*; Series 904–916.

win the nation's wars but must not be so strong as to subvert the democratic values of the nation it defends.[14]

A balance permits the military to maintain a professional orientation toward fighting future wars but demands in return a partial sacrifice of the military's autonomy from civilian society and civilian "missions." This is not merely a compromise where each side gets a bit of what they desire. By sacrificing a measure of autonomy, the professional military may gain in return a greater measure of civilian support and respect. Likewise, while some civilian leaders in peacetime might discount almost entirely the possibility of the return of major war and thus support the military only insofar as it can be made useful in operations other than war, the civilian population is protected nonetheless—or at least it is more protected than it might otherwise be, because the professional military is permitted to prepare for war, if only "on the side."

A balancing of the interests of civilian and military leaders after war might even lead to better military preparations for future war. At the least, it should be observed that the *quality* of military policies has not always been diminished by departure from objective control; and in fact, objective control can lead to rigid and inflexible policies, even if they are the policies preferred by autonomous military leaders. The familiar story of the U.S. Army's reluctance to give up its horse cavalry, even in the face of the development of mechanized infantry, can be read as a cautionary tale for those who would assume the military's leadership always knows what is in the best interest of their profession.[15] Similarly, it is worth noting that the person who exerted perhaps the most positive influence on military professionalism in the twentieth century was a lifelong civilian, Secretary of War Elihu Root. In achieving his reforms, moreover, he was opposed by the famous army stalwart, General Nelson Miles.

In using a positive sum balance as the dependent variable, this study necessarily relies on historical analysis and judgment. The interests of the military and of civilian elites in different eras cannot be adequately identified except through historical analysis. They cannot be described except through historical narrative. Nor can different outcomes along such measures as postwar budgeting and force size be analyzed except in relation to sometimes subtle differences in the threat environment faced by the nation after its various wars. Furthermore, making the concept of balance operational involves making judgments about civilian as well as military priorities at particular times in the nation's history. If it is right and proper for the military to advance the non-war-fighting interests of the nation in peacetime, we must know what those interests are before we can assess whether the military is effective in their promotion. We must also be able to distinguish core national interests from peripheral interests of civilian pressure groups.

The perspective adopted in this book is that the enduring themes of American civilian interest in peacetime have been *national integrity* and *unity*. Because of the trajectory of America's social and economic development, "integrity" has been linked historically to expansion. Expansion, a central theme in American history, has occurred not only in geography but in democracy as well. In both realms, the military has made important contributions in peacetime. In fact, maintaining and building upon expansions in these domains has been a principal mission of the U.S. armed forces after war.

After the Revolutionary War and throughout the ensuing century, the physical expansion of the nation was achieved through diplomacy and warfare. Either way, the armed forces were called upon in peacetime to explore, negotiate, build roads and other infrastructure, and provide civilian protection—and sometimes government itself—while settlement took place. The army had the crucial role, but the navy was also assigned a task in expanding the domain of American trade, often through such civilian tasks as the negotiation of treaties.

In the twentieth century, the prevailing sentiment in the nation promoted expanding its wealth and influence. Again, the military contributed in peacetime as well as wartime, and accepted a measure of transmutation in the bargain. This occurred, as we shall see, in the early years of American imperialism, when the military applied its traditional expertise in frontier work to the nation's new colonial possessions. In the Cold War, military preparation became an open-ended commitment, and the difference between peace and war lost its former clarity. In this setting, the armed forces were less clearly a benefit rather than a cost to civilian America's non-war-related interests. Even so, in numerous ways, from defending trading partners to spurring the development of new technologies, the military was called upon from the 1950s through the 1980s not only to contain communism but to aid the nation in its historic "pursuit of happiness."

A similar story is told in this book of the military's contribution to the democratic expansion of the nation. In the Revolutionary War, approximately five thousand African Americans served in integrated units in the Continental forces. (Approximately one thousand fought for the British, who were first to offer freedom to blacks in exchange for military service in this war.) In the peacetime environment of the 1820s, the secretary of war was pressured by southern members of Congress to exclude blacks from enlistment in the army. The sheer need for troops during the Civil War, coupled with political considerations, forced a change in policy, and black troops made up nearly ten percent of the Union army and one-fourth of its navy.[16] Even larger proportions of the army were made up of foreign-born Americans, many of whom took a shortcut to citizenship through war participation. More recently, the success of modern civil rights owed a great deal to the Cold War, and though the fact often goes overlooked, civil rights in the late twentieth century achieved some of its greatest success within the U.S. Army.

Applying the Criterion of Balance

The realignments in the United States after war can be categorized as shown in Table 5.

From the perspective applied in this table, it is not so much who, as *what* wins that matters. What sort of policy outcomes are achieved?

In the worst realignments, there was political turmoil in which military factions took part. Reconstruction was not fated to fail, but it lacked a political consensus in its support. As a consequence, the program was eventually abandoned. By that time, however, the military, despite the efforts of many of its leaders to avoid Reconstruction duty, was despised by roughly half the civilian population. Service to the nation—redeeming the sacrifices of the war through the peacetime use of the forces in the South—fell short of its goals and was not balanced during the early postwar period by comparable attention to the need for reform. Army and navy leaders eventually achieved considerable progress in reform later in the century, but it was a decimated, if educated, military that next returned to war in 1898.

In the aftermath of the Vietnam debacle, the professional military went through a period of collapsing morale and, at first, reluctant reform. The chief reform of the era, the ending of the draft, was forced upon the services by civilian authorities. Once the professionals regained their footing,

Table 5.   *Outcomes of U.S. Civil-Military Realignments after War*

Null Set	Post–Vietnam Post–Civil War	Post–WWI Post–WWII Post–War with Mexico	Post–War of 1812 Post–Revolutionary War Post–Spanish-American War	Null Set
Disastrous: Military Occupation (self-occupation, in a coup, or occupation by an adversary); civil-military relations are uncontested because the civilian sphere has been over-run.	**Poor:** The military is oriented toward civilian tasks without compensatory autonomy; or the military turns inward and rejects legitimate civilian desires to use the military in peacetime operations.	**Fair:** The professional military yields to civilian pressures for service but sees its capacity for war eroded. Inexpensive reforms, especially in military education, may be achieved.	**Good:** The civil-military bargain is struck: the professional military helps the nation achieve core interests, while maintaining the potential for a return to war.	**Perfect:** The end of war. Civil-military relations are serene because the military is no longer needed.

they exerted considerable effort to reform. Unfortunately, the essence of the new professionalism that began to emerge in the late 1970s was embodied in the "never again" school of thought on the Vietnam War. Never again would the professionals let civilian authorities push the military into a war they might not win or that might never end. Never again would the president be able to send a large number of troops into combat without mobilizing the people. Eventually, these attitudes would lead to the political involvement of military professionals in post–Cold War conflicts over the use of the military for missions that reminded some too much of Vietnam. In this instance, reform was not balanced by a due consideration of the military's duty to advance the interests of the nation by providing service in non-war-fighting missions that civilian authorities wished to pursue.

In the aftermath of the War of Independence, the War of 1812, and the Spanish-American War, a productive balance of service and reform was achieved, and the false choice of either one or the other rejected. In each instance, reforms increased the professionalism of the forces, while the military simultaneously helped to expand the nation and pursue its interests. Civilian and military leaders working together earned the backing of a political majority in favor of competent peacetime forces.

After the Revolutionary War, the Washington administration overcame considerable ideological and constitutional obstacles to create an army capable of defeating hostile Native American forces in the Ohio Valley and repressing internal dissent in western Pennsylvania. This practical force was not a match for the British in the return to war in 1812, but that is an unreasonably high standard to apply to this earliest American military. What it accomplished in service to settlers and the government was complemented by a considerable improvement in its professional standing. Simply winning congressional support for a standing peacetime army was a significant reform. After the War of 1812, as after the Spanish-American War, the military was set to work expanding the borders of national control, while at the same time its leaders looked inward and improved the profession of arms.

In the aftermath of the world wars, and the War with Mexico, a mixed record was achieved. In each instance, political consensus on the necessity of preserving military strength was lacking and the issue of contemporary service was muddied by partisan conflict that military professionals could not escape.

As a final note, what is missing from Table 5 is as significant as what is depicted: there are no instances of either a wholly satisfactory or a wholly disastrous postwar realignment in the United States. In analyzing the history of American civil-military relations, there is no escape from nuance. Objective and subjective means of control have been employed simultaneously, and inward-looking reform has sometimes been accompanied by outward-looking service. At times, in fact, it has been the civilians who have led the military to undertake necessary reforms. Likewise, it has been members of the military elite themselves who have sometimes taken the most keen interest in civilian-minded service.

Conclusion

The scholarly debate over the nature of civil-military relations in the United States and over the significance of civil-military tensions since the end of the Cold War can be advanced by comparing postwar transitions. By hypothesizing a trade-off between the pressures of transmutation and extirpation, a criterion for the evaluation of postwar eras has been developed that will now be applied to differentiate among periods in U.S. history that previous theories of civil-military relations suggest were essentially alike. In case studies of postwar transitions, the succeeding chapters seek to demonstrate the utility of a dependent variable in civil-military relations that pays as much attention to the question, "What wins?" as to the classic question of "Who wins?"

CHAPTER TWO

Successful Realignments

In the most successful postwar realignments, military policy achieved a balance between inward-looking reform and outward-looking service. Professionalism was advanced, and the autonomy of military professionals to make certain decisions about their services was respected. Military professionals were not given discretion, however, over the choice of jobs to be done. The reforming armed forces were ordered into civilian-like service to the nation. This limited the extent to which professional standards and training could be accomplished, but it did not make such improvements impossible. Overall, the balance of reform and service kept the military at a safe distance from the extremes of both alienation *against* and absorption *by* civilian society.

After the Revolutionary War, the War of 1812, and the Spanish-American War, political majorities supported the usefulness of the armed forces to address immediate problems, and to prepare for future war. Such political will did not simply emerge, of course, but was created through negotiation and debate. As Michael Desch's theory suggests, in the context of weak internal and external threats, a premium is placed on the military leadership's adaptability. The ability of military leaders after these wars to articulate credible and pragmatic doctrines for their services was noteworthy. Such leaders accepted limited transmutation and committed some portion of their forces to civilian tasks. By doing so, they helped overcome the deep-seated hostility of many Americans to a professional

soldiery. After these wars, military and civilian leaders cooperated in promoting "dual use" projects that advanced the nation's defense along with
its territory and power.

Post–Revolutionary War

In 1783 a peace treaty was signed bringing the War for Independence to a
close. Also in that year, the United States began its first postwar realignment. The navy was essentially sold, the army was momentarily left with
an eighty-man "force," and a faction of bitter officers schemed to undermine the new republican government.[1] The readjustment continued until
1802, with the establishment of the United States Military Academy. The
creation of this center of military professionalism by none other than
Thomas Jefferson, a longtime military skeptic, signaled that a consensus
had been achieved in national policy. The armed forces would be oriented
toward dual-use projects and frontier work in peacetime, but they would
not be denied the opportunity to develop professional values and expertise even as they helped to develop the new nation.

Key Events

The key events of this realignment included, naturally, many "firsts" for
U.S. military policy. In 1787, partly in response to the military ineptitude of
the nation under the Articles of Confederation, the government was
placed on the stronger foundation of the Constitution. As Emory Upton
wrote later, the Constitution explicitly granted to the national government
"every war power the most despotic ruler could ask."[2] The states lost their
right to engage in foreign diplomacy, to field standing forces in peacetime,
or to go to war unless invaded. They also thereby lost any claim to legiti-
macy in resisting the imposition of national laws. Article I, moreover,
granted the national government many specific military powers, including
the right to declare war, to raise a military force, to authorize limited warfare ("issue letters of marque and reprisal"), and to levy taxes to wage and
prepare for war. A commander in chief was designated in Article II. The
difficulty, of course, was that these powers were intentionally fragmented
among competing branches. The affinity of the president with the military
was presaged in the Constitution, however, as the presidency joined the
armed forces as the only truly national institutions of early American life.[3]

In 1790, the first full year of George Washington's first term, the military underwent its first reorganization under the Constitution. The army was strengthened, but not sufficiently to prevent disaster in the field that year and the next. In the encounter over possession of the Ohio River Valley, General St. Clair of the U.S. Army witnessed his militiamen running in retreat through his line of regulars. On that occasion he lost 632 soldiers in an even fight against Native American warriors.[4] In response to these humiliations, the Legion of the United States was created, following the recommendation of Baron General von Steuben of Revolutionary War fame. The Legion was authorized at a strength of 5,414, with new categories of officers (adjutant, inspector) and enlistees (saddler, sergeant major).[5]

This represented a substantial improvement in the army's strength. As the outgoing commander of the Continental army, Washington had issued what he thought was a very restrained report, calling for a peacetime force of 2,600 men. Instead, the nation got 700 militiamen to be loaned to the federal government for one-year enlistments. Though the Confederation Congress gave 40 percent of its budget to the army, the amount was so meager that offensive operations against hostile Indians were banned in the Ohio Valley for want of men.[6] Under mounting pressure from settlers in that area, and with the government's mechanism for taxation and military organization established in the Constitution, Washington, now serving as president, was at last rewarded by Congress with an army of almost eight times the size of the initial "force."

Also in 1792, Congress passed a Uniform Militia Act. The act proved utopian in its very title, but it expressed the values of the citizenry. Military service was considered a duty of "every free able-bodied white male 18 to 45," at least in theory. Two years later the militia played a minor but celebrated role at Fallen Timbers when the Legion, along with 1,500 mounted rifle militia from Kentucky, avenged defeat. The militia had a greater role to play in 1794 in putting down a domestic threat in the Whiskey Rebellion. Under the control of the central government and regular officers and led into western Pennsylvania by President Washington himself, a multistate militia force quelled an anti-tax revolt that threatened to disable the new government.[7] Also in 1794, Congress passed the first act to support a navy in the United States, appropriating funds to pay for six frigates and to construct coastal defenses.[8]

In 1796, the last year of the Washington administration, a true military peace force was established. The army was maintained and its duty to police the frontier explicitly recognized. Naval plans were diminished in response to success against the Barbary pirates, but three frigates then under construction were completed. This represented the apex of professionalism and military strength in the early republic, for when Alexander Hamilton and other advocates of a bigger military sought in 1798 to establish a "New Army," the project was ridiculed by political opponents and the press and undermined by President John Adams himself. The New Army was officially disbanded in 1800, the year of Thomas Jefferson's election to the White House.[9]

Reform

The reforms achieved in military policy in this first realignment were considerable. First, in the creation of the Constitution, the military potential of the nation was enabled, though not guaranteed. The new government was a cumbersome instrument, but when the will for building military strength emerged, the Constitution delineated the processes whereby such will could be exercised. In this period the president was typically the proponent of the military, while Congress alternately supported and restrained executive plans. Considerable increase in force levels occurred, and five thousand men became the new peacetime norm. Furthermore, a practical peacetime orientation for the army and navy was established at this time. The navy was to have limited expeditionary capacity. Its principal role would be to aid the expansion of U.S. trade abroad and to assist in coastal defense at home. The army was to train and prepare for war but simultaneously to explore and police the frontier.

The results of these reforms could be seen in military professionalism, as defined by Huntington, who identifies three core components to professionalism: responsibility, expertise, and corporate identity.[10] What was the status of these in the first postwar realignment?

The corporate identity of the military was strengthened in the battles that they won. For the army especially, this period was critical: it seemed to show the disaster that befell a poorly trained force and the victory that could be achieved with sufficient force and adequate preparation. The expertise of the military was enhanced during this period as difficult assignments on the frontier provided valuable lessons to the officers and troops. Most importantly, the Military Academy began its work of inculcating professional values in generations of army leaders. The responsibility of the military, finally, was negotiated at this time. Ultimately, success proved convincing to critics of a standing army in peacetime. As a consequence, the army and navy accepted their responsibility to the expanding nation and its commercial and material interests. The army accepted a further responsibility for peacekeeping (or "stability operations") on the frontier.

Service

And what of the military's service to the nation during this period? Even those framers of the Constitution who were suspicious of a standing army acknowledged its usefulness. "The Support of the Federal Union," according to George Clinton, was the "first and Principal Object of an army." The Union was yet fragile, and in the short term it was made more so by the settlers' urgent desire to expand the union's borders westward. Republicans and Federalists alike accepted the need for military deployments to the West, though some Republicans agreed to this policy only to isolate the military from the bulk of society and to increase revenues from federal land sales. As for the army itself, its officers typically owned land in the West, thus contributing a private motive to a public one in underpinning their frontier endeavors.[11]

The army's western work was not completed, moreover, once their battles with Indian adversaries were concluded. Indeed, in some ways, the victory at Fallen Timbers was merely the end of the beginning of the first postwar realignment. When the soldiers in the West were not fighting, what were they doing? The army was busy providing aid to peaceful settlement. Soldiers earned fourteen cents a day extra pay for construction work (and extra liquor for sixty days or more of such labor).[12] In addition to construction work at forts, army units were essentially available for hire by local communities. The federal posts thus became nodes of activity and development on the frontier.

At the same time, the army in the West was tasked with the difficult and often unpleasant job of trying to keep peace between white settlers and Native Americans. Sometimes this meant taking sides against the settlers, which naturally tended to alienate the local white population against the soldiers. In his Seventh Annual Address to Congress, George Washington emphasized the importance and delicacy of this task for the army.[13]

The navy too had its part to play in this first postwar period. In President Washington's last yearly message to Congress, he made the first executive recommendation for naval policy, and in so doing, he stated his vision of the purpose of the sea force in a time of peace. In addition to enforcing the nation's contemporary foreign policy of neutrality, he said, naval forces were "indispensable" to "an active external commerce."[14] The helpful role of the navy in expanding commerce was similarly noted in 1798 by Secretary of War James McHenry. The naval and land forces combined, he observed, were necessary "to secure our trade, defend our territory in case of invasion, and prevent or suppress democratic insurrection."[15]

The importance of the army in service to the nation was advanced further by Thomas Jefferson as president when he created the United States Military Academy. Such an academy had been recommended by strong nationalists for years, and President Washington had restated his support for an academy in his last annual message to Congress. That very quickly after taking office Jefferson earned the distinction of founding the institute came as a surprise because Jefferson was one of the most pacific-minded presidents of the early republic. In the caustic commentary of Henry Adams, "Few men have dared to legislate as though eternal peace were at hand, in a world torn by wars and convulsions and drowned in blood; but this is what Jefferson aspired to do."[16] Unfortunately for Jefferson, however, he could not live up to these aspirations as president. The military was too much needed to be disbanded.

Consequently, Jefferson sought to Republicanize the army by advancing the sons of his supporters into the officer corps through West Point. The most careful historian of Thomas Jefferson's relationship with the Military Academy argues that this was Jefferson's deepest motivation. It was patronage politics, in other words, that moved Jefferson to found and then expand West Point. Jefferson himself kept lists of the party affiliations of officers, and by the time he left office, he could note with pride that he had succeeded in the "chaste reformation" of the U.S. Army. The majority of the officer corps were men he had commissioned, and a majority were Republicans.[17]

The Republicanization of the army under Jefferson was not as dangerous for the army as it might have been because of changes in the partisan environment of the nation. Essentially, the Republicans became the hegemonic party. At a time when virtually everyone was, or was soon to become, a Republican, it hardly mattered that army officers were too. Ironically, the final demise of the pro-military Federalists resulted from that party's opposition to the nation's next war, the War of 1812.

While eroding the old association of the officer corps with the elite Federalist Party, Jefferson nevertheless employed the military in much the same way as did his predecessors. He aspired to as small a navy as possible but discovered that naval strength was imperative to protect American vessels against piracy and to enforce his unpopular embargo. Under Jefferson the army, meanwhile, built dual-use roads along the Natchez Trace, handled the transfer of Louisiana from France, explored the Far West (the famous Lewis and Clark were captains in the "Army Corps of Discovery"), and continued to keep the peace between settlers and Native Americans.[18]

The Jeffersonian-Washingtonian consensus held for the remainder of the post–Revolutionary War era, until the nation went back to war in 1812. In the final years leading up to the War of 1812, however, military policy did not expand at as rapid a pace as the nation. At the same time that American legislators observed American interests coming under increasing threat from Great Britain, they did nothing to enhance the nation's capacity for war. As for West Point, the Academy became in time "like a foundling, barely existing among the mountains, and nurtured at a distance out of sight, and almost unknown to its legitimate parents."[19] The War Department likewise failed to keep pace with the demands on the army.[20]

A price was paid in the next war, but how could it have been otherwise? To criticize this realignment for leaving the military unprepared for a war that was rashly entered into is to hold military policy in the infant United States to an unreasonably high standard. The ideological and political opposition to any peacetime force at all was considerable, and it was an accomplishment to gain agreement on the modest naval and ground forces that were created and maintained. Had the military not made themselves so useful to civilian society, it is doubtful that this consensus could have been achieved. As was suggested in the prior chapter, a partial transmutation is at times the price to be paid for a reasonable, if not ideal, degree of professional strength and autonomy.

The Realignment after the War of 1812

The post–War of 1812 realignment likewise can be characterized by its beginning; its end; and its key events, reforms, and service. In this instance, the adjustment to peace began in the Fourteenth Congress, elected in the final year of the war. This Congress worked to "remedy the weaknesses which the War of 1812 had revealed, and to preserve what the war had fostered."[21] Congress continued into peacetime some of the new taxes passed to fund the war and extended the life of the national bank, internal improvements, and tariff protection. The party of Jefferson had truly made peace with the necessity of a military establishment and a government strong enough to support it. Ex-president Jefferson himself took note and attempted to stoke the anti-martial spirit of his followers, commenting that "it is nonsense to talk of Regulars. They are not to be had among a people so easy and happy at home as ours. We might as well rely on calling down an army of angels from heaven."[22] But just as Jefferson could not dispense with Regulars as president, neither could any other responsible national leader during his lifetime.

The period's end can be said to have occurred in 1833. In this year, Congress responded to the problems of the postwar army by increasing pay and conditions to stem desertions, which had reached near-epidemic proportions, in part in response to the employment of soldiers for civilian work on the frontier. Simultaneously, Congress authorized the creation of the Dragoons, whose necessity the professional army had learned in the Black Hawk War.[23] Again, service was balanced by reform.

Key Events

Key events of this period were numerous. In 1816, in the immediate aftermath of the war, a major seacoast fortification plan was enacted and naval building increased. A plan to expand the navy was passed, appropriating one million dollars per year for eight years. The amount actually proved more than the navy and the nation, with its premodern organizations and limited skill at manufacturing, could manage to spend.[24] The U.S. Military Academy at West Point also received encouragement from Congress, and the professional leadership of the Academy began a successful four-year defense of its institution against civilian-minded cadets who charged the institution with violating their individual liberties.[25]

Also in 1816, John C. Calhoun took office as secretary of war and began his tenure as the most successful military secretary in the century—a leading proponent of military strength and military service to the nation. Consistent with the plans of the new war secretary, Congress directed the department in 1818 to report a plan "for the purpose of opening and constructing such roads and canals as may deserve and require the aid of government, with a view to military operations in time of war." The next year, Calhoun's report was submitted, and work began.[26]

By 1821 a new peacetime equilibrium had been achieved in the strength of the army. Calhoun had indicated his philosophy on peacetime preparation for war in a paper delivered to Congress on 12 December 1820.

"However remote our situation from the great powers of the world," he wrote, "and however pacific our policy, we are, notwithstanding, liable to be involved in war; and, to resist, with success, its calamities and dangers, a standing army in peace, in the present improved state of the military science, is an indispensable preparation."[27] A peacetime army of approximately six thousand men "remained essentially the same in force down to the time of the Mexican War."[28]

In the mid-1820s army professionalism received two additional boosts. First, in 1824 Fortress Monroe was established as a post-graduate institution for instruction in artillery. Then, in the next year, legendary army professional Winfield Scott published a new set of army regulations.

Reform

Notable reforms were achieved through these important innovations. Force levels were maintained adequately, even winning the retrospective praise of Emory Upton, who noted that the army of this time was "fairly proportioned to the wants of the country."[29] Taking to heart the lessons of the late war, the management function of the War Department was improved through changes in the supply system and the reconfiguration of the management branches collectively as the "General Staff" of the army. Through this last change, the civilian secretary and the leading professionals of the military were placed in continuous high-level contact in the nation's capital. West Point was rejuvenated, becoming more selective in admissions and strict in discipline. A Board of Visitors was appointed, which maintained pressure on the Academy to maintain its standards. Through the actions of Secretary Calhoun and Commanding General Scott, army practice and training were improved.

The limits of reform during this period were also revealed, however. First, the management of the army, though improved, still left much to be desired. The General Staff acted not so much as a collective body to advise, as a collection of generals each jealously guarding his discretionary authority over his own "fiefdom" within the services. In manpower policy, the relation of the regular force to the militia continued to be problematic. The militia had proven itself largely inept in the recent war except when led by exceptional commanders. As a result of the disinclination of citizen soldiers even to report for duty in the War of 1812, ten thousand militiamen were assessed fines. However, collection and prosecutions were extraordinarily lax, reflecting civilian distaste for compulsion. Eventually, the effort

to collect fines was simply given up, and the militia law of 1792 was continued, unchanged and unenforced.[30]

Calhoun had the practical wisdom, nevertheless, to accept that the professional force would never be so large in America that it could fight a real
war without a marked mobilization and reliance upon citizens at arms.
His desire was that the peacetime army be so staffed and organized that it
was in practice "expansible" to meet wartime needs. In this way, the citizen
soldiery that would by necessity be called upon to fight in war would be
led at every rank by professionals. Dispersed around the country in companies in peacetime, the officer-heavy expansible army would coalesce
into brigades and divisions in the event of war. Calhoun and other reformers thus made the most of what was a difficult situation. A steady
state military "capable of dealing with domestic disturbances, fighting Indians, and maintaining open sea lanes" was so organized that it could rapidly be transformed into a force suitable for war.[31]

Military professionalism improved during this period. The corporate
identity of the military was enhanced as heroes of the war were added to
the pantheon of military professionals. Moreover, new leaders replaced
the retiring generation of Revolutionary War veterans, who still held most
of the commands in the services at the start of the war. The expertise of the
forces was addressed in several of the changes noted above, including the
issuance of new regulations and the institution of improved education
and training. The responsibility of the military for the nation was, moreover, acknowledged and proclaimed by leading civilian and military proponents of a stronger force. The nation's forces, proclaimed Calhoun,
must prepare for "future wars, long and bloody," while also expanding and
safeguarding the country's expansion through settlement at home and
trade abroad.[32]

Service

Services rendered by the military during this period were in line with the
philosophy of Secretary of War Calhoun. Along the southeastern frontier,
General Jackson followed up his heroics of 1815 with a semi-private war for
Spanish Florida. This operation was of doubtful legality but was tremen-
dously successful in expanding the area of national settlement. Pre-
dictably, it saddled the regular army with the frustrating task of fighting
hostile Indian populations and lawless settlers in protracted "peace operations" on the coastal frontier.

Out west, Calhoun chastised his critics for displaying "more of timidity than wisdom" and ordered the army to build new posts in advance of settlement. The purpose, to Calhoun, was clear. The "permanent security of our frontier," he wrote, "is considered by far of the greatest importance" in these new posts. They would also, he contended, bring considerable gain to the nation, which, with army help, would win a monopoly on "the most valuable fur trade in the world."[33]

Calhoun overreached in the army's Yellowstone, or Missouri Expedition, which was eventually scaled back and moved eastward, closer to the actual line of settlement. Nonetheless, Calhoun believed that the nobility of the army's service to the nation would not be lost on either the nation or the average soldier. "The American soldier," he wrote, "actuated by the spirit of enterprise, will meet the privations which may be necessary with cheerfulness combined with the importance of the service. The glory of planting the American flag at a point so distant, on so noble a river, will not be unfelt."[34] Until it was abandoned in 1827, Fort Atkinson enjoyed the distinction of being both the largest garrison in the nation and the most advanced outpost of America in the West.

Because the army was sometimes placed beyond the support of the civilian population, soldiers were tasked not just with exploring, building, and defending, but with farming as well. From 1818 to 1833, military posts were ordered by the War Department to engage in extensive agricultural production. From a reduction in costs and improvement in health, General Scott himself anticipated "the most favorable results" from this unpopular order.[35]

Roads of "national importance," meanwhile, were surveyed, planned, estimated, and to some extent actually built by the army during this period as well. Arguing that the geographic enormity of the country demanded an expansive role for the army, Calhoun became in effect the nation's "geographer in chief," as well as its secretary of war.[36]

The responsibility of the army to the nation, as articulated by Secretary of War Calhoun, was endorsed by a succession of postwar presidential administrations. James Monroe wrote of the importance of the army and navy "to prevent war" as well as "to diminish its calamities when it may be inevitable." Calhoun's dual-use roads would help the nation achieve both aims.[37] John Quincy Adams, who followed Monroe in office, had an especially expansive view of governmental responsibility. His vision encompassed a generous scope of action for the army. "In a period of profound peace," he wrote in a message to Congress, the conduct of war "forms but a very inconsiderable portion of the duties devolving upon the administration of the Department of War." To the War Department "are attributed other duties, having, indeed, relation to a future possible condition of war, but being purely defensive, and in their tendency contributing rather to the security and permanency of peace." Such duties, the president elaborated, included the building of forts on the frontier, the distribution of pensions to veterans, the maintenance of Indian relations, and the superintending and performance of surveys and internal improvements.[38]

Did the service of the post–War of 1812 military go too far? Certainly the Inspector General (IG) of the army thought so. There were often so many soldiers on construction or agricultural duty at isolated postings, he observed, that they forsook drill and parade. Soldiers sometimes joined in the IG's discontent. "I went into the army to *avoid* work!" complained one soldier. The irony (and balance) in the situation, however, is underscored by the fact that the position of Inspector General was created in the flurry of reforms following the war.[39]

The balance between service and reform in this period did not erase the inevitable tensions caused by mixing subjective and objective control mechanisms. Ironically, during this time military professionals often expressed their concern that the isolation of soldiers in western posts cut them off too much from civilian society. Artillerists "remote from the healthful influence of public opinion," consequently sought relief from isolated postings. New graduates of the Military Academy, "unsuspicious, confident in the strength of [their] morals," similarly were said to suffer in remoteness "from the absence of good society."[40] The military-minded secretary of war worried about the opposite problem: too much reliance upon subjective control, coming from too great an exposure of military personnel to civilian habits. The nation, Calhoun lectured Congress in 1818, need not fear so much its military "members being hostile to liberty" as they should worry about effects "of an opposite character—that both officers and soldiers will lose their military habits and feelings, by sliding gradually into those purely civil."[41] James Monroe, as president, sided with the civilian-minded military, asserting that having soldiers work in civilian capacities was of too great a benefit to be compromised, for "the military will be incorporated with the civil, and unfounded and injurious distinctions and prejudices of every kind be done away."[42]

Overall, a blend of civilian-oriented missions and inward-oriented education and training became part of army doctrine in this period. This balance was accepted even by the highly professional Commanding General Edmund P. Gaines in the late 1830s. Gaines was prescient in recognizing that the advent of steamships made America's extensive seacoast insecure. His proposed remedy was a massive public works project to build five transcontinental railroads to speed the movement of men and supplies to wherever they were most needed in case of attack, and a flotilla of floating batteries, essentially forts on barges, which likewise could be maneuvered to advantage in time of war. In speeches, official reports, and pamphlets, General Gaines urged "the young men of the States of the American Union, civil and military," to join in this endeavor. The entire operation, which Gaines described as "the most useful, and the most magnificent work known to ancient or modern history," would be under the direction of officers of the U.S. Army.[43] Gaines never won Congress's approval for his ambitious plans, but he was authorized to take modest steps in the direction of greater war preparations. To better prepare for war, the ultra-professional Gaines ordered his soldiers to clear roads and dredge canals, and his officers to become proficient in the making of surveys and topographic maps. Through such means the army deepened its connection with the nation while preserving sufficient expertise to win the next war.

After the Spanish-American War

The realignment following the war with Spain in 1898 was similar in many respects to that after the War of 1812. For one thing, a pro-military civilian led both realignments. Like Calhoun decades before, Secretary of War Elihu Root assumed leadership after a war that had revealed serious deficiencies in the military establishment. President Theodore Roosevelt chose Root, a New York corporate lawyer, for the position largely on the basis of his legal talents. The War Department had won possession of overseas territories and would need to administer them. The legal complexities were considerable. Moreover, Roosevelt admired Root's knowledge of corporate affairs and hoped that his appointee would bring efficiency to a cumbersome bureaucratic organization. Military professionals interested in reform looked on with approval, while those fearing reform hoped to control the new appointee.[44]

In Root's case, the war just past had also left a legacy of greatly expanded responsibilities. The nation had become an empire and required an imperial military. A historian of the period draws out these changes in contrasting the army establishment over which Root assumed leadership with that of 1897, the year before the war: "Instead of 25,000 soldiers scattered in small detachments over the Continental United States, the army Root took over consisted of almost 100,000 men, two-thirds of them deployed at overseas stations and more than 30,000 engaged in or on their way to combat in rice fields and jungles half a world away. Its generals governed Cuba, Puerto Rico, and the conquered portions of the Philippines, shouldering as they did a weight of responsibility and a range of duties unequaled since Reconstruction."[45]

The appointment of Root in August 1899 marked the beginning of this realignment. Its end came in February 1913. In that month, the lame-duck president, William Howard Taft, called upon U.S. troops to respond to violence in Mexico. With a single telegram, Taft mobilized 20,000 fully equipped soldiers, who quickly moved to the border. This feat was unimaginable before the reforms of the Root era and was the product of organizational innovations made in the post–Spanish-American War reform. The new War College had made advance plans for just such a mobilization; the new General Staff had the efficiency to carry it out. With this demonstration of the army's skill, lame-duck Secretary of War Henry Stimson so impressed the incoming secretary of war that the latter agreed to continue the reforms that had made it possible. Incoming President Woodrow Wilson confirmed the bipartisan accommodation behind an improved military policy when he announced that General Leonard Wood, the leading army modernizer of the time and a villain of anti-modernizing interests within the military itself, could serve out his term, remaining in office as army chief of staff until April 1914.[46]

As after the Revolutionary War, military improvement was a political issue that eventually won bipartisan support. As after the War of 1812, career military leaders joined with interested civilians to advance reforms. As after both prior examples of successful postwar realignment, the military was put to work performing non-war-fighting, civilian-oriented missions.

Key Events

The key events of the post–Spanish-American War readjustment were concentrated in the immediate aftermath of the war. New realities in military responsibilities demanded rapid changes in strategy, doctrine, organization, and management. In 1898 the Civil War general and railroad executive Grenville Dodge was appointed to head a commission to investigate the sensational failures that had marred recent military victory. The Dodge Commission convened on September 24 and held hearings for five months. In this investigation, the major lines of conflict between reformers and their opponents were drawn. Commanding General Nelson Miles emerged as the chief antagonist of military modernization. He was backed by the Grand Army of the Republic, a Civil War veterans' organization.[47]

The Dodge Commission's eight-volume report publicized many problems.[48] The bureau system within the army and navy was criticized, as was the ambiguity of the command structure. Miles, meanwhile, made headlines with his charge that troops in Cuba had been provided with "embalmed beef." His charges turned out to be as false as they were scientifically meaningless, and his attempt to derail change could not match the pressures for serious reform. Secretary Root appointed the Governor of Havana, Brigadier General William Ludlow, to study the broad subject of army reform in light of the Dodge Commission's revelations.

Critical support for Ludlow came from his civilian superiors. Civilian officials gave support as well to Leonard Wood, who was promoted Governor of Cuba over hundreds of other officers of greater seniority. His rank increased by virtue of the appointment from Captain Surgeon to Major General of Volunteers. Secretary of War Root was so impressed by Wood and Ludlow that he heralded their activities in conquered territory as being of greater significance than even the triumphs of battle. What impressed Root was the diverse range of accomplishments of Wood and his fellow military proconsuls. Their activities blurred the distinction between military and civilian roles and identities as soldiers built schools, superintended censuses, reduced yellow fever, and otherwise improved the lives of America's new "subjects."

The next year, in 1900, the public endorsed the new direction in national policy by resoundingly defeating William Jennings Bryan for president. Bryan was the flag bearer in that election for the Democratic Party. Four years earlier, he had been the nominee of both the Democrats and the Populist Party. His 1900 campaign focused attention on the issue of America's emergence as an imperial power. During his run for office, he sought to rekindle an ancient American suspicion of all things military. "Military rule," he declaimed, "is antagonistic to our theory of government. The arguments which are used to defend it in the Philippines may be used," he warned darkly, "to execute it in the United States." The growth in army strength, he similarly argued, shifted men "from the ranks of the wealth creators to the ranks of the tax consumers," and placed "force against reason in the structure of our government." The army, Bryan reasoned, represented the "impersonation of force. It does not deliberate; it acts. It does not decide, it executes, it does not reason, it shoots."[49]

A majority of voters apparently thought otherwise, for the result was a landslide in 1900 for the Republican Party. This was, in fact, one of the most significant elections in American political development, placing Republicans firmly in power in the national government and mandating the president to reconstruct old institutions.[50] With the election behind him, Secretary of War Root was able to characterize the guerilla war in the Philippines as "minor in character" without concern for a political backlash.[51]

Also in 1901, Secretary of War Root and President Roosevelt took a major step forward in military professionalism with the creation, by executive order, of the Army War College at Carlisle Barracks, Pennsylvania. The War College became the capstone of a coordinated hierarchy in military education and promoted a uniformity of leadership culture within the army. Moreover, the War College was a planning body as well as a school. The War College repaid its debt to army reformers, led by Root, by issuing reports and recommendations that challenged the government to increase the military and permit continued improvement in military organization and leadership.[52]

In January of 1903, Congress passed the first major reform in the relationship between the regular army and the citizen armies of the militia (known by now as the National Guard). The Dick Act, named after Representative Charles Dick, a former president of the National Guard Organization, represented a historic compromise. The army wanted the Guard to be subordinated to the regulars as a secondary reserve force. The War Department, after considerable wrangling, accepted the inevitability of the Guard as the nation's first reserve force in a return to war; but in exchange, the Guard accepted federal funding, joint U.S. Army-National Guard exercises, War College instruction for part-time officers, and consistency in equipment and doctrine.[53]

Shortly after the passage of the Dick Act, the General Staff Act was signed into law. The chief of staff now would "supervise" the staff bureau chiefs, the formerly all-powerful lords of the services. The General Staff would at last be worthy of its name, providing direction for the army at the highest level, planning and coordinating the newly expanded duties of a global force.

There were, of course, setbacks for the reformers as well. They wished to consolidate the supply work of the force under a single head but were defeated in this attempt. They wished to undermine the power of the Old Guard within the military leadership, represented by the position of the Adjutant General (AG). But their victory over the AG's post and its inhabitant, General Fred Ainsworth, was costly. Ainsworth was forced out of his job in 1912, but Congress retaliated by reducing the General Staff, or, as its critics called it, the "General Stuff."[54]

Overall, the direction of change enhanced the military power of the nation. As he exited the White House, Roosevelt listed what he believed to have been his greatest achievements as a peacetime president: doubling the size of the navy and sending the fleet on a round-the-world show of force; "taking" Panama; mediating the war between Russia and Japan; conserving natural resources; regulating big business; and increasing the strength and alertness of foreign policy. Every one of these measures was designed to enhance the nation's military power. The increase in naval strength, the U.S.-sponsored revolt in Panama, and the strengthening of foreign policy, were explicitly related to war and war preparedness. The mediation of foreign conflicts, especially the war involving Japan—for which Roosevelt was awarded the Nobel Peace Prize—was also in service of American power. "It was essential," the former president wrote in his memoirs, "that we should have it clearly understood by our own people especially, but also by other people, that the Pacific was as much our home waters as the Atlantic."[55] Peace in the Pacific would curb Japanese power so that the United States might extend its influence in its new home waters. Similarly, by husbanding the country's vast resources and directing them into intelligent uses, the government ensured the necessary supplies, including minerals, for war. And by forcing the owners of industry to behave with a modicum of respect for their laborers, Roosevelt hoped to increase the feeling of unity that was a necessary underpinning to any successful use of force.[56]

As the president himself saw it, the expansion of the nation's capacity for military action was the very foundation of change in government policy after the Spanish-American War.

Service

After the Spanish American War, the military performed both traditional domestic and newer colonial roles. With regard to the latter, General Wood was far from unique in wishing to bring all the resources of American Progressivism to bear on Cuba's problems.[57] Moreover, like his illustrious patron, Theodore Roosevelt, Wood was forceful in putting himself and his work before the public. "We in America," Wood once complained, "understand too little the work of the army, too little of what it has done to save life, and we talk too much of it as a destructive force."[58] Wood wished for the public to understand and appreciate the work of the army in peacetime.

Wood's Cuban experiment included a Department of Agriculture, Commerce and Industry, which sought to promote economic investment. Tariffs were reduced in the interest of both Cuban consumers and North American producers. In the jails, conditions were made to conform to the newest theories of North American reformers. For young offenders, the army built reformatories and trained their wardens in nonpunitive techniques.[59] In Puerto Rico, Wood's disciples went so far as to look for inspiration to the ultra-Progressive Henry George, the guiding spirit of officers' efforts to classify all land in the new possession as to its "social usage."

Even Nelson Miles, who loudly criticized American policy in the Philippines, accepted army responsibility in the Caribbean. Puerto Rico, he reasoned, might in fact be annexed with the assistance of soldiers. In evaluating the military's role in performing constabulary duty in Puerto Rico, in fact, Miles raised what he thought was the *positive* precedent of Military Reconstruction after the Civil War.

The Philippines were different, Miles reasoned, because they were far away and the job of subduing rebels was difficult. The army's role there exposed it to the prospect of military defeat. Moreover, Miles continued, casually mixing traditional professional concern not to expose the forces to defeat with a more civilian-minded concern for making good use of the army in peacetime, the army could be put to better use at home! "Roads, not empire," he proclaimed, should be the government's priority. Money saved by quitting the Philippines might be spent at home in the construction of "internal improvements," a subject with which the Old Army had considerable experience.[60]

In the Philippines, the push for reform was mitigated by the need for continued war-fighting, and regular officers clashed with their civilian government head, William Howard Taft. Still, military leaders in the Pacific sometimes took to their new missions with the same enthusiasm as they had in the Caribbean. General John Schofield, like Miles, invoked the example of Reconstruction. Unlike Miles, he thought the example applied in the Pacific as well as closer to home and creatively responded to the problems of a mixed civil and military operation. Veterans' letters home from the Philippines demonstrated as well an emotional depth of satisfaction in service.[61]

Because the regular army was still needed to fight guerilla forces, however, some of the most civilian-like police work in the Philippines was delegated to "Scouts"—soldiers who stood organizationally between the regular army and the indigenous constabulary. Scouts were Filipino soldiers, commanded and trained by personnel from the U.S. Army. The Scout's civilian duties were supposed to be temporary, but typically they were not.[62] Service with the Scouts was hard, and to make matters worse, Scout officers were treated like second-class citizens in the U.S. Army. Their pensions were lower than those of non-Scouts; their opportunity for advancement was poorer; and they were not eligible for membership in the private veterans organization, the Military Order of the Carabou.[63] Scout leaders continued with their work nonetheless.[64]

Traditional domestic service in the United States at this time also continued and received consensual praise from military and civilian authorities. Particular pride was expressed in army and marine performance in the aftermath of the San Francisco earthquake and fire of April 1906. Camps for displaced inhabitants of the city, dumps for refuse, sanitation facilities, and other structures were built by Regulars. It was, remarked observers, merely bringing home (again) the recent experience of the soldiers abroad. "All shoulders went willingly to the wheel," proclaimed one officer with pride, looking back on his duty in San Francisco.[65]

The satisfaction that military professionals took in civilian service was reflected by the editor of the *Infantry Journal*, who wrote: "Being, after all, human, we like the waving of handkerchiefs and clapping of hands as we march in parade, eyes to the front, so that, when occasionally the public sees that there is virtue in us, we are glad." After all, the editorialist continued, "the Army is a part of and belongs to the nation." The army was therefore urged by the professional journal of the infantry to maintain readiness for disaster while increasing readiness for war.[66] In this editorial, moreover, the writer merely echoed a familiar theme from his publication's pages. The utility of helping civilians and thus helping to undermine "the foolish and the pessimistic ones, who are always with us in this land, crying about the danger of militarism," was widely acknowledged by military professionals.[67] The civil-military "bargain" was a good one for the professionals.

The Scouts in the Philippines encapsulate the mixture of subjective and objective control mechanisms that characterized this postwar period. They were led by regular officers but were oriented toward peacekeeping and police-type work. Regular army enlistees in the Philippines and the Caribbean also engaged in civilian duties and accepted such jobs as appropriate expressions of their expertise and responsibility. So long as the army was not forced to *fight* in the manner that civilian authorities sometimes wished them to—with less use of force than officers thought necessary—they were able to incorporate their new service into their self-identity as military professionals. The army experience in Reconstruction and, more recently, in frontier work was frequently looked to for precedents.

Meanwhile, especially at the highest levels of the military, objective control was utilized in creating "space" for the discretionary exercise of authority by the new General Staff. The military's leaders gained leverage against anti-modernizing elements both within their own ranks and within Congress. The modernizers' allies within government were the president and his secretary of war.

Political consensus emerged at the end of this realignment, providing a foundation for future professionalization and enhancements of strength. The professionalizers' power was far from absolute, but it was sufficient to withstand the return to power of a Democratic president and his appointment of a pacifist to be secretary of war. One reason was that military reforms had expressed the general interest of the nation during this period in modernizing and improving efficiency. Military reforms in the early 1900s were in fact so closely intertwined with the broader governmental and societal changes of the era that it would have been incredibly difficult to undo what Root and Roosevelt had accomplished without undoing all the changes in the nation's nonmilitary policies as well.

Conclusion

If we had looked merely at whether "the military" or "the civilians" prevailed in making policy at these times, we would not have learned a great deal about what makes for productive civil-military relations. Evaluating the substance of policy inescapably requires the use of judgment. The subjective nature of the judgments offered in this chapter would not be mitigated, however, but in fact increased, if instead we were required to declare definitively "who won." Who spoke for the military professionals after the Spanish-American War? Was it Nelson Miles, the highest-ranking army general, or the civilian secretary of war? Was it the army renegade, Leonard Wood, or his antagonist, the army stalwart, Fred Ainsworth?

In fact, in the realignments studied in this chapter, civilian leadership and military flexibility were both important. With regard to the role of civilians, George Washington as president was as important to the establishment of a sound military policy and good civil-military relations as was George Washington as commanding general. Similarly, the realignments that followed the War of 1812 and the Spanish-American War owed a great deal to civilian secretaries and presidents. With regard to the role of the military, in each realignment the services were put to work advancing the peacetime mission of civilian America. Though wary at times of advancing too far toward civilianization, the military leadership in these postwar periods made peace with the fact that they were needed in peacetime and could not spend all their time preparing for war.

CHAPTER THREE

Poor Realignments

Analysis of the periods after the Revolutionary War, the War of 1812, and the Spanish-American War in the previous chapter demonstrated that political and societal consensus in addition to civilian and military cooperation are important in bringing about a balanced realignment. The cases examined in this chapter show the importance of these factors through negative examples. After both of the world wars, there was a lack of political and societal consensus and uneven cooperation among senior civilian and military leaders. These factors undermined the prospects for a satisfactory equilibrium in military policy.

After World War I

The realignment to World War I began with congressional consideration of a new national defense policy. The result was the National Defense Act of 1920. This act reflected a compromise between the interests of the professional military establishment and the anti-martial impulses of a nation eager for "normalcy." It was, nonetheless, a clear ratcheting upward of military strength, especially for the army, and it propelled military leaders to seek peacetime continuance of the exuberant support that the public gave the armed services during the war. The fundamental constraint that the military's leadership encountered was the reluctance of civilian society and its elected leadership to take the recent world war entirely seriously.

The war, many people came to believe, was all a big mistake, and the United States would do well to avoid repeating it by retreating from foreign entanglements and military preparedness.

The conclusion of the realignment came in Franklin Roosevelt's lengthy presidency. The second President Roosevelt was famously pragmatic, and he placed a priority in the early and mid 1930s on responding to the crisis of the economy. For the military, this meant a focus on service and homeland defense even while its professional expertise deteriorated. The tensions of 1920s military policy, between the professionals' desire to prepare for war and a skeptical population's desire to domesticate the small force, were preserved rather than resolved in the early Roosevelt administration. The army poured manpower into the Civilian Conservation Corps (CCC), while the navy benefited from increases in naval construction—which the practical president construed chiefly as a public works program. Veterans' benefits were cut as an economy measure.

At the end of the decade, FDR at last led the nation to accept responsibility for war preparations. "Dr. New Deal," Roosevelt proclaimed, had become "Dr. Win the War." The interwar focus on homeland defense was abandoned, but even so, it took the surprise attack of the Japanese to propel the United States formally into World War II. The citizen army that was mobilized to fight the war was not as large or as professional as the reformers of the interwar period had hoped it might be, but it included a great many graduates of the CCC and the Reserve Officer Training Corps (ROTC), post–World War I innovations in military training. As a precise date for the termination of the postwar era, September 1, 1940, serves well. That was the date of Congress's enactment of the nation's first peacetime draft.

Key Events

Key events of the postwar transition occurred in two waves, the first immediately after the war, the second about ten years later. Even before the National Defense Act of 1920, there was, to begin with, the 1920 presidential campaign. In this election season, the military rushed to the center of attention as General Leonard Wood very nearly won the Republican Party's nomination for president while still on active duty. General John "Black Jack" Pershing was also interested in the office; however, he was a political novice compared with Wood, and his Dewey-like bid for the nomination ended as miserably as had the admiral's. The significance of these generals' bids for office in 1920 is that they belie the myth that the country simply turned away from all things military after the war. Wood's nomination was, in fact, spoiled only after numerous ballots at the Republican convention, which he entered as the leading candidate. His candidacy was ultimately rejected, not because he was too military, but because he had been accused in the primary season of not being his own man—of taking excessive contributions from William Cooper Procter, a wealthy soap manufacturer.[1]

It was Warren Harding, however, who won the nomination and the presidency in 1920 and who accepted the results of the eventful Naval Conference of 1920/1921. Naval progressives had enlarged the navy before and during the war. Naturally, navalists wanted to keep the trend in naval strength going upward after the war. However, costs had grown considerably along with technology and armaments. Whereas it had cost about five million dollars to build a battleship earlier in the century, by the end of the war, each battleship cost nearly forty million.[2] In the face of such inflation and with the return to peace, Iowa Senator William Borah called for an international disarmament conference. Senator and former Secretary of War Elihu Root warned against the idea. The nation, however, was in no mood for an expensive preparedness campaign. Moreover, Root's pro-military position was undermined by the support that leading military officers, including General Pershing himself, gave to Borah. *Collier's Magazine* joined the chorus, offering readers "Tell the President" cutouts, which came into the White House at the rate of a thousand a day.[3] With unemployment increasing and the navy hurt politically by intraservice conflict over the future of surface warfare, the conference was organized, and Secretary of State Charles Evans Hughes was given the job of chief U.S negotiator.

At the conference, Hughes brokered a treaty that achieved U.S. naval parity with Great Britain while setting Japanese naval strength at 60 percent of that of the United States and Great Britain. This result has been criticized for decades, but it was hardly a feeble navy that resulted. The chief difficulty with the conference results was not, in any event, the strength of naval forces, but it was the U.S. agreement not to convert territory west of Hawaii into major naval facilities. The Philippines, as a consequence, would remain a hostage to events in the Pacific.[4]

Ground force issues were settled in the same year in Congress. In making their decisions, the Senate Military Affairs Committee utilized the services of Pershing's number one aide during the war, Lieutenant Colonel John McCaully Palmer. Palmer was a West Point graduate, but also the son of a citizen-soldier hero of the Civil War. He had a strong distaste for the regular army's patron saint, Emory Upton. The disciples of Upton wanted to fashion the army as an expansible force under the control of a top-heavy cadre of career officers. Because the peacetime army would have so many officers, professionals would maintain leadership of the expanded force in the event of war. The bulk of enlistees would be taken from among the population at large. To ensure that the men of the nation would be up to the task, the Uptonians wanted to prepare all men during peacetime for the eventuality of war.

Palmer liked the second part of the plan, the part about universal military training. But he disliked the part of the plan that would bar citizen soldiers such as his father had been from army leadership during war. The neo-Calhounian expansible army plan, he thought, was "not in keeping with the genius of American institutions."[5]

Palmer's hopes for universal military training were as idealistic as was his denunciation of the expansible army. The adoption of his preferred system of military training, he insisted, would transform "the great outlay required by the war will" into a "a permanent investment . . . effective for any future emergency whether it be ten years or a century from now."[6] The senators used the reformer to help knock down the expansible army plan but ignored him when it came to universal military training.

The National Defense Act nonetheless gave the proponents of preparedness a partial triumph. The peacetime army was authorized at about 280,000, half of the force level requested by the General Staff but much larger than the prewar norm. It was to be organized, not as an expansible force, but as a garrison for outlying territories and as a pool from which to draw men for small expeditionary forays around the globe. Should a large ground war come again, the necessary land units would be built from the ranks of the citizen militia, with the acknowledged likelihood of conscription. Universal military training was rejected, but the Defense Act permitted the army to support and train volunteers at citizens' military camps along the prewar Plattsburg model.

Two final features of the National Defense Act built on reforms made before the war in the modern management of the army. The General Staff was enlarged, and the old Land Grant plan, making military instruction available to college students outside of the service academies, was expanded. The new plan, Reserve Officer Training Corps (ROTC), made military instruction of civilians an important mission for the professional army.[7]

About a decade later, after the Great Depression had shaken the nation, another key event in the post–World War I realignment took place. In May of 1932, while President Hoover was in his final year of office, 15,000 veterans of the late war marched on Washington, D.C. The soldiers were among the victims of the economic contraction, and they demanded that the government convert their promised bonus certificates into ready cash thirteen years before their certificates were to mature. In June Congress, in keeping with the bipartisan consensus that government economy would help restore the economy, rejected the veterans' demands. Most of the marchers returned home, but about two thousand remained in makeshift camps in the District. Fearing that the marchers were under communist control, President Hoover ordered the army into action. On July 28, Chief of Staff Douglas MacArthur personally led troops who employed tear gas and riot tactics to destroy the marchers' shacks and force them beyond the city's limits. The result was a public outcry against the president and the army.[8]

The change in administrations brought a change in approach to government action generally. While President Roosevelt at first shared his predecessor's great concern for government economy, he was willing to experiment and loath to employ force at home. Ironically, the civilian-minded President Roosevelt suffused his administration with war analogies. In New Deal rhetoric, "internal preparedness" became a core objective of the government.[9] From this perspective, World War I was no longer a mistake or a tragedy but was a great proving ground. "The ordeal of war," proclaimed Rexford Tugwell, a member of Roosevelt's Brain Trust, "brings out the magnificent resources of youth. . . . The ordeal of depression ought to try your mettle in similar ways. . . . The feeling which shook humanity during the War and which after War reshaped the entire civilization of mighty nations is called for again."[10] The crisis of the day, Roosevelt agreed, "calls for the building of plans that rest upon the forgotten, the unorganized and the indispensable units of economic power, for plans like those of 1917 that build from the bottom up and not from the top down."[11] Some of the most popular New Deal programs, in keeping with the tone of Roosevelt's rhetoric, mixed martial and civilian themes.

Franklin Roosevelt, according to his biographer, James McGregor Burns, was interested in the Civilian Conservation Corps (CCC) "as much as [in] any single measure" of the New Deal.[12] The CCC was launched during the famous first Hundred Days of Roosevelt's presidency in which a Democratic Congress eager for leadership created dozens of new agencies and programs proposed to them by the executive. MacArthur was not a fan of the CCC but reluctantly took it on. It was a considerable innovation, though less than what some more activist members of Congress desired: the direct use of the military to provide relief to the population.[13]

During the day, CCC workers were supervised by men from the National Forest Service, the Soil Conservation Service, or some other federal civilian agency. In the evenings and during off-duty hours, military personnel were in charge. Army reservists, a great many of them out of work themselves, comprised the bulk of the supervisory personnel, though the army, navy, and marines all sent men from among their professional ranks. By the summer of the bill's enactment, over a quarter of a million men were enrolled for a six-month "hitch" in more than a thousand camps. By the time the program ended nine years later, some three million men had served in the CCC.

The CCC was suffused not just with military personnel, but with military frameworks of evaluation and judgment as well. Critics complained of a high "desertion" rate early in the program's history. Friends of the program boasted of its effect in "making men" of the enrollees and even in rounding out the campers' physiques. (An average weight gain of eight pounds did not go unnoticed by federal inspectors in these lean times.)

When the nation moved from ersatz to earnest war, 90 percent of the men who had at one time or another been in the CCC served in uniform during the war, along with approximately 50,000 reserve officers with CCC experience. In September 1940, as the administration prepared for war, the CCC was reoriented toward training for wartime. Ironically, this often meant that CCC men were taken from healthy work out of doors and corralled indoors to learn how to work with radios, repair automobiles, or cook and bake for a thousand men at a time. The program ended when the real war made it obsolete.[14]

Reform

What were the consequences of these events for military reform? Two central issues were manpower and "the relationship of the elements of the Army of the United States to the federal government and each other."[15] In 1919 the General Staff submitted to Congress a plan for a half-million-men regular army and universal military training overseen by regular officers as a means of providing the mass for a return to any future war.

On the issue of manpower, the postwar period provided the usual setbacks to plans for a much-enlarged peacetime force. Congress authorized a force of "only" 125,000 men, and actual figures lagged behind authorizations. This was recognized as such a problem that the army designated the effort to increase the regular force "Major Army Project No. 1." The army achieved a scaled-down goal of 165,000 personnel only in the late 1930s.[16] Still, at just over 130,000, the postwar force of the mid-1920s was about one-third larger than the prewar norm. The marines saw similar results, increasing to 16,000 from a peacetime level of about 10,000.[17]

To build interest in army manpower, military reformers attempted to work with the old prewar preparedness lobby and the new veterans' organization, the American Legion. The "enemy" was identified by the preparedness lobby as the "ladies of both sexes" who talked of pacifism and further defense cuts. The "rush to defenselessness" must stop, proclaimed Brigadier General Hugh Drum, with War Department backing. Thus, on September 12, 1924, the military organized a Defense Test Day. All able-bodied men were asked to turn out to take part in exercises. 17,000,000 citizens were reported to have participated. However, when the hoopla was over, there was no resultant increase in the military's budget or its manpower levels. The president, whose priority was the economy, was as pleased as the military's leadership was disenchanted.[18]

On the issue of the organization of the army and its source of manpower, the military reformers had reason to be even less happy. The preparedness campaign of the prewar effort was reestablished on a smaller scale after the war, but its interest in military training for average citizens was not received with enthusiasm. The postwar preparedness lobby even had to face the embarrassing revelation of its chief organization's financial distress.

The army's plan to train all male citizens for wartime service did not prevail. But there were significant reforms nonetheless. The most significant innovation was probably the creation of ROTC. In the decade following World War I, more than three hundred ROTC units were established in which 125,000 students were trained and to which at any one time about 5 percent of the army's officer corps were assigned as instructors.[19] ROTC represented a successful compromise between the extreme of universal military training and a return to prewar practices.

Also important were changes in military management. The evolution of the General Staff during this period included the disaggregation of the Staff into units responsible for personnel, intelligence, operations and training, supply, and plans.[20] In the coordination of military management with civilian policy, reforms were not as successful. No regular coordinating body was established until 1938 to formalize civil-military relations at the top level. This was not for lack of effort on the part of the professional military. The Joint Planning Committee of the Joint Board made numerous requests to the civilian secretary of state for the creation of such an organization, but its efforts were repeatedly rebuffed.[21]

Reforms of this period were in keeping with the general consequence of peace on government operations and innovations. The result was too much change for some and not enough for others. Quick cuts and dismantlements from wartime levels of effort wounded the War Department. The Department had 4 billion dollars in outstanding and unfilled orders on Armistice Day. More than half of these were cancelled by the government in the month after peace was proclaimed. This level of drawback was generous by some standards, however. With regard to all government building programs, more than 70 percent were cancelled with the termination of the war.[22]

Similarly, in contrast to the war's effects in Europe, the war failed to stimulate a permanent change in domestic social policy. In the United States, the War Industries Board was quickly dismantled, as was the U.S. Employment Service.[23] Still, the postwar policies restraining a naval arms race and creating a more professional, if still citizen-reliant army were viewed in retrospect as great successes by none other than General Pershing, speaking from retirement in 1932.[24]

The influence of reform could be seen on military professionalism. The corporate identity of the military was reinforced as the war provided exemplars of military values. The war was memorialized broadly in the United States, and in the military itself, war heroism was remembered in typically American fashion. In an egalitarian gesture, American cemeteries used identical markers for the graves of enlistees and officers, and in typical American fashion, each fallen soldier received an individual marker. Unlike older American war cemeteries, however, Great War cemeteries in France contained no regional memorials and few state markers.[25] The war had marked a step forward in the nation's progress toward a self-conscious unity. The army's identity as a national force was enhanced as a result. However, army morale languished in the 1920s. While the army officially made manpower its number one priority, some army leaders saw morale of those already in uniform as an even bigger problem.[26]

The expertise of the military was enhanced during this period in the reorganized General Staff. In the Marine Corps, significant innovations were made by Commandant John A. Lejeune, who pursued the development of an amphibious landing capacity for his service. Because of the marines' continued deployments to policing operations around the globe, especially in Latin America, not as much attention could be spent on planning for war as Lejeune would have liked, but the results of the marine's limited experimentation with new techniques in amphibious fighting were instrumental to U.S. success in World War II. At the same time, military aviation was advanced by mavericks within the army, especially the popular Billy Mitchell, who risked court martial to propagandize for the future of air power.[27]

Finally, with regard to the professional virtue of responsibility, military leaders were sometimes forced to guess what they were supposed to be preparing for. In the absence of direction from civilian authorities, they hit upon defense as the answer: first for the homeland; then, in the 1930s, for the hemisphere. To be consistent, army planners even made a vain attempt to persuade their civilian superiors (and their peers in the navy) to drop the pretense of being able to defend the Philippines. As for preparation for offensive operations, military planners tended to share civilian assumptions that, as World War I had been a colossal mistake, it was unnecessary to prepare for a World War II. Difficulties arose, however, as some military leaders believed the army's defense of the homeland required defense of its morals as well as its territory.

Military Service to the Nation after World War I

Old-style military service was still relevant and accepted by military leaders and civilian authorities after World War I. General Leonard Wood was sent to Illinois in the immediate aftermath of the war when pent-up labor demands erupted into riots. Reflecting his belief that foreign-born radicals were behind the unrest, Wood proclaimed his support for a "ship or shoot" policy. Similarly, the army was employed at the biggest site of unrest to respond to the violence of a general strike in Seattle.[28] General Pershing at the start of the decade, and his successor, General Charles

Summerall, at the end of the decade, both spoke proudly during this period of the army's old-style service to the nation, encompassing riot control and much more.[29]

The ubiquity of army service during the decade helped to insulate the military from yet deeper cuts during the fiscal constraints of the late 1920s. Congress liked the distributive benefits offered by military appropriations, and the nation appreciated the services rendered. Among other good works, the military operated the main barge line on the Mississippi River, mined nitrate for munitions at dams along the Tennessee River, operated and extended cable and telegraph lines in Alaska, operated steamship and canal services in Panama, and responded to natural disasters.[30]

At the same time, new-style service was embraced. In the wake of anti-immigration politics and the postwar Red Scare, the military leadership proclaimed the armed forces' responsibility for moral defense and uplift. As late as the National Test Day of 1924, the army's leadership used the Red Scare as a backdrop to advertise the value of an enlarged armed force.[31] Palmer, whose plans for army accession policy were not followed, nevertheless stated the premises of the army's new-style service orientation in a memorandum to his boss, General Pershing, before the war had been won. "Our Army will, in fact, become in peace what it has been during the present war—a National Army. The people of the country will be kept in close touch with their Army, because the people will in fact constitute the Army."[32]

The "New Era" seemed to call for a "New Army." Such a force should be imbued with a spirit of education and improvement. Consequently, the educational and vocational work of the army, which Pershing and other defense leaders had emphasized even during the most militarily stressful moments of the war, was stressed in peacetime. "The educational, vocational, recreational and character-building system is not a temporary one," explained Secretary of War Newton Baker. "It has been designed to form a permanent and essential element in the New Army." "It would be unpardonable stupid of the Army," Baker continued, "not to use every means to spread this idea."[33] Baker was highly enthusiastic about the allegedly uplifting influences of military service. In raising the force needed for the war, fully one-half of the nation's men had been judged "physically subnormal." To Baker, this was a problem that the army was well situated to address, along with such related problems as the "older boy problem" (juvenile delinquency).[34]

Such a devotion to the broadest conception of "national strength" could, of course, be taken too far. Peyton March and the officers of the General Staff tended to scoff at Secretary Baker's most enthusiastic statements.[35] Still, the army's top leadership took the idea of the "New Army" seriously. Pershing summed up the professionals' perspective when he wrote, on his retirement, "The Army's attitude toward its job has changed since the War. Service in peace or war has become the goal of its training, whether it be blazing an air route around the world or lending trucks and men to help a harassed and Christmas-package smothered postmaster."[36]

The service orientation of the New Army was maintained through the 1920s. Regular army officers continued to work with the federally funded Citizens' Military Training Camps, teaching military ideals and citizenship. In the army's public statements on its mission, acceptance of postwar reorientation was restated in numerous documents. A pamphlet, "The United States Army as a Career," proclaimed in 1926, 1929, and 1931: "The Army of the United States is the best fed, the best paid, and the best kept Army in the world. The soldier's opportunity for advancement, mentally and physically, is the best. The true soldier is a self-respecting, well-balanced and loyal citizen worthy of the respect and esteem of the Nation he serves."[37]

Did this mean that subjective control was the norm in the 1920s? To an extent, yes. The military was "controlled" by the embrace of civilian values, including the value of teaching citizenship and uplift to the young men of the nation. Military leaders were themselves in the lead, embracing the values-orientation of the New Army and pleading the case for gratitude and support from the nation on the grounds of such service.

Objective control, however, was also evident, though limited. Tight budgets and the popular wisdom that World War I was a mistake rather than a precedent restrained the gains army leaders could make when looking inward during this time. Equipment improvements and acquisition, professional training and experimentation, and planning for the return to war were all handicapped in the postwar period. But these items were constrained not so much by the competing demands of outward service to the nation as by the political and fiscal environment, which was hostile to military preparedness. Service was embraced, but in this postwar realignment, such service was not enough to earn for the military sufficient money or "space" to deepen its initial reforms.

After World War II

The realignment after World War II got its start on Christmas Day 1945. On that day, the "Army Mutiny" of the winter season erupted in the rioting of four thousand soldiers in Manila. The troops wanted to go home, and the government was judged dilatory in returning them to the United States, despite the wholesale demobilization of American forces following the war. At home, "Bring Back Daddy" clubs organized to pressure members of Congress. Soldiers flooded Congress with postcards stamped with the simple message, "No Boats, No Votes."[38] President Harry Truman captured the mood when he cautioned the cadets of West Point in 1946, "People are going to be sorry they ever saw a soldier or a sailor or a marine." "It is nothing new," the president reported with regret.[39] The end of this postwar period was the clearest of all such terminations. On June 25, 1950, North Korea began its invasion of South Korea and the nation returned to war.

Key Events

Events in this brief readjustment represented "five years of political upheaval in defense policy."[40] During the war, the need for better organization led to the creation of a Joint Chiefs of Staff to advise the president and to coordinate military plans and operations. Also during the war, intelligence activities became more centralized, and the army's air forces became virtually autonomous. These innovations established starting points for negotiation after the war. The navy sought to maintain its autonomy and feared the loss of its air component and perhaps even of the marines. The army desired a unified department of war in the Cabinet and wanted the Joint Chiefs of Staff to propose the military budget to the president, usurping Congress's constitutional role. Congressional committees, private "think tanks," and the president joined in the conflict with the service chiefs.

The result, two years into the realignment, was one of the milestones of military policy, the National Security Act of 1947. This legislation reconfigured the defense apparatus of the government. From Thomas Jefferson's administration through World War II, the Secretary of War had served in the Cabinet with the Secretary of the Navy. With the passage of the 1947 bill, the last Secretary of War, James Forrestal, became the first secretary of defense and the head of a newly named "National Military Establishment." The Establishment encompassed the Joint Chiefs of Staff (JCS) as the collective principal military advisors to the president and the secretary of defense, though with no budgetary authority. In addition, the act that created the National Military Establishment set up the autonomous United States Air Force, the Central Intelligence Agency, the National Security Resource Board, and the National Security Council (NSC). The NSC's membership, as written into law, consisted of the president, the vice president, and the secretaries of state and defense.[41] A Joint Staff of high-ranking officers from all services was created to assist the JCS.

In 1949 the National Security Act was amended to strengthen the position of the secretary of defense, to establish a chair of the Joint Chiefs of Staff (CJCS), and to increase the size of the Joint Staff. At the same time, the name of the apparatus was changed from the National Military Establishment to the Department of Defense.[42]

Several further developments in military policy took place in 1948. The Women's Armed Forces Integration Act was passed, establishing a modest foundation on which further increases would be made in the integration of women into the military; President Truman issued his famous executive order desegregating the armed forces; and, lastly, the draft was reenacted.

The reenactment of the draft was a compromise and, it was hoped, a temporary departure from peacetime tradition. Military leaders and the president wanted, again, universal military training. The public seemed supportive, at least to judge by public opinion polls. The experience of the war, after all, had made universal military training a near reality, as eight of ten age-eligible men had served.[43] But Congress would not support it. The bottom line was that universal military training was more coercive than a selective service draft, and America's liberal ideology looked with skepticism on compulsion, even in service to the nation. Opponents of universal military training succeeded because they moved the debate to the plane of a philosophical conflict between American values of individualism and liberty on one side and compulsion on the other.[44]

Supporters of universal military training after the war included, again, John Palmer, who argued that it was in fact in keeping with the American militia tradition. Besides, added Palmer, it was only training, not actual military service, that was at issue. Most Americans, however, disagreed. "Conscription was still conscription, even if it involved only a year or six months of drill and of military training in the United States."[45] Reluctant to endorse universal military training but sensitive to the army's plea for help in filling its demobilized strength in the face of a booming economy, Congress passed a "temporary" draft reinstatement in 1948, after a brief hiatus in which no draft law was in force (March 1947–July 1948).

As Aaron Friedberg observes, "But for Korea it is quite likely that by the beginning of the 1950s, the United States would have completed the transition to an entirely voluntary military format."[46] Indeed, before the Korean War began, most draft boards in 1950 were open only part-time. Voluntary enlistments had picked up, and a new peacetime manpower equilibrium seemed to have been established.[47]

Truman's order to desegregate the services was tied to the reinstatement of the draft. The point was to make the draft more politically palatable. Truman's order was nevertheless opposed by the army's leadership. An army board headed by Lieutenant General Alvan Gillem argued that "practical" considerations should prevail. Blacks, the Gillem Report concluded, should be kept separate and assigned solely to support units.[48] Truman, looking ahead to the election of 1948 and personally moved by stories of African American soldiers attacked by racists upon their return home, ignored professional advice and stopped explicit segregation within the ranks. Still, it took five years for even training camps to be integrated, and much longer for leadership integration to occur.[49]

In 1949 interservice rivalry and strategic uncertainty collided in the "Revolt of the Admirals." U.S. Navy brass sounded off against the budget slashing plans of Secretary of Defense Louis Johnson. Johnson cancelled plans for a new super-carrier and supported the air force's ambitions to be the key player in providing air power projection with its strategic bombers. The revolt was an embarrassing moment for the professional military, but it had its value. In the words of one historian, it "lifted the veil on a defense policy that was expanding military commitments worldwide while simultaneously undermining the war-making capacity of the armed forces."[50]

Civilian proponents of a stronger national security were making much the same argument at the time, most famously in the landmark study by the National Security Council, NSC 68, which argued that the nation's postwar responsibilities had grown well beyond its capacities. Massive rearmament and defense increases were imperative, the NSC concluded. The budget-minded president and his secretary of defense "would have burned NSC 68 gladly," but the Korean War necessitated that they embrace, in war, its proposals for peace.[51]

Reform

Through such key events, reforms were made in the management of defense, military manpower policy, and the integration of military interests into civilian society. Centralization was the theme of management reform as encapsulated in the National Security Act of 1947 and its 1949 amendment. When it came to manpower, the needs of the era were only partly addressed in what was to be a temporary reinstatement of the draft. As NSC 68 made clear, from a risk-averse perspective, the nation needed to do much more to address the growing potential threat of the Soviet Union. This was a clear case of doctrine—the Truman Doctrine articulated in 1948—running ahead of reality, even though it was Truman himself who proved a key stumbling block to closing the gap.[52] Congress, for its part, cut the defense budget below levels that even Truman was willing to accommodate.

According to one analyst, the result was "a lopsided foreign policy" in which Congress passed the Marshall Plan and at the same time "defeated the administration's military manpower programs meant to underpin American foreign policy in Europe."[53] Indeed, in 1948, the year that Truman articulated his famous anticommunist doctrine, manpower and defense spending fell to their lowest levels in this postwar period.[54]

Compromise was also present in manpower policy in the integration of formerly excluded persons. The military went along with the government generally in supporting policies that sent women back home after their wartime mobilization. But women's sacrifices did help achieve the limited enfranchisement represented in the new policies of 1948. The military's leadership was even more clearly opposed to the integration of blacks in the services. Against military advice, Truman pursued a more inclusive line of policy, in part to prepare for the anticipated resumption of an all-volunteer force.

The military's leadership envisioned a prolonged battle, not just against the Soviet Union, but against domestic indifference to the armed services. Thus, former Army Air Force Major General James H. Doolittle was tasked with heading a commission, the Doolittle Board, that investigated changes in the relation of the armed forces with civilian society.

The Doolittle Board worked with a private advertising company to promote a more civilian-friendly view of military service. Though in 1947 there was only one officer assigned to the voluntary enlistment program in the Pentagon, the Board's recommendations led to some lasting changes in personnel policy.[55] Pay was increased, merit was given greater emphasis over seniority in promotions, and the rights of individuals were expanded within the military justice system. On the last point, the Uniform Code of Military Justice was promulgated, replacing in 1949 the age-old Articles of War.[56]

Despite these movements toward greater integration with civilian society, the military did not, in this postwar period, take a central role in the postwar Red Scare. Still, President Truman's loyalty program was a significant endeavor, and the military participated in teaching citizenship to its own personnel. The services did not, however, seek a leading role in educating the civilian population this time around.[57]

Service

Beyond preparing for a return to war, what was the postwar military to do? First, in order of the postwar chronology and in terms of manpower devoted to the task, was the constabulary task of policing Japan and Germany. Ironically, given General Douglas MacArthur's reactionary political views at home, he and his staff looked to the New Deal for inspiration in the wholesale transformation of the Japanese political economy. They widened the distribution of income, broke up financial cartels, and encouraged labor unions.[58] In both Japan and Germany, U.S. occupation forces assaulted militarism and redesigned the defeated countries' armed forces along more democratic "American" lines.[59]

Second was the traditional job of training citizens to be soldiers, perhaps through universal military training or the continuation of the draft or through a return to voluntary enlistment. Of course, the prewar ROTC program was also continued. Third, a new dimension was added by the unprecedented scale of the war effort, which enlarged popular expectations of government and made the military a familiar institution.

The soldiers, sailors, airmen, and marines of the war would "serve" their nation now simply by returning to civilian life. Perhaps because the experience of war was the nearly universal experience of a generation, there was little popular fear of returning soldiers after this war. In fact, popular culture extolled the virtues of the veteran, and government programs to assist the veteran in his return to civilian life reached unprecedented levels of generosity.

To capitalize on the human talent of the war effort, the "GI Bill" was passed after considerable lobbying by the American Legion. The consequences for civilian America were huge. From 1944 to 1949, the government paid out over $4 billion in GI unemployment benefits, education, and job training. Half of the college students in the United States in the first three years after the war were beneficiaries of the GI Bill. More than ten million veterans of the war eventually received benefits in education and job training. In addition, more than $50 billion in home loans were made to veterans.[60] At the elite level of the military, veterans poured in unprecedented numbers into top positions in industry and civilian government.[61]

Permanent Incomplete

The balance between reform and service in this postwar period deserves a grade of Permanent Incomplete. Several issues that were not resolved before the Korean War put an abrupt end to the realignment. The gap between foreign policy doctrine and military capabilities was not addressed. The military was underfunded and undermanned for its ostensible worldwide responsibilities. Second, though service did not outrun reform in this instance, reforms themselves were not complete by the end of five years. The famous Key West accord did not satisfactorily resolve the issue of military coordination and joint responsibility in war-fighting.

As for the peacetime service performed by the military in this period, one important step was taken. This was the first postwar period in which no national political figure blasted a "standing army" as an affront to American liberties. A large peacetime military was at last acknowledged to be a necessity. To make it more enticing to volunteers, changes were made in the direction of civilianization. The military lobbied for higher pay and a better quality of life, while the president ordered that greater opportunities to enjoy these things be granted to women and to African Americans. Even after the return to war cut short the transition to an all-volunteer force, these steps toward subjective control were not retraced.

Conclusion

In the realignments after the world wars, service and reform were held in an imperfect balance, constrained by political circumstances. In some respects, the military was in a situation similar to that after the War with

Mexico. In that conflict, the military had won in impressive fashion, thanks largely to the professional leadership offered by its West Point graduates. The civilian leadership of the nation acted sensibly after the war, even recognizing the principle of an expansible army, the old dream of Secretary of War John C. Calhoun. As a consequence, when Indian troubles in newly won territories required more force, the president was able to expand the regular army in 1853–54 by 3,500 men without adding any new officers. The army's service to the nation expanded as well in the familiar ways: road building and explorations, helping in the westward expansion of the nation.[62]

Military reform after the War with Mexico was limited, though, because all knew that the army might soon be called upon to take sides in a civil war. Military strength was acceptable out West but was politically divisive anywhere else. This was not exactly the case after the world wars. Still, something similar was seen in both periods. After World War I, many people questioned the relevance of the military because they too did not want to consider the likelihood of a return to war. President Wilson had warned the nation in 1919 that the recently completed world war might soon be termed the "First," but most Americans, if they believed him, thought that a second such war, if it came, need not involve the United States. Building up military strength, critics alleged up to the very start of World War II, would only drag the nation into war.

After World War II, a majority of the voting public and leaders of both parties at last accepted the inevitability of American involvement, even military involvement, overseas on a regular basis. But the need for reform and manpower were too great to be met in the short time available before the next war broke out. One can only wonder how weak the U.S. military might in fact have become had it not been for the North Korean attack on South Korea.

These problems, however great they were, were slight compared with the twists and turns of military policy following the Civil War and the American portion of the Vietnam War. In those cases, military professionals became not merely the companions to, but the antagonists of, significant domestic political interests and parties. The military's leadership was ultimately forced by open civilian hostility to abandon the pretense of political neutrality and fight to preserve its identity and expertise. In both cases, the results were near disasters.

CHAPTER FOUR

Two Near Disasters

The realignments after the Civil War and the War in Vietnam were the least successful of all postwar readjustments. In the Civil War, an excessively new and unsupported turn toward service in the defeated South led the army to question its identity and responsibilities. Eventually, after more than a decade, the experiment of Military Reconstruction was halted, and the military turned inward to focus on reform. Something similar happened after the war in Vietnam when military leaders faced the near collapse of morale and a challenging domestic environment that gave voice to anti-military sentiment. The result was instability in military orientations. From a regrettable advertising campaign featuring the slogan "The Army Wants to Join You," the service's top leaders went on to enunciate a doctrine characterized by distrust of civilian authority. "We'll Call the Shots" was the unspoken message of the brass as it sought to incorporate the "lessons of Vietnam."

The similarity in these realignments is striking but perhaps not surprising. Both were, after all, the products of defeat. Whereas the defeat in Vietnam was clear to all, "defeat" in the Civil War is a more challenging concept. That war was a victory, certainly, for the Union army and the Union itself; but after the war, the nation faced the task of reintegrating the defeated South into the body politic. The gradual reabsorption of the defeated half of the nation undermined the attempt to use the military to reshape the South. Southern leadership won increasing gains in politics and weakened the nation's will to use force in peacetime. In both realignments, the armed forces became hostage to, and took an unusual interest in, partisan politics.

After the Civil War

The start of the post–Civil War realignment is difficult to pinpoint. The army began peacekeeping in defeated states, in fact, even before the war was concluded.[1] And at the very moment that peace was achieved, the army was already called upon to face a conventional threat from a European rival.

As Generals William Tecumseh Sherman and George Gordon Meade marched their armies to Washington, D.C., for the Grand Review that symbolically marked the termination of hostilities, the War Department sent General Philip Sheridan to command 80,000 troops in the vicinity of Arkansas. Sherman led his army south into Texas. The "free defense" that America supposedly enjoyed during this period because of its distance from Europe and the friendship of England had been revealed as a myth during the war when the British failed to block the French conquest of Mexico. Eventually a diplomatic solution, backed by the threat of force, forced a French retreat.[2] As quickly as this threat dissolved, however, so did the means to meet it. The volunteers that provided the overwhelming mass of the army during the war were rapidly discharged from duty, leaving the regular army with a slight, though short-lived, pre-1898 peak of about 57,000 men in 1867.[3]

At the same time as the War Department responded to a conventional threat, its work elsewhere in the South was consolidated in the War Department's new Freedmen's Bureau, and need in the West for its service continued as before. With regard to this last traditional peacetime task, in 1866 alone, the U.S. Army engaged in combat with Indians on at least fifty-two occasions and took 165 Indians prisoner, while killing 568 and wounding 161. In these battles on the frontier, in places as disparate as Grief Hill, Arizona; Crazy Woman's Fork, Dakota; and Camp Watson, Oregon, ninety-nine enlistees and six officers of the U.S. Army were killed in action.[4]

The end of this period of readjustment is similarly difficult to identify. Military Reconstruction came to a halt in 1877 as the result of the contested presidential election of the prior year. But in 1877 the army also was ordered into unprecedented levels of activity in responding to domestic labor unrest. The army's unpopularity with the Democratic Party—the consequence of its wartime victory plus its postwar works—handicapped its ability to perform strike functions, and the states stepped in with an invigorated militia.

In the 1880s the shunned military turned to reform, gaining sufficient momentum to continue making improvements after the retirement of the innovative Commanding General William Tecumseh Sherman. 1882 can stand, for want of a better date, then, as the terminus of this realignment. That was the year in which the War Department made its first systematic effort to study the crippling problem of desertion. The results of this self-study included practical reforms aimed at improving the quality of life for those remaining in the nation's service.[5]

Key Events

During this extraordinary period, after President Andrew Johnson declared martial law at an end in 1866, commanders throughout the South followed their commanding general's lead in quietly disobeying the president. General Grant at first kept as much distance as he could from the party politics of the age, but he could not turn a blind eye to the situation that officers faced in the South, where they were sometimes forced to appear as defendants in civil suits seeking redress and compensation for actions taken during the war.

Following President Johnson's declaration of the end of martial law, Congress began to assert increasing power over the situation in the South, passing four Military Reconstruction Acts in 1867–68, including the "Command of the Army Act." Military officers in the South were essentially given the power of conquerors to organize new governments and to bypass their reluctant commander in chief in the White House.[6] Grant, as commanding general, protected the army while preserving his political future. The novelty of the situation could be seen in the fact that Grant at one point simultaneously exercised the functions of both secretary of war and commanding general.

During the legislative session of 1871, the frustrations and contradictions of this postwar mess intensified. First, on March 9, Massachusetts' abolitionist senator, Charles Sumner, was forced off the Senate Foreign Relations Committee. Supporters of President Grant shared the war hero's wrath over Sumner's refusal to back Grant's plan to use force to annex the

Dominican Republic. Then, one month later, Congress passed an "enforcement" act, authorizing the president to suspend the writ of habeas corpus and to enforce the Fourteenth Amendment by the use of federal troops, an authority that President Grant no longer desired. The postwar government was not united on military policy. The executive had an occasional idea to use force (abroad), but Congress often balked; while Congress's efforts to use force (at home) were hampered by presidential opposition or ambivalence.

In 1873 an economic panic fueled the traditional postwar mania for retrenchment and dampened the prospects for a moderate Republican North-South alliance. The crisis in the economy consequently made the postwar realignment even more highly sectionalized politically than it otherwise might have been. In 1876 an embittered and regionally divided Congress turned on the army, which was now paid back for its role in Reconstruction. As a consequence, it took a special session of Congress in 1877 just to appropriate pay for army personnel. Officers had to borrow or rely on their own savings during the intervening period of no pay. Enlistees typically had to make do with their rations. Many calculated the risks and benefits of the situation and deserted.

Reconstruction did not end gracefully for the military. When Rutherford B. Hayes took office in 1877, there were only two Republican governors left in the South, in Louisiana and South Carolina, and they controlled only so much of their states as their meager detachments of federal troops could patrol. Hayes's claim to the presidency rested on the contested returns from just these states (plus Florida), and he did not want to appear ungrateful. But the Democrats now controlled the House and Senate, and in the last year of the outgoing Grant administration, they had refused to appropriate any funds whatsoever for the army.

In some accounts of U.S. military history, this event is portrayed as an example of the nation's casual cruelty toward its military. 1876 was the year, Colonel R. Ernest Dupuy wrote in his 1956 classic of U.S. Army history, that "the regular army really tasted the full bitterness of national indifference."[7] But Congress was hardly indifferent about the army. The Democrats who controlled the institution were violently opposed to the army so long as it remained, even in part, an agency of Military Reconstruction.

With the army reeling from a cutoff of funds, and with 1876 Republican losses in key non-Southern states, Hayes and his supporters can hardly be blamed for not searching for a military option that no longer existed.

Instead, Hayes signaled his willingness to compromise. He called the Fortieth Congress into special session and watched with approval as Republicans negotiated with Democrats for the resumption of army appropriations upon the termination of military support for the contested Southern governments.

At roughly the same time, the nation was faced with intensified demand for the army's services in the Indian Wars and for the use of troops in response to labor violence. Both situations gave the army's leaders leverage in resisting outright extirpation in the aftermath of Reconstruction. In both situations, though, the post–Civil War army's weaknesses were exposed.

In the same year that Hayes "won" the presidency, the army suffered a humiliating setback at Custer's "Last Stand." Custer's defeat spurred the military thereafter to adopt a harsher policy toward Indian adversaries. The army eventually won its war in the West, but it was not an easy affair; nor was it brief.[8]

In 1877, the Great Railroad Strike called forth a military response. After four trunk lines of the East called off a rate war, they agreed to recoup their losses by cutting wages 10 percent. The result was the first nationwide strike in the United States, which temporarily halted rail traffic in much of the country. Because of the limited size of the army (24,000), and because they were working that year without an appropriation, Hayes had to be cautious in responding to state calls for troops. The president adopted a policy of sending in troops only when requested to do so by a governor or federal judge, and even then ordering into action a force that would supplement but not supplant a state's militia.[9]

When ordered into a conflict, regular army troops and marines performed admirably in strike duty across the nation. These trained men, "by their presence alone," General Winfield Scott Hancock reported, could disperse most crowds.[10] While militiamen were accused of killing rioters, no striker was killed by a regular army soldier or marine. The use of federal troops was effective because outside of the South the public generally perceived the soldiers as they were—professionals who would do their duty without prejudice.[11]

Although the military was once again proving itself useful to civilians in peacetime, civilian hostility continued into the late 1870s. Hayes's cautious use of federal troops looked reckless to some, and in 1878 a coalition of Southern Democrats, still reeling from the Civil War, plus pro-military

Northerners concerned about soldiers being forced to operate outside the chain of command, came together to place new limits on the armed forces. The Posse Comitatus Act, passed in 1878, prohibited the army from aiding civil officials in enforcing the law unless expressly ordered to do so by the president. As a consequence, and because of the political impossibility of building up the national army in any event, the militia in many states were reorganized and buttressed into a "National Guard" of state forces. The army had become identified, not with the interest of the whole nation, but with a region and a party. Even when new domestic threats gave the army non-war-fighting missions that were less regionally divisive than Reconstruction, the military's status could not quickly be restored.

Reform

To fight the Civil War, volunteers had rushed into the services. The officer corps changed as a result, becoming less professional. In 1867, less than 30 percent of army officers were graduates of the Military Academy. At the war's start, more than 68 percent of officers had been West Point graduates. The ban on Confederate veterans in the army also drained the military of a portion of its professional experience. The new army was in fact officered by new men.[12]

The new army did not, of course, last for long. General Grant wanted a regular army of approximately 80,000 personnel.[13] What Grant and the army got was a force of about 57,000 in 1867, which then was reduced to 37,000 in 1870. The economic panic of 1873 led to a further reduction to a new equilibrium point of approximately 25,000 men, where army strength stayed into the 1890s. Parallel changes occurred in the navy, which reverted to canvas sail. A sailing navy was weak compared to potential foreign adversaries but was adequate for seaport defense and the support of U.S. trade. The major constraint was money. In fact, Andrew Johnson, in his various tactics to reduce the military as a threat to the South, found his greatest success with the simple argument that the new-sized military cost too much. Congress's plan to "govern the Southern states by military force," he warned, "may finally reduce the Treasury of the nation to a condition of bankruptcy."[14]

The bipartisan concern for economy helped, in fact, to fracture the Republican Party's support for the military. The Radical Republicans, the self-professed moral wing of the party, were increasingly charged with immoral economics. Overspending, warned leading Reform Republicans, would lead to inflation, which in their view would rob the creditor class for the benefit of debtors. In the atmosphere of the late 1860s, "the friends of sound money and sound morals" came to believe, in the words of Iowa's Republican senator James W. Grimes, that "the great question in American politics today is the financial question," which "ought to override" the continued support of Reconstruction.[15] By 1869 reductions in army strength met with virtually no opposition within Congress.

War's legacy also squeezed out new investment in the military. By 1889 it took 1,500 clerks in the D.C. Pension Office to take care of the massive paperwork involved in caring for the war's soldiers and widows. Pensions to veterans were the government's biggest expenditure item for decades.[16]

Organizational changes could often be accomplished without new funds, however, and were significant in this period. The need for reform along some lines was, moreover, impossible to ignore, as desertions drained the strength of the smallish army that Congress could agree to pay for. In 1867 when the army was authorized at 54,138 enlistees, it suffered more than 14,000 desertions. By 1871 fully one-third of the army, now at an authorized strength of about 26,000, deserted. This pattern was not reversed until the economic panic of 1873 made military service more attractive. But by the 1880s desertions again increased, reaching about 40 percent of the yearly gain from recruitment in an average year for that decade.[17]

As a consequence of these numbers, the military's efforts at reform were sensibly aimed mostly at retention. This was not exactly what the military's more innovative thinkers desired. Reformers within the navy wanted technological experimentation; they would continue to sail under wind power long after more warlike powers converted to steam. Forward-thinking officers in the army wished to increase the power of line officers. Increasing the relative status of the line against the staff, however, did not promise to resolve the issue of desertions. Staff leaders would maintain their traditional superiority.

The tone of reform in the late 1870s and the mid-1880s was captured in an article from the *Army and Navy Journal*. "In our young days," the author observed, "the recruit was looked upon as an obnoxious animal . . . with no beneficent military authority to provide for his many wants down to a pocket handkerchief. We live and learn."[18] Quality-of-life improvements for enlistees included vocational education and athletic opportunities, uniform retirement pay, new and renovated barracks and forts, and improved pay. To the disgust of professionals such as General Sherman, Sunday inspection and dress parade were discarded.

The first edition of the "Soldier's Handbook," issued in 1884, expressed the realigned army's new solicitude for the enlistee. Its tone was friendly, and it included numerous items of advice for the soldier's health and happiness. There were also reminders in the handbook for the officers who were to lead the new user-friendly army. "Military authority," the handbook noted, "is to be exercised with firmness, but with kindness and justice to inferiors." "Superiors of every grade," the booklet continued, "are forbidden to injure those under them by tyrannical or capricious conduct, or by abusive language."[19] Civilianization was the obvious theme of these reforms.

Though this period was not favorable for far-reaching changes, the army departed from tradition in two areas: the integration of African Americans into the regular army, and the improvement of officer education. African Americans had served in all of the nation's wars, beginning with the War for Independence. They had, however, been relegated to segregated volunteer units, since regulations restricted service with the regular army to "free white males."[20] In 1866, Republican Senator Benjamin Wade of Ohio successfully sponsored a bill to create within the regular army a limited number of regiments composed of African American soldiers, officered by whites. African American cavalry troops, nicknamed buffalo soldiers, served on the western frontier and earned a reputation for bravery and discipline. An effort to create regiments of Native Americans later in that era was, by contrast, so unpopular in the army and so weakly supported in Congress that the experiment was terminated after five years.

The most far-reaching military reforms after the Civil War came in the field of education. In 1874–75, during a self-imposed exile from Washington, D.C., where the corruption of the Grant administration was reaching the War Department, General Sherman digested the lessons, not just of the Civil War, but of the recently completed victories of the Prussian army. These ruminations confirmed Sherman's belief that the United States needed a more professional army leadership. The path to increased professionalism in America, Sherman believed, was education.

The army must itself become a "school," "organized and governed on true military principles." With a fortuitous change in the secretary of war,

Sherman was able to implement his ideas. General Schofield, a West Point graduate who shared Sherman's interests, was ordered to West Point, and the U.S. Military Service Institute was founded, with Sherman's aid, as a civilian lobby to support professionalism in the army.

The results of Sherman's emphasis on education were numerous. At West Point, the power of the Corps of Engineers was at last reduced so that the academy could provide a more rounded education, combining liberal arts and military instruction with the traditional focus on engineering skills. Specialized schools for postgraduate education were also strengthened or established. Fort Leavenworth in particular was the site of an important advancement, the School of Application for Cavalry and Infantry. Its work marked a step toward consolidation of doctrine within the army. Sherman also supported the career of Emory Upton, whose writings established an ideal toward which future reformers would look for inspiration, though he thought Upton was overly harsh toward civilian America. Sherman also set a personal example for the army's other senior leaders by refusing to be drawn into politics and by instructing the public at every opportunity of both the need to prepare for war and the need to do everything possible to avoid it.[21]

The influence of these changes on army professionalism overall was mixed. The corporate identity of the military came under assault during this time. The influence of formally schooled officers was weakened with demographic changes in the officer corps. Volunteer veterans who sometimes remained in the army at high positions spoke derisively of "book learning" and extolled the virtues of the untutored American as a natural fighter. The pressures and ambiguities of Reconstruction, meanwhile, fragmented the army and dragged some of its leaders into political contests either to extend or retract Military Reconstruction and the work of the Freedmen's Bureau. Sherman himself blamed the Republican Party for "every law that could be devised to put down and oppress the real soldier." Real soldiers, thought Sherman, belonged either in school or in the West, not in the defeated South.[22]

The expertise of the military was eventually advanced in Sherman's educational campaign. But this renaissance did not extend to realistic training opportunities for the small and dispersed army. In the navy, technological improvements were retarded for a long time.

With regard to the military's responsibility, there was a clear conflict. Was the army a fit instrument of political redemption in the South? Could the South, in any event, be redeemed by force? The losses had been so great that it was only natural that many political leaders thought so. But most of the army's leadership had no such interest in Reconstruction.

Service

Old-style frontier service in the West continued to be important after the Civil War. A chronological history of the army's Indian actions published by the army in 1891 takes fifty-five pages of small type to list all the battles with Indian forces from the end of the war to the date of publication.[23] However, despite its extensive service in the West, Military Reconstruction in the South was central to the army's experience in this period.

The postwar army was sent to the American South on an extraordinarily difficult mission. The most novel of its experiments involved the Freedmen's Bureau, an agency within the War Department officered and staffed by regular army personnel. The Bureau was one of the government's most important tools for governance within the defeated states from the end of war to 1872. Its history encapsulates the possibilities and frustrations of the transition from war to peace. It was the tool for the fondest hopes of some leading reformers of the time, including its leader, General Oliver Otis Howard. Its demise was at the hands of political divisions and military intransigence.

The Freedmen's Bureau was an outgrowth of wartime efforts to protect former slaves and to regulate the transition from a slave-based economy. Its commissioner, General Howard; its seventeen assistant commissioners; and virtually all of its inspectors and agents were regular army personnel.

Money problems in the Freedmen's Bureau shaped its early structure. Because Congress had neglected to appropriate funds for the Bureau at the time of its creation and afterwards sometimes neglected to appropriate money for salaries, there were few civilian employees. Even the most civilian tasks in the Bureau, such as placing values on confiscated property, reviewing the fairness of labor contracts, and designing school curricula, became jobs for soldiers. By thus employing army personnel and by renting abandoned or confiscated lands that President Johnson's policies had not yet returned to private hands, the Bureau eked out an existence.[24] The money problems of the government as a whole limited its ability to draw on even an adequate supply of military personnel, who were in typically short supply and needed elsewhere. At the high point of Bureau staffing at the end of 1868, 901 men worked for the agency, about one-third of them in purely clerical positions. By comparison, this was about half the number of civilian teachers employed by freedmen's aid societies in 1867.[25]

The effect of this parsimony was magnified by army reluctance to embrace a novel task. General Meade, in remarks uttered after the North's acceptance of Southern surrender, spoke for many in his profession when he said, "We of the Army have done our work."[26] In part, this reflected the officers' professional principles. It also coincided with their partisanship, which tended towards moderate Republicanism. They would not tolerate disrespect toward the United States and would not abide physical harassment against freed blacks, but they tended also to believe, in sympathy with Southern whites, that freedom had a baleful effect on the recently freed.

Secretary of War Stanton and General Howard were more true believing than this, and they managed to secure a leadership for the Freedmen's Bureau that was more radical than the army as a whole.[27] Still, the bureau was not where the army's more ambitious soldiers typically cared to serve. As a consequence, turnover was high in the upper ranks; and at lower ranks, Howard had sometimes to contend with the dregs of units whose commanders responded to the War Department order to detail to the bureau a certain number of men in the same manner that some of the colonies had responded to English militia calls in the 1750s.[28] With such problems, what the Bureau accomplished is remarkable.

During the Freedmen's Bureau's operation and as a result of its cooperation with hundreds of transplanted New England school teachers, approximately one of every ten blacks in the South attended school. In W. E. B. DuBois's estimation, in fact, the Bureau's most impressive accomplishment was providing constabulary support to what he termed "the crusade of the New England schoolma'am." The Bureau's educational emphasis was spurred by its leader's intense interest in the subject. Indeed, while commissioner of the Bureau, General Howard labored to establish a university open to all, including freed slaves. That university, in Washington, D.C., bears his name to this day. Fisk, Atlanta Clark, and Hampton Universities were also founded with help from the Freedmen's Bureau.

The Bureau also worked until 1869 to relieve the suffering of freed slaves and poor whites (the "refugees" of the enabling act's title) by distributing millions of rations.[29] Bureau doctors, meanwhile, tended to over half a million patients by 1869. Bureau agents accomplished other tasks as well, administering the payment of bounties to freedmen who had served in the

Union army, transporting freedmen to places where they might find work, and regulating labor contracts for freedmen with their employers. In hindsight, the Bureau's eagerness to put freedmen to work—often for their former masters and often at hopelessly low wages—seems a failure.[30] Still, to DuBois, the "labor bureau" of Howard's paternalistic officers was "successful beyond the dreams of thoughtful men."[31]

The Bureau's success was largely a result of the personal interest that General Howard took in his work. Howard was known in the papers as the "Christian General." His rectitude had been a prominent feature of his character since his youth. At the Military Academy in the 1850s, he was shunned by his classmates for his entire second year due in part to his outspoken religiosity. The impression Howard thus made on some of his contemporaries, both before and after graduation, was not flattering. "If he was not born in petticoats he ought to have been, and ought to wear them," was the sentiment of the famous Civil War leader, Joseph Hooker.

Hooker may not have appreciated him, but in the Civil War, Howard proved an able commander and was helped along by Sherman, who chose him to command the army of the Tennessee. Before the war's end, Howard began working with voluntary organizations active in the areas of his postings and wrote numerous letters to the War Department urging greater action on behalf of the former slaves. Because he had thereby gained the backing of the influential voluntary organizations active in freedmen's relief, Lincoln selected him for the Bureau's leadership.

Before he accepted the job, Howard received what proved to be prophetic advice from his mentor. "I hardly know," Sherman wrote, "whether to congratulate you or not, but of one thing you may rest assured, that you possess my entire confidence, and I cannot imagine that matters, that may involve the future of four millions of souls, could be put in more charitable and conscientious hands." The problem, as Sherman went on to point out, was that "though in the kindness of your heart you would alleviate all the ills of humanity it is not in your power. Nor is it in your power to fulfill one-tenth part of the expectations of those who have framed the bureau." But Howard thought the appointment providential. He had no choice but to accept, and he believed earnestly that he could erase the hostility between the races "if we can only bring the whites to do the Negroes justice."[32] Howard's conviction that he was doing God's work was probably what gave him the strength to withstand the difficulties he encountered as commissioner of the Freedmen's Bureau.

After the Bureau's end, Howard had to defend himself against a Court of Inquiry, a political tool of conservative Republicans who wished to discredit his work. From the point of view of these racially conservative Republicans, the Bureau had accomplished its greatest possible good in the presidential election of 1868 when General Grant won election with the votes of 450,000 blacks in a contest where the margin of victory was just over 300,000.[33] While Howard was found guilty of no wrongdoing, he had to spend thousands of dollars of his own money to defend himself before this inquiry and against several civil lawsuits alleging injury from Bureau decisions.

The Bureau's greatest failures were those it shared with the army as a whole. The military occupation of the South, of which the Freedmen's Bureau was an agent, ultimately failed to secure even those minimal changes in the South's racial hierarchy that would have brought the region into conformity with the Constitution, as newly amended. The Bureau's most active period ended at the close of 1868. From 1869 to the end of June 1870, the Bureau's only work besides the paying of bounties was the furtherance of education for blacks. In the summer of 1870 the appropriation from Congress for even this task was exhausted and was not renewed. The work of non-Bureau military personnel in Reconstruction continued, however, for several more years.

There were about twelve thousand regular army troops in the South in 1868, about six thousand the next year, and from 1872 to 1877, about three thousand.[34] Their duties overlapped considerably with those of the Freedmen's Bureau personnel. In fact, for so long as the Bureau remained in operation, the position of district commander in the occupation army's military zones and assistant commissioner within the Bureau were combined in the same person.[35] As such, army personnel were the enforcers, when they had the capacity for the job, of the Bureau's orders.

Army personnel within and outside of the Bureau sought to implement the government's Reconstruction policies regarding voting registration, election balloting, labor contracts, the regulation of commerce, and other decidedly civilian items. Often, officers had to divine for themselves what the government's policy might be, because all three of the government's branches would sometimes weigh in on an issue, such as precisely who was eligible to hold office or to vote in a Southern state.[36]

The demise of the army's role in Reconstruction is often dated as the moment of the political bargain that sent Hayes to the White House after the muddled presidential contest of 1876. But Military Reconstruction had by that time all but ended anyway. The evidence was in plain sight. The government's "enforcement" acts, outlawing the Ku Klux Klan and similar organizations, went unenforced. In state after state, whites staged vigilante rebellions against Reconstruction governments and black voters, "redeeming" state governments after the military withdrew. Sometimes, as in Georgia from 1869 to 1870, a state was returned to military rule; but the military could only maintain justice so long as they remained physically on guard. In the 1870s, and especially after the economic panic of 1873, neither the president nor most elements of the northern Republican Party favored the military's use in the South.

The gradual withering of political support for the military in the South caught some brave southerners off guard. In North Carolina, for a prominent example, the Reconstruction governor, William Holden, declared two Piedmont counties in rebellion in 1870 and sent state militia to take control. The militia succeeded but incited charges of mistreatment from whites. To quell the unrest, Governor Holden asked three times in 1870 for federal troops to be sent to the region. Each time, President Grant evaded the request. Finally, Grant ordered that six companies of army troops be sent to Raleigh and that a small number from this force be dispatched to trouble spots as needed. The commanding officer in Raleigh was ordered, however, not to permit his troops to be enrolled as a police force.

Fearing that locally controlled juries would be overly solicitous of the fate of rebellious citizens arrested by the militia, Governor Holden suspended the writ of habeas corpus and ordered military tribunals to try the men. When the defendants won a federal order overruling the governor, President Grant backed up the order.

During this standoff in the hills, state elections in North Carolina returned large majorities for Democrats, except in the two counties where regulars stood guard at the polls. The new legislature promptly impeached and convicted Governor Holden. Seeking aid in Washington, Holden found his pleas unanswered by the president.[37]

This scenario, with variations of locale and actors, was played out many times. Several years later in Texas, for example, a West Point companion of President Grant, General Joseph Reynolds, sided with Reconstruction Republicans in a dispute over election returns. The result was a victory for Radical Republican candidates in the election of 1869. In subsequent campaigns, however, whites in Texas put Radicals on the run. In a final effort to save the Reconstruction government, armed Republicans fought Democrats for physical control of the capitol following the gubernatorial election of 1873. In response to requests from local commanders for permission to use their forces to quell the violence, President Grant again refused to intervene.[38]

Grant may have been callous, but he was not indifferent. He acted as he did, or refused to act, because he was a peacetime politician; and peacetime politicians, especially when they have no particular agenda to pursue, go where the people lead them. By the time of the Texas controversy, the Republican Party of the North had all but written off the Reconstruction governments of the South.

Reconstruction governments had developed two principal liabilities. First, they could no longer be counted on to deliver votes when needed. If the Freedman's Bureau had been able to achieve General Howard's dream of a reconciliation of the races in the South, the Republican regimes in the defeated states might have developed roots in the region, but this did not happen. Republican votes from the South could be had, but only at the price of persistent and costly military enforcement of racial justice. With the rise of liberal Republicanism in the North and Midwest in the 1870s, this price began to seem unduly high. But why not continue to use force, or even escalate the reliance on force, to eradicate at least the threat from the redeemers and the Ku Klux Klan? This question points the way to the second great obstacle to indefinite military performance of peace operations in the South: to use the military in this way was unseemly.

Liberal Republicans thought Reconstruction unseemly because it violated their principles of economics. It promised government help to freedmen, but only free and unfettered competition in the marketplace could assure justice to those who labored. In articulating this belief in the sanctity of market competition, liberal Republicans voiced a conviction, associated before the war with the Free Soil Party, that slavery was an injustice to whites, who by being forced to compete with slaves, lost dignity along with a portion of their wages. Liberal, or Reform Republicans, were particularly anxious to avoid the creation of a class-based politics in the South. Radical Republicans who espoused land redistribution and who extolled the work of the Freedman's Bureau in negotiating favorable labor contracts for African Americans were, to men such as Francis Lieber, Edward Godkin, and James Russell Lowell, "Red Rads" out to create a black "proletariat" in the South. "What is bad among ignorant foreigners in New

York," declared Lowell, "will not be good among ignorant natives in South Carolina."[39]

Even radical Republicans recoiled at the ugliness of their task. Sometimes they went so far as to rationalize an end to forcible Reconstruction as an act of charity to southern blacks. So long as Congress funded the armed occupation of the South, white redeemers would be moved to acts of terror against blacks. One can imagine many in the North asking: "Might it not be better, ultimately, for everyone, if the trouble were stopped?" To such minds, the violence of the Klansmen and their like acted as a form of extortion. Reconstruction, from this perspective, became intolerable because it was so plainly military.

The inescapably violent nature of Reconstruction became a national issue with events in Louisiana. With a 50 percent black population and prominent black and racially mixed gentries in New Orleans, Louisiana was perhaps the preeminent battleground of Reconstruction. In 1871 and 1872, rival factions within the state's Republican Party fought for control. President Grant tried to tread lightly because James Casey, the husband of Grant's wife's favorite sister, was prominent in one of the factions and because he did not want to drive non–Radical Republicans over to the Democrats in the 1872 election. After Grant's reelection, however, the rival gangs and a resurgent Democratic Party continued to clash, sometimes violently, and always with pleas by the radical forces for assistance from the army. In 1874, seemingly inspired by the infamous "White League" slaughter of blacks in rural parishes, some 4,000 armed anti-Radicals in New Orleans took to the streets and captured the City Hall, the statehouse, the state arsenals, and police stations before barricading the city's streets. Under orders from Grant and with the dispatch of three gunboats and five thousand additional troops, the insurgency collapsed until November's state elections.

The election returns of November promised further trouble: forty-six Democrats and forty-six Republicans won seats in the state legislature, with five contested spots to be awarded by the new, presumably deadlocked legislature. To head off the possibility of more violence, Grant ordered General Sheridan to investigate and to take command of federal troops in the area if necessary. At the legislature's first convening, Democrats seized power by kidnapping several Republican legislators and bodily laying hold of the speaker's rostrum. Thereupon Sheridan took command of federal troops in the area and awarded the government to the Republicans. Sheridan recommended to President Grant that all supporters of the White League in Louisiana be arrested as "bandits" and tried in military tribunals.[40]

Sheridan's recommendation was received with no enthusiasm in the White House. In fact, the general's brusque action, which included bringing armed troops into the statehouse and taking over the position of sergeant at arms, led to a furor in the North. Vice President Wilson, House Speaker James Elaine, Secretary of State Hamilton Fish, and a chorus of other prominent Republicans expressed outrage. In a presidential message of January 13, 1875, Grant apologized for this distasteful and illiberal event. Later that year, the Washington National Republican, a loyal administration paper, proclaimed the Reconstruction Amendments "dead letters" in the South.[41] In the balance of Northern opinion, injustice to blacks, especially now that the taint of slavery had been lifted from the re-United States, was outweighed by shame that army troops should be the arbiters of an election.

In 1877 the army made a partial turn toward a new peacetime role: strikebreaking and riot control. But police duty did not come to occupy much of the army's energy because Democrats in Congress were still wary of the army. Nonetheless, the army proved itself capable and even sometimes eager for such service. Even the quintessential reformer Upton extolled the utility of the army in responding to the problems of the time. "During the late riots," wrote Upton, "had there been available from twenty-five to fifty battalions of national volunteers, commanded by regular officers, it is possible, and probable, that much of the bloodshed and loss of property might have been avoided."[42]

Overall, this realignment reflected an over-extension of an under-supported redirection in military responsibility. The eventual turn inward led to a renaissance in military thinking but without a commensurate reform in operations, strength, or plans.[43]

After the Vietnam War

The post–Vietnam War realignment began when a reform-minded Congress took action on the nation's security apparatus. In 1973 Congress passed the War Powers Resolution and focused attention on covert operations and intelligence gathering. Earlier in the Cold War, and throughout most of the Vietnam War, the legislature had done penance for its old isolationism. With defeat in Vietnam, Congress sought to reclaim its prerogatives over military policy.

The War Powers Resolution is familiarly analyzed as proof of the "resurgence" of Congress. In fact, it has proven a weak restraint. Its constitutionality has never been acknowledged by a U.S. president. Its "clock," meant to force a president to quit an engagement or seek Congress's approval, was started by Congress only once (12 October 1983). Ironically, the War Powers Resolution may even have strengthened the president's hand in military operations by formally recognizing the president's power unilaterally to send troops in harm's way for at least a limited time. It thereby "legalizes a scope for independent presidential power that would have astonished the Framers," observes a respected analyst of executive-congressional relations.[44]

Of greater consequence in 1973 was the end of the draft and the movement toward a more integrated and reserve-reliant military force. The All Volunteer Force (AVF) was a response both to liberal criticism of the conduct of the Vietnam War and to a rising libertarian/conservative critique of national government power. From the libertarian perspective, the draft was an illegitimate expression of the government's power to compel obedience. The draft, said libertarian-minded reformers, was merely a form of "taxation."[45] Selective Service, eased in the early 1970s, was terminated in 1973. How, in the absence of the draft, would the military be able to meet its personnel needs and at the same time remain closely linked to the nation's broad middle class?

The answer was the "Total Force." Military professionals who joined with civilian reformers to implement the Total Force Concept "papered over recruitment shortfalls" to ensure that the military would never again be ordered into war without the mobilization of the nation—a presumed prerequisite when reserve forces are to be used in combat. Reserve units were, as a consequence, integrated into the nation's war plans, with key functionality located among reservists.[46]

Another part of the effort to meet manpower needs in a volunteer force was the greater integration of women and minorities into the services. In 1967 the formal ceiling on the proportion of the service that could be female (2 percent, set in the aftermath of World War II) was abolished. In 1972 the ban on women in ROTC was likewise lifted, and in 1976 women were admitted to the service academies for the first time. The proportion of the services accounted for by women rose rapidly to double digits.[47]

Similar increases were observed in the proportion of blacks in the services, especially the army. The proportion of black NCOs rose from 14 percent of the army in 1970 to 26 percent at the end of the decade.[48]

This realignment came to a troubled and incomplete end in the Persian Gulf War of 1990/91, which marked the end of explicit post-Vietnam planning and reactions. President George Bush stated in the aftermath of that war that Vietnam had at last been exorcised from the nation's conscience. In fact, the war suggested that the ghost of Vietnam, though weakened, still haunts the Oval Office.[49]

The president, guided by his national security team—and in particular Colin Powell—accepted a trade-off in the war that made sense in light of Vietnam but that left the security of the region in doubt, as became evident in the presidency of George W. Bush. The overthrow of Saddam Hussein was a desired end product of the first Gulf War but not a goal. The president reportedly expressed his personal desire for "some kind of Ceaucescu scenario."[50] It was, in other words, a thing merely to be hoped for. In fact, when rebellious Shiite Muslims in the south and Kurds in the north revolted against the Hussein regime in the aftermath of the Iraqi defeat in Kuwait, the American response revealed doubts as to whether the Bush administration truly wished Hussein out of power. It all depended on the costs involved. If it meant the "Lebanonization" of Iraq, that was perhaps too high a price to pay. If it meant protracted U.S. military involvement, in the words of CIA Director Robert Gates, "Therein lay Vietnam, as far as we were concerned."[51]

This was surely a prudent course to follow, but it left many Americans unmoved. It also revealed some of the fine print, so to speak, in the post-Vietnam civil-military bargain. A president may have his war, but the military must have a clear-cut victory. Objectives that might lead to a murky end state are to be avoided, even at the cost of leaving large security issues unresolved.

Key Events

Key events during this period were relatively few in number. Defeat chastened the nation in the use of its forces. The first two post-Vietnam presidents, Gerald Ford and Jimmy Carter, used the military only in operations to evacuate or rescue Americans from trouble.[52] Even in Ronald Reagan's administration, characterized by a pro-military attitude, the Vietnam legacy restrained possible military use. As after the World War I, the public was still skeptical of the use of the armed forces, though more positive about those who served. Isolationist sentiment flourished in the United States and found new voice in domestic politics. In addition, a popular myth evolved that the nation had been duped into the entire Cold War. Government leaders were assailed by the new isolationists for their alleged lack of credibility and their subservience to the "Merchants of Death."

The adversary culture of the 1960s matured in the post-Vietnam era. Floating in a sea of affluence, who wanted to fight a war? "Make Love Not War" was more than a slogan. In a humorous reflection of the interconnectedness of the era's transformations, Vietnam Veterans Against the War grew into a national organization after Playboy magazine donated space for a full-page advertisement.[53]

For the armed forces, restraint was forced upon a military establishment that was in no condition to be adventurous in any event. In real dollar terms, defense spending began to decline in Fiscal Year 1969, and "by the end of the Nixon-Ford administrations, had dropped 25 percent below pre-Vietnam levels. The defense budget share and defense GNP share dropped sharply as well, with both declining to pre-Korea levels."[54] The Reagan administration built on a midterm turn in military policy under the Carter administration. In Reagan's first four budgets, inflation-adjusted rates of spending increased by an average of more than 7 percent each year.[55] Still, the purported lessons of Vietnam clung to the military.

In the Reagan years, even when armed forces were used, they were restricted to short, decisive operations. Beirut in 1983 began to promise a lengthy mission and thus was terminated in haste. Grenada in 1983 and Libya in 1986 were model post-Vietnam engagements, extremely limited in duration and in exposure of U.S. troops to the risk of casualty. In problem areas where force was called for but the conditions of rapid use and limited casualties did not appear to hold, the United States merely provided weapons and some training, as in Afghanistan, Nicaragua, and El Salvador. In these last two countries, military leaders reportedly blocked what might have been the introduction of U.S. troops into combat situations.[56]

Despite this prevalence of non-events, three key moments of decision deserve to be highlighted. First, in 1979 Army Chief of Staff General Edward "Shy" Meyer declared that the nation was protected by a "hollow army." His assertions were made, not just to the president in private, but to Congress in public testimony. This was the opening wedge of the period's focus on inward reform and a new self-identity. With General Meyer's backing, the army introduced a new, more professional recruitment and advertising campaign. A new emphasis on training for war was given concrete expression in the National Training Center.

In 1984, in the midst of the "Second Cold War" of the Reagan administration, Secretary of Defense Casper Weinberger, guided by his military aide, General Colin Powell, set forth a six-part statement of conditions on the use of force (the Weinberger-Powell Doctrine). As paraphrased by an analyst, "Essentially they were: (1) Vital interests of the nation or its allies must be at stake; (2) A clear commitment to victory must exist; (3) Political and military objectives must be clear; (4) Forces must be properly sized to achieve the objectives; (5) Reasonable assurance of public and Congressional support must be secured prior to intervening; and (6) Force must be used only as a last resort."[57]

This doctrine's publication stemmed from a controversy within the Reagan administration over the use of forces in Lebanon, where after "mission creep," 241 marines were killed in a single terrorist bomb assault. In making his statement, Weinberger fulfilled the familiar role of the military-minded civilian reformer, championing the military professional's point of view. Like the military chiefs he ostensibly led, Weinberger worried that the buildup in military capacity of the 1980s might loosen the post-Vietnam restraint on the use of force.

In 1986, finally, the Goldwater-Nicholls Act was passed after years of hearings and controversy. This act strengthened the chairman of the Joint Chiefs of Staff. The chairman's role went from that of facilitator to leader, from soliciting the votes of the other chiefs to consulting with them and, if need be, merely keeping them informed. The entire Joint Staff now worked for the chairman, as did the vice chairman.[58] The reform directed the chairman to utilize his staff to advise the secretary of defense on budgets, programs, and requirements, providing the legal as well as practical foundation for the chairman to become the key player in the design of the armed forces.[59]

Most of the chiefs lobbied hard against this reform. The chief of naval operations even warned of following a "Prussian" example. But the ineptitude of the military to perform joint operations had recently been on display at Desert One (1980) and Grenada (1983), making the chiefs' complaints appear insensitive to a real need for change.[60]

The result, according to those who judge the change favorably, was a restoration of needed balance within the Pentagon, putting senior military leaders on a more equal footing with the civilian secretary of defense, whose role had been strengthened in the 1960s by Secretary of Defense Robert McNamara.[61] Inter-service cooperation, "jointness" in military lingo, was further promoted by a requirement that candidates for promotion to general officer perform joint duty, and that general officers, once promoted, attend a mandatory capstone course at the multi-service National War College.

Reform

Reform got off to a rough start in this era. Of those who entered the military from 1972 to 1974, only 16 percent felt positive about the military, compared to 64 percent of those who entered in 1961–65.[62] Even so, the move to the All Volunteer Force (AVF) and related changes worked better than most observers thought possible. Even as late as the mid 1980s, thoughtful analysts wondered whether the AVF would ever succeed. In fact, Eliot Cohen concluded in a 1985 publication that AVF had already failed. Among other criticisms, he noted that in 1980, 48 percent of recruits had been brought in at the lowest acceptable mental category.[63]

Other commentators noted at about the same time, though, that a change in the nation's attitude towards the military was in progress, led by the pro-military Reagan administration. Reagan was committed philosophically to the AVF. He had, in fact, criticized the Carter administration in his campaign of 1980 for "letting down the nation's defenses" and for seeking to bolster them "by taking steps to restore the draft" (Carter's largely symbolic decision to require Selective Service registration).[64] The later 1980s provided evidence that the military and the nation had found a way to make the AVF work. Enlistee morale, recruitment success, and the quality as well as the quantity of the forces all improved.

In the Gulf War, the soldiery of the AVF proved its willingness to fight, and its commanders demonstrated their ability to make good use of the Goldwater-Nicholls Act's changes in command. The services fought jointly under the strong leadership of the chairman of the Joint Chiefs of Staff. The weaknesses of the AVF and the Total Force Concept (TFC) were, however, also seen about this time. By 1989, more of the army's manpower was in the reserves and the National Guard than in the active force. But in the Gulf War, the much-talked-of fighting contribution of the TFC's National Guard "round-out brigades" was nugatory.[65] If they had truly been required, the largely political rationale behind their creation would have been rightly subjected to intense scrutiny.

Women in the Gulf War served throughout the forces and served well, by most accounts. However, the Gulf War did not provide a critical test of the post–Vietnam War reform integrating women more fully into the services. Only a war in which U.S. forces faced daunting casualties could provide such a test. Ironically, the experience in the Persian Gulf nonetheless bolstered the political leverage of the proponents of further female integration into the remaining gender-exclusive areas of service.

The influence of post-Vietnam reforms on military professionalism was complex. The military certainly overcame a crisis in morale and identity. Near the end of the war, the army in particular was no longer functioning well, with alarming rates of drug abuse, insubordination, "fragging" of officers, and assorted other problems. The war in Vietnam had to end, said one officer troubled by such incidents, for the army to be saved.[66]

The termination of the draft seemed to confirm the suspicions of military professionals that the country had turned its back on the services.[67] Though the end of the draft did not, in fact, signal anti-military hostility, it did threaten military identity in a more subtle way. By treating military service as merely a "tax," the civilian reformers who introduced the AVF put forth a model of "service" that made a mockery of its very name.[68] If serving in the military were just a job like any other, by what right did officers impose their will upon subordinates? Why should anyone take a job that did not promise good pay and advancement opportunities? Why take a job where discipline was required twenty-four hours a day?

At first the army, with its large manpower needs, jumped on the civilianization bandwagon, promising recruits a more relaxed, validating experience. In time, with the change in zeitgeist witnessed in the 1980s, observers of the AVF came to believe it suffered from an excess of corporate identity: those who served too often had an elitist attitude and had become dismissive and even contemptuous of the civilian nation they were meant to protect. The problem of over-identification with civilian society had transformed into its opposite. At the end of the 1990s, the tensions between civilian values and the values of the military were the subject of an intense debate over an allegedly dangerous "gap" between two cultures (discussed in a later chapter).

Even military leaders with positive feelings about contemporary civilian culture worried in the 1990s that the civilians did not really support their men and women in uniform. "The mercenary issue is an important one for us," commented a senior member of the Joint Staff in a confidential interview with this author. At the close of the post-Vietnam transition, the corporate identity of the services was strong but was headed into trouble; the link of the military to civilian society would become a central issue of military policy.

The expertise of the military was enhanced as a result of reforms made in the aftermath of the Vietnam War, with one big unresolved problem. The army came back from its "hollow" stage; the navy prospered under strong leadership in the 1980s; the marines set the pace in their emphasis on values instruction; and the air force capitalized on tremendous improvements made in the 1980s in the accuracy of its munitions. The ability of these services to fight together was enhanced. Commanders became better leaders as they served longer command tours and were subjected to the harsh testing of the National Training Center. So where is the unresolved issue? It is back, so to speak, in Vietnam.

Did the military at the end of the decade have the necessary expertise to fight and win a similar war if it had to? The military leadership's reluctance to return, even in doctrine, to Vietnam was striking at the close of this realignment. The Vietnam War was a footnote to studies at West Point, and the armed service's guiding principles of engagement seemed to mark Vietnam or anything remotely like it "out of bounds."

The conventional military critique of the Vietnam War castigated civilian leadership instead of looking inward to assess how well or how poorly the military's leaders faced the challenges of such a war. The "Praetorian Critique" of the war might sometimes mete out criticism of military commanders, but only for alleged complicity in civilian mistakes, not for a failure to establish a winnable strategy for limited warfare.[69]

In terms of its responsibility to the nation, the post-Vietnam military was guided by the Weinberger-Powell Doctrine. The military, said its leaders and defenders, was to be used for "real" wars or not at all. Once the Cold War ended, nationalist violence flared up in parts of the former Soviet Union. The result was a dramatic increase in warfare, but not in the sort of big, mechanized war that the U.S. military preferred to fight. The Weinberger-Powell Doctrine therefore established the groundwork for certain conflict between the nation's reluctant warriors and any commander in chief who hoped to shape with force the new world order emerging from the ashes of the Union of Soviet Socialist Republics.

Service

If the military was responsible to the nation, how was it to demonstrate its responsibility? The irony was that the services were not often called upon in the 1970s, once the pullout from Vietnam was completed. Despite this, some critics thought the armed forces were overly receptive at this time to "stimulus to overinvolvement in efforts to maintain social relevance."[70]

Just as after World War I, the military's brass proclaimed a "New Army" and threw its energies into such programs as vocational training for soldiers, alcohol and drug rehabilitation, and various forms of uplift. Especially controversial was the continuation into peacetime of Secretary Robert McNamara's "Project One Hundred Thousand," designed to lift that many people into a better life by bringing them into the army despite failing to qualify. Some critics thought that such efforts might even get an unfortunate boost after the war, as the Special Forces and their commanders brought their "nation building" expertise back home with them. Indeed, a small Special Forces program was launched in Appalachia after the Vietnam War. But the overall pattern was not one of overuse of the services for civilian purposes. Instead of being overused, the services suffered the indignity of being ignored.

Civilian indifference reflected ignorance, according to some military critics. "One could almost make the case that we have done our job too well," wrote the celebrated Lt. Col. Harry Summers in 1976. "We have protected the American people from the horrors of war so well that many believe that such horrors do not exist."[71] As Summers noted, the tendency of the military when faced with such indifference was to "play hedgehog." This, in effect, is what happened. The Weinberger-Powell Doctrine was the ultimate credo of the military hedgehog.

The drift in military service was toward elitism over the course of the latter half of this realignment. The military could "serve" the nation by being more military than it was before; by turning even the AVF into a thoroughly professional organization. Pay, benefits, and quality of life generally would be addressed over the 1980s; but philosophical and doctrinal changes pulled the military apart from, rather than closer to, civilian

America. "One role of the American military establishment," suggested a veteran in the journal of the Army War College, "may be to become stewards of values that, neglected by the country as a whole, may yet revive if continuity is to be preserved." So that it might hold up to the nation a reflection of its better self, the services must fight, the author continued, the "yearning for popular esteem."[72]

Ironically, the greatest actual service the military provided the nation in the post-Vietnam era was perhaps its sheer cost. The rebuilding of the military that occurred in the second stage of this realignment helped expose the inefficiencies of the Soviet Union to its own leaders. Perhaps not surprisingly, the military's elite was as unprepared for the end of the Cold War as it was in the 1980s for a return to limited warfare. The consequences linger in the post–Cold War environment. "We are very blunt" with our students, reported an instructor at West Point in the year 2000, "that in the future their experiences will be closer to Vietnam than to Desert Storm. At the same time, for our policymakers, the Vietnam Syndrome is still there." When pressed, however, neither this instructor nor his colleagues interviewed for a *New York Times* story on West Point saw any way the U.S. Army could have won in Vietnam.[73]

One wonders what these future army leaders were being taught: that they should try to avoid at all costs being ordered into the very sort of engagements that they are most likely to face? that there is little hope they could actually win such battles if they are forced to fight them? that it is all the civilians' fault? The military was not "over" Vietnam when the Gulf War ended, and they were not "over" it as the century drew to a close.

Conclusion

What did not work in these two near disasters? In one, an excessive reliance on subjective control mechanisms. The experiment of Military Reconstruction was so radical that it divided the army against itself and ultimately alienated a large portion of the civilian population against the regulars. The professionals turned inward after their rejection in politics and accomplished much, but what they achieved was largely on the plane of theory. It would take another war and another century to align a renaissance in thought with meaningful reforms in organization, manpower, and capabilities.

In the more recent case of Vietnam, there was the opposite problem: an excess reliance on objective control. Of course, the civilians did not exactly pick this method of control. Its choice was made by the military's leadership with the significant help of civilians such as Secretary of Defense Weinberger. The consequence was a highly professional force but one that was to some extent alienated from civilian society and hence often skeptical of civilian command.

CHAPTER FIVE

Military Reform and Service in the 1990s

The previous three chapters have shown a range of possibilities for postwar periods. These chapters have provided historical detail to help "operationalize" the concept of "good" civil-military relations for the postwar period and understand what conditions contribute to such relations. Achieving balance between military reform—looking ahead to the next war—and military service to the nation in peacetime—which embraces more than war preparations—was defined in Chapter 1 as the ideal of postwar transitions. The cases demonstrated what balanced and imbalanced reforms have looked like in practice and suggested that balance requires that military professionals struggle to maintain a core of professional identity in peacetime.

At the same time, we saw that military professionalism can be maintained and even enhanced when service leaders accept a partial redirection of time and energy toward tasks on which civilians put a high priority, even if they are not tasks military leaders are enthusiastic about. This is particularly the case when such tasks address a vital interest of, even if not a threat to, the nation. The performance of such tasks keeps the military in touch with core national commitments and underlines for a skeptical public the present value of military organizations. In short, performing civilian-oriented tasks in peacetime sustains the armed forces' connection to civilian America.

What conditions are most conducive to this happy state of affairs? How have military and civilian leaders in the past achieved balance between subjective control, inherent in the redirection of military effort toward civilian tasks, and objective control, enshrined in military efforts at professional development and preparations for war? What, in more theoretical terms, are the independent variables associated with the dependent variable of good civil-military relations? Identifying such independent variables was a primary motivation for the case studies just completed. What, then, have we found?

First, cooperation among civilian and military leaders has been an element of each successful reform. The reorganizations of the military after the War of 1812 and the Spanish-American War, in particular, were products of military-minded civilian leaders working with reform-minded military professionals. Given the military's absolute reliance in the American system on civilian political support, there is only so much—such as the educational initiatives of the post–Civil War army—that can be achieved without this cooperation and support.

Second, political consensus has been vital, especially to sustain support for peacetime missions. This was difficult to achieve after the Revolutionary War, but the emergence of consensus underlay the role of Thomas Jefferson as a supporter of the military profession. The lack of consensus on the contemporary utility of the military has, by contrast, led to disastrous failures in peacetime, as in Reconstruction. Without consensus, military involvement in civilian affairs has led naturally, and regrettably, to involvement in partisan politics. Involvement in politics has left the military at the mercy of the shifting winds of partisan change.

In this chapter, we turn to the first decade of the post–Cold War transition. As we saw in the Introduction, no clear resolution in civil-military relations was achieved during this time. The subjects that caused controversy among military planners in 1989 were the same subjects that caused serious divisions in 1999. Should women be allowed in ground combat? Should the services be open to homosexuals? What is the military's responsibility for missions other than war? Should the military services be redesigned and reconfigured for peace missions and/or for new types of war? The model developed in this study of civil-military relations and of what contributes to good relations suggests that to the extent that such questions remained open at the close of the decade, the reasons lay in the status in this decade of our independent variables. In other words, the reasons were a lack of civil-military cooperation and an absence of consensus on the role of the armed forces.

Beginning and End

The realignment after the end of the Cold War started with Pentagon planning efforts. In 1989, as the Berlin Wall fell, military leaders began to plan in earnest for a post-Soviet-threat environment. The chairman of the Joint Chiefs of Staff, General Colin Powell, took the lead in these efforts, beginning the planning process that took shape in the Base Force Plan—the minimum requisite force of a superpower, even a lone superpower, Powell thought. The end of what we may term stage one of this realignment occurred symbolically as the same General Powell, now in civilian attire, was sworn in as secretary of state for the second President George Bush in January 2001. Stage two, which encompasses events of September 11, 2001, and the debate over a strategic doctrine of preemption, will be addressed in Chapter 6.

Key Events

The decade of the 1990s was a busy one. Key events occurred in the areas of operations, planning, and policy.

Operations

The decade began with the Persian Gulf War of 1990/1991. Although the war was a massive undertaking, the repercussions on the home front were limited, in part because the war was such a lopsided event. Iraqi military casualties numbered in the tens of thousands; United Nations forces lost 200 men and women from hostile fire. More than half a million Americans served in the war, yet combat losses among American personnel were 122 from the army and marines, 6 from the navy, and 20 airmen. The loss rate in the air was, in fact, below the normal accident rate in combat training.[1]

The war did, however, make a media celebrity of General Colin Powell, chairman of the Joint Chiefs of Staff at the time. Powell achieved the status of a folk hero for his impressive performance on the Cable News Network (CNN). In one of his televised briefings, Powell announced: "Our strategy to go after this army is very simple. First we are going to cut it off.

And then we are going to kill it."[2] Tough talk was in keeping with the dictates of the Weinberger-Powell Doctrine's renunciation of half-measures.

Despite carnage in Iraqi bunkers and tough talk in Washington, "for much of the country," David Halberstam observed in 2001, the Gulf War "was a kind of virtual war, something few people were engaged in or had sacrificed for. Thus, like many things celebrated in the modern media, it was distant and oddly non-participatory; when it was over, it was over, leaving remarkably little trace."[3]

In the world wars, homes displayed gold stars to signify the loss of a family member. In the Gulf War, yellow ribbons and American flags decorated homes and cities, representing more often a painless patriotism rather than a personal sacrifice.[4] Voters demonstrated the limited impact of the war on the home front. On the theme of "It's the Economy, Stupid," the decidedly non-military Bill Clinton won election to the presidency. Adding insult to injury, in 1995 a French cultural critic, Jean Baudrillard, offered an account of the war as a postmodern simulacrum, under the title *The Gulf War Did Not Take Place.*[5]

The army had gotten the message even before the president. While President Bush rhetorically framed the Gulf War as the opening of a New World Order, military planners recognized it early on as a false starting point. The U.S. military would not often fight against so inept a commander and with a collective force that everyone knew was going to be dismantled in the post–Cold War drawdown. Still, this war had consequences for military policy. The Goldwater-Nicholls Act proved its worth to most observers, as did the All Volunteer Force (AVF) and the Total Force Concept (TFC) that provided its domestic foundation of support. The proponents of the "Revolution in Military Affairs" took inspiration from the performance of precision-guided munitions, while detractors warned of the illusion of "clean" warfare. Perhaps the most enduring legacy was, ironically, a new if somewhat arbitrary standard by which to measure proposed reductions or reconfigurations of forces. The "Gulf War equivalent" was a shibboleth of military planning throughout the 1990s.

During the eight years of the Clinton administration, numerous military deployments led to a remarkable increase in the tempo of operations and the demands on military personnel. Over the course of the decade, the rate of overseas deployments increased 300 percent. There were no fewer than thirty-five "small scale contingencies" to which the U.S. military was required to respond in the 1990s. As a consequence, the average soldier or marine was deployed 140 days out of the year away from his or her home station in 1996; the navy routinely kept half its ships at sea; and the air force saw a 400 percent increase from Cold War norms in the rate of personnel deployed away from home base. The reserves were increasingly called on to contribute to such missions. In fact, reserve force contributions to active-duty missions increased 1,200 percent in the decade.[6]

As one group of analysts observed, "The very competence the U.S. military has displayed in successfully responding to a wide variety of contingencies seems to have encouraged its further use."[7] At the same time, the U.S. Air Force suffered a significant decline in the number of overseas bases from which to launch such missions.[8] The particular missions that engaged the military during the 1990s included Somalia, Bosnia, Haiti, and Kosovo.

In Somalia, 25,000 American military personnel were sent by President Bush in 1992 to take a leading role in what began as a United Nations humanitarian mission. The usually reluctant military leadership virtually volunteered to send troops on this humanitarian mission. In the words of one observer, this was "Powell's way of doing something humanitarian but, equally important, *not* sending troops to Bosnia."[9] However, there was tension from the outset between the military's perspective on what might be accomplished and Secretary of State Madeleine Albright's optimism. Albright described the operation as "an unprecedented enterprise aimed at nothing less than the restoration of an entire country as a proud, functioning and viable member of the community of nations."[10] Under the pressure of such unrestrained idealism, and in response to "mission creep" on the ground, Delta Force commandos and rangers found themselves ambushed during a raid on a Somali war lord's temporary headquarters. On October 3, 1993, eighteen American soldiers were killed, and television cameras relayed to the world the sight of one of the dead being dragged through the streets of the Somali capital.

The president and congressional leaders, anticipating a public demand for withdrawal (despite public opinion polls that demonstrated perseverance in the face of this incident), announced that the United States would pull out by the end of March 1994.[11] President Clinton's first secretary of defense, Les Aspin, was forced to resign, having failed to provide the forces in Somalia with tanks and armored personnel carriers, the use of which might have averted the disaster on the ground. Aspin's departure conveniently shifted criticism away from the decisions that the president and his

secretary of state had made about the United States' overall policy in Somalia.

The Bosnian operation appeared at first considerably more dangerous.
It too was inherited by President Clinton from his predecessor. In June
1992 a UN protection force had been deployed to keep a fragile peace in
a growing civil war. There had been considerable debate over the wisdom and necessity of U.S. involvement. President Bush, supported by the
chairman of the Joint Chiefs of Staff, Colin Powell, resisted direct U.S.
engagement. The public had difficulty in maintaining clarity over who was
fighting whom and for what purpose in the former Yugoslavia, and there
was an atmosphere of exhaustion in the White House following the Gulf
War. General Powell, meanwhile, continually gave the president the highest plausible estimate of how many Americans would be needed *on the
ground* should the United States commit to intervention.[12]

Candidate Clinton, unable to criticize the incumbent over the popular
and generally successful Gulf War, occasionally took time away from his
economic agenda to promise air strikes and "heat" in Bosnia. Once in office, televised violence and the incapacity of the European Union to resolve the crisis eventually forced President Clinton to give form to these
promises, amid criticisms of "foreign policy by CNN."[13]

In Operation Deliberate Force, a U.S.-led NATO force, working with a
Bosnian ground offensive, forged the conditions necessary for a peace
agreement. At an air base in Ohio, the presidents of Serbia, Croatia, and
Bosnia-Herzegovina agreed to a new partition of the Balkans. The Dayton
Accord, signed November 21, 1995, would be implemented by some 60,000
soldiers under NATO command. The U.S. role included contributing
20,000 troops to the Implementation Force (IFOR). Though this was only
a tenth of the troops that General Powell had said the United States might
need to deploy, the administration still felt the need to downplay the commitment. The troops would be withdrawn in a year, administration officials promised Congress. This was understood for what it was, a political
fig leaf to cover the operation through the 1996 presidential election. At the
end of the decade, approximately four thousand U.S. ground troops were
still "keeping the peace" in Bosnia. The NATO force in Bosnia is now
tasked, in fact, with an open-ended "Trusteeship," trumpeted by NATO as
"a new weapon in the armoury of international interventions."[14]

The Haitian mission in 1994–95 was driven in the first instance by U.S.
domestic politics. President Clinton, responding to pressures from mem-

bers of his party in Congress and to Florida politicians fearing an "invasion" of Haitian refugees, sent a force that, at the last minute, halted their advance while former President Jimmy Carter with the ubiquitous General Powell, at that moment in retirement, brokered an agreement on the island. Haiti's military dictators were permitted to stay in the country, but U.S. forces were able to wade onshore facing TV cameras instead of small arms fire. A U.S. intervention force of 20,000 remained in Haiti from September 1994 to March 1995, during which time Jean Bertrand Aristide returned to the country to resume his elected presidency. More than 2,000 U.S. troops were left in Haiti after March 1995 as part of a 6,000-person UN peacekeeping force. In congressional testimony, U.S. commanders criticized this indefinite assumption of a constabulary role in a barely functioning state as futile and wasteful.[15]

In Operation Allied Force, U.S. air power was used, beginning March 24, 1999, to "demonstrate NATO seriousness," to "impact the Yugoslavian military," and to deter a wider Yugoslav offensive against an ethnically distinct population in the province of Kosovo.[16] At first, Yugoslav forces intensified their offensive in the wake of U.S.-NATO air strikes. President Clinton seemed to invite trouble when he publicly declared, "I do not intend to put our troops in Kosovo to fight a war." Nevertheless, in early June 1999, after eleven weeks of bombing and with a ground offensive by the rebel Kosovo Liberation Army, coercive diplomacy once again seemed to work.

The tensions and disagreements within the administration, including disagreements between civilian and military leaders and among military leaders themselves, over getting involved in Kosovo in the first place and how to fight the "war" for its liberation, were still plainly evident at the operation's conclusion. General Powell and other military commanders called it "Madeleine's War," making reference to the interventionist secretary of state.[17]

Even victory could not erase the considerable antagonisms that had built up over Kosovo within the military. The commander in the field, General Wesley Clark, the Supreme Allied Commander in Europe, had become enamored of coercive diplomacy while serving as chief military deputy to Richard Holbrooke, the civilian negotiator who engineered the Dayton Peace Accord. Clark, according to his own account, had to struggle against a reluctant Pentagon at every step of the intervention, especially when it came time to plan for the possibility of ground combat.[18] To the contrary, argues Andrew Bacevich, Clark wobbled dangerously in the planning and conduct of his operation. In the planning phase of the operation, he refused to take seriously the threat that his strategy might force the United States into a costly ground war. Once it became clear that he had put false hope into his ability to predict his opponent's reactions, he lobbied strenuously to begin preparations for a ground offensive and to deploy, toward this end, attack helicopters. Clark's miscalculation had caused the United States, according to Bacevich, to "blunder into an open-ended conflict against an unpredictable, surprisingly defiant foe and with the future of NATO hanging in the balance."[19]

The Pentagon's senior military leadership worked behind the scenes to slow down the operational availability of the attack helicopters. In the air campaign, because the U.S. government "was, for all practical purposes, unwilling to countenance the loss of a single American soldier," the United States waged its war from high altitude, giving "the principle of noncombatant immunity" "short shrift." The role of the U.S. military in Kosovo, as a consequence, was not to fight battles but "to deliver ordnance."[20]

After the bombardment had ceased and before an Apache helicopter had fired a shot in anger, the Joint Chiefs of Staff squeezed Clark out of command in Europe prematurely.[21] At the end of the Clinton administration, the fate of Kosovo was still in question, and approximately 6,000 U.S. forces remained on the ground.

Planning

While these and yet other operations were ongoing, military planning underwent three waves of comprehensive reassessment. From 1989 to 1993, Chairman Powell was clearly in charge. The result was the Base Force Plan. Powell was motivated, he explained, by a desire to do things right "for a change" in an American retreat from war. Pentagon watchers were already clamoring for a "peace dividend" from the end of the Cold War.[22] Powell was determined not to permit a wholesale destruction of Cold War forces. To finesse the issue of threat, Powell turned the Pentagon toward capabilities rather than threats as the central concern of planners. The biggest threat of all, Powell warned, was the absence of a clear threat![23]

The two most important changes in strategy announced in the Base Force Plan were a reorientation toward regional conflicts and the need to fight "come as you are." The United States could not, that is, count on having the luxury of mobilization or "reconstitution" when facing threats from rogue states or nonstate actors. In addition, President Bush explained in a major address on the new policy delivered on August 2, 1990, American security would require continued high levels of investment in research and development. To support these plans, the Base Force called for twelve active duty army divisions, eleven active air force tactical fighter wings, three marine division equivalents, and twelve aircraft carrier groups, plus a substantial but reduced reserve component for each service.

Les Aspin, a critic of the Base Force Plan while serving in Congress as chair of the House Armed Services Committee, was appointed secretary of defense by incoming President Clinton. At the Pentagon, Aspin sought a "Bottom Up Review" (BUR) of defense needs, releasing a statement of his plan in September 1993. The BUR rationalized further reductions in forces from Base Force levels by emphasizing the reduction in threats since the Gulf War's end. In planning force levels, the BUR turned away from capabilities and back to threats. The standard was a "two Desert Storm equivalent," meaning that the United States would need just enough forces to fight simultaneously two wars equal in intensity to Desert Storm. In this way, Aspin and his civilian policy staff rejected the strategic caution that had underpinned the Base Force Plan.

The BUR gave priority to near-term threat scenarios, especially from Iraq and North Korea, but it was essentially silent regarding potential longer-term conflicts that might emerge from China and Russia. In truth, though, neither the threat scenarios that were specified nor those that were not drove the BUR's conclusions. Rather, in the words of a longtime Senate staffer involved in defense legislation, the BUR was motivated by the need to "downsize the Base Force to fit into a lower budget ceiling. Strategic rhetoric had to be superimposed on a budget-driven exercise."[24]

Despite the fact that the Clinton administration's national security strategy emphasized the importance of "shaping" the international environment and "engaging" rather than reacting to or containing potential adversaries, the BUR offered little rationale for military involvement in such efforts and thus undersized the ideal force for the United States.[25] To paper over the gap between stated objectives and contemplated resources, the Clinton administration assumed reliance on the United Nations for peacekeeping and shaping exercises. Even so, only under the most optimistic assumptions could the BUR force accomplish its stated objective of confronting two "nearly simultaneous" major regional conflicts. The difficulty of maintaining readiness for even one such event while using the same personnel and equipment in numerous smaller scale contingencies was largely ignored. Despite these flaws, the BUR targets for force structure were accepted by Congress. Shortly thereafter, however, the Republican Party returned to power in Congress, having campaigned in part on the need to reinvigorate the military.

Republicans in Congress focused attention in committee hearings on what they saw as an alarming decline in military readiness, but divisions among Republicans prevented Congress from offering a forceful critique of the Clinton administration's direction in military planning. Defense budget resolutions for the last half of the 1990s closely followed presidential requests. As David McCormick noted in his 1998 study, *The Downsized Warrior*, "1995 was most notable for the fact that surprisingly little changed. As the consequence of a split between deficit hawks and defense conservatives within the Republican Party, the defense budget resolution for fiscal years 1996–2000 passed by Congress in June 1995 was similar in content and scope to Clinton's own budget proposal."[26]

In 1995–97 Congress did, however, provide the initiative for the last of the decade's reviews of military planning by requiring the secretary of defense to undertake the first Quadrennial Defense Review (QDR).[27] By forcing the Clinton White House to show its hand on defense, the Republicans in Congress provided themselves the opportunity to criticize administration planning and actions, especially Clinton's use of armed forces in peacekeeping. The QDR also provided a forum for military planners and interested civilian experts to debate the overall direction of military reforms. Outside analysts in particular alleged in this process that both the Base Force and the BUR had been budget-cutting exercises disguised as strategic planning. If anyone or anything was in control, they alleged, it was inertia and incrementalism.

The QDR nevertheless did take some additional steps toward the inevitable rethinking of defense in a radically changed international environment. It announced a planned reduction of active military personnel to 1.36 million, from a mid-1990s baseline of approximately 1.5 million and a 1989 reference point of 2.1 million. The force structure, however, was anticipated to be essentially the same as called for by the BUR. A procurement budget increase to 60 billion dollars per year was set as a goal to be achieved in 2001. In keeping with Clinton administration strategy statements, the QDR was premised on a policy of engagement in which military forces would be used, not just in defense of vital national interests, but also of those deemed "important but not vital." For humanitarian missions, the QDR envisioned the use of U.S. forces in cases where a catastrophe "dwarfs the ability of civilian relief agencies" and where risks to U.S. military personnel is "minimal."

Congress, still under Republican control, mandated in 1996 that the secretary of defense fund his own critics who would critique the QDR. The National Defense Panel, a group of academic and military experts critical of Clinton-era defense policy, issued a report in December 1997. It criticized the QDR for giving insufficient attention to asymmetric threats from terrorists and rogue states and for understating the problems of readiness, procurement, and cost reductions.[28]

Policy

In terms of military policy, important events likewise occurred in the 1990s, especially in terms of personnel. The recent gains of women in the services, as indicated earlier, were tied to the introduction of the AVF. With the end of war, the alleged "costs" of further opening the military to women were obscured, and old restrictions seemed suddenly as archaic as the Cold War itself. By the end of the decade, 99.4 percent of U.S. Air Force positions and 80 percent of military specialties overall were open to women as well as men. The changes in the navy and marines were most dramatic. Before 1993, 61 percent and 33 percent of positions in these services, respectively, were open to women. At the end of the decade, the figures were 90 percent and 62 percent.[29] The remaining restrictions, including Special Forces, infantry, heavy artillery, and submarines, were all being debated at the end of the 1990s. Even with the Cold War drawdown in effect, the Department of Defense was the nation's number one employer of women by the middle of the decade.

With women comprising almost 14 percent of the total force by the late 1990s, the Defense Department under President Clinton strongly supported the greater integration of women in the military. A commission appointed by Secretary of Defense William Cohen in 1997 to study gender-integrated training came out strongly in support of such training, despite a series of damaging sexual harassment claims lodged against male instructors by female recruits in gender-integrated environments. The reality was both that women were vital to the military's operations and that women might well sustain heavy casualties in future combat.[30]

On a different manpower issue, the Clinton administration erred tactically when it devoted its first week to a different issue of personnel policy, the role of gays in the services. President Clinton had made a campaign promise to lift the ban on gays, but when he attempted to fulfill that pledge, he discovered that his power over military personnel policy was far from absolute. The Joint Chiefs of Staff, openly siding with conservative members of Congress from both parties, rejected Clinton's proposal.[31] The resultant compromise, "Don't Ask, Don't Tell," was crafted chiefly by Senator Sam Nunn. By the end of the decade, that policy was still controversial, and discharges from the military on account of sexual orientation were in fact on the increase.[32]

Reform

As big as what did happen was what did *not* happen in the 1990s. There was no equivalent to the National Security Act of 1947 or the National Defense Act of 1920 in the rethinking of national security structures. Instead, the Goldwater-Nicholls Act provided a reference point for more modest reform. As chairman of the Joint Chiefs of Staff, Colin Powell leveraged his authority within the parameters of the act and took unprecedented leadership over military planning and policy. His leadership was so transparent that critics charged he had contributed to a "crisis" in civil-military relations. Powell vehemently denied that there was a crisis, but in the official Joint Staff history of the Base Force Plan, Powell's role is emphasized, and the comparative weakness of civilian authorities is described in almost gloating detail.[33]

Despite Powell's leadership in planning, President Clinton ultimately was responsible for decisions on the use of "Powell's" forces. In the eyes of some analysts, Clinton's decisions constituted a coherent, if flawed, doctrine.[34] The goals of the Clinton Doctrine were engagement and enlargement.[35] Engagement of potential adversaries—which meant many things but not, presumably, warfare—was identified as the path to the enlargement of democracy. The Clinton Doctrine envisioned the use of U.S. forces, moreover, not just to promote "vital interests" of the United States, but "important interests" and "humanitarian" objectives as well, provided the potential costs were not too great. The armed forces therefore incorporated the reality of its use in missions other than war in successive planning statements over the 1990s. In a Joint Publication issued just weeks before Powell's retirement as chairman, the Joint Chiefs, in fact, set forth a military rationale for limited operations, arguing that the use of *decisive* force can at times undermine the long-term objectives for which U.S. forces might have been employed in the first place.[36]

In July 1996 a new chairman of the Joint Chiefs of Staff, General John Shalikashvili, issued a comprehensive planning statement for the military's post–Cold War development. *Joint Vision 2010* embraced seemingly all missions, old and new, and provided the template for a force that would be capable and prepared to engage in politically complex international situations limiting the use of force.[37] The emphasis of *Joint Vision 2010*, however, was on war fighting. Its tenets, as identified by a "Red Team" analysis headed by Air Force Colonel Charles Dunlap, are "technological preeminence and an uncompromising faith in the superiority of the individual [American] soldier."[38]

The army's own vision statement, "Army After Next," showed that their leaders, too, wanted to "do it all." "Maintaining and shaping the peace," the Army After Next project observed, "is a continuous task." The use of the term "shaping," prevalent not just in this army document but throughout late-Clinton-era planning statements, suggests the military's growing savvy in meeting, at lest rhetorically, the demands of the 1990s. The pace of "shaping" missions, the Army After Next team acknowledged without complaint, might well increase in the future.[39]

The navy, meanwhile, changed its orientation from deep water to littoral operations, while the air force broke the Cold War paradigm that associated "strategic" weapons with nuclear devices. The air force, moreover, took concrete steps to increase the efficiency with which it could undertake a high tempo of operations. After spending several years resisting nonvital missions and even curtailing training, the air force "finally got the message," proclaimed Air Force Chief of Staff General Michael Ryan on August 5, 1998. "Some of these contingencies are not going to go away," he observed at a Pentagon briefing. In response, the air force reorganized its active duty, guard, and reserve components into ten teams, two of which would be "ready to deploy quickly on any kind of mission, remaining on alert for a 90-day period every 15 months."[40]

At the highest levels of command, civilian wishes were gradually incorporated into military doctrine throughout the 1990s. The power of the president over the selection of the military's "upper management" is surely important here. President Clinton's final chairman of the Joint Chiefs of Staff, General Henry Shelton, seemed to warn the incoming Bush administration not to anticipate radical changes in the Clinton Doctrine when he stated publicly after the election of 2000: "It is naïve to think that the military will become involved in only those areas that affect our vital national interests."[41]

At lower levels among the officer corps, however, there was an overwhelming sense in the decade of waiting out the storm. "If only" Bill Clinton were not so ignorant of the military, "if only" we got a combat veteran back in the White House, "if only" the top brass would resist co-option by the White House, things might be different.[42]

One thing junior and senior officers agreed on was that the forces were underfunded.[43] Budget constraints clearly motivated major changes in force structure and strength, though they did not greatly influence the president's ability to employ forces in missions other than war. Under the Base Force Plan, active duty army personnel were expected to drop from 750,000 in 1990 to 535,000 by 1997, with more modest declines elsewhere, resulting in an overall reduction in active-duty forces from 2,009,500 to 1,632,000.[44] The BUR projections further reduced force levels, with troop reductions coming close to 200,000 fewer than Base Force levels, keeping with Clinton's campaign promises. Army divisions were to drop from 18 to 10, not 12. The QDR, for its part, envisioned reductions in the military building blocks of only the air force, from 13 to 12 fighter wings. The budget slashing had begun to stabilize. The architects of the QDR envisioned a year 2002 end strength of 1.36 million personnel, a 34 percent drop from the height of the Second Cold War in 1987, accompanied by a 32 percent reduction in Department of Defense civilian personnel and a 22 percent reduction in the reserves.[45]

These downturns in force planning reflected a real decline in the military's share of GNP, from 7 percent in FY1987 to 3.2 percent in FY1998. The military was receiving the smallest share of the federal government's budget by FY1998 since Pearl Harbor (15 percent, compared to 28 percent in FY1987).[46]

Still, these reductions were more sensible and orderly than in any other twentieth-century postwar period. In part, this probably reflects real increases in the professionalism of the Defense Department and the strength of the national security decision-making apparatus. However, it also almost certainly reflects the strange way in which the Cold War was "won." The Reagan years reflected a form of military mobilization, but it was slight compared to what might have been had the Cold War had a "hot" ending. From this perspective, the post–Cold War drawdown was modest because levels of spending fell from a comparatively modest height. It was also significant that the military rallied at the end of the Cold War with momentum from post-Vietnam reforms. Military planners were more determined than ever to have "no more Task Force Smiths" (in addition to no more Vietnams).[47]

The budgetary and non-budgetary changes in the forces witnessed through the various rewrites of the 1990s were challenged by critics. Republicans alleged that the first QDR, just like the Base Force and the BUR, had failed to face the difficult task of setting boundaries around what the smaller forces of the United States could and could not do in the future. "All things to all people," complained the Republican chairman of the House National Security Committee, Floyd Spence. Democrats, for their part, wanted even more radical accommodations to peace. There were, from the Democratic point of view, too many nuclear weapons in our post–Cold War arsenal; too much spending, which might encourage potential adversaries to enter an arms race; and too little effort spent on "shaping" initiatives. Such was the criticism offered by Ron Dellums, the ranking Democratic member of the same committee, in hearings on the QDR.[48]

Academic critics of the reform process of the 1990s questioned the seriousness of the military's professed ability to conduct two Major Regional Contingencies (two Desert Storm equivalents) simultaneously. Also, outside analysts wondered aloud about why the military remained enamored of force projection as a priority and why they persisted in using "force on force" thinking as the basis for war planning. Homeland defense, not war fighting abroad, some experts warned, might emerge as a critical military mission if rogue states or terrorists decided to launch comprehensive attacks on the United States.[49]

At the end of the decade, military policy was relatively stable as the nation awaited the outcome of the presidential election of 2000. Many officers were hopeful that a change in administrations might bring about a change in attitudes and priorities and thus provide an opening for a new emphasis on preparing for "real" wars. If this suggests poor civilian and military cooperation, or even military foot-dragging, that is in line with Michael Desch's analysis of civil-military relations during this period. From 1990 to 1997, Desch "coded" only four "wins" for civilian leadership in civil-military disputes in the United States. The civilians had their way, according to Desch, on only the selection of a strategy for the Gulf War, the FY 1994 budget reductions, the Haitian "invasion," and air force responsibility for the Khobar Towers bombing in Saudi Arabia. The military, in Desch's view, prevailed in seven other conflicts: Bosnian intervention in 1992, gays in the military, strategic change from win-win to win-hold-win, the military pursuit of Bosnian war criminals, restrictions on land mines, and the conditions of the discharge for an adulterous air force officer. Desch codes the conflict over women in combat as providing a mixed result, with neither party prevailing over the other. This pattern is markedly different from what Desch observed during the Cold War and from 1938 through World War II, when civilians almost always prevailed in such disputes.[50]

To Desch, this shift represents the indeterminacy of the structure of civil-military relations in the strategic environment of that decade. Peter Feaver analyses the pattern of civil- military relations in the Clinton administration similarly, though in terms of principal-agency theory. Military leaders were emboldened during this period to shirk their responsibilities to their commander in chief because the perceived benefits to the profession outweighed the perceived costs of such a course of action. The president, for his part, was a peculiarly weak commander in chief and lacked the informal authority to keep his military chiefs under firmer control.[51]

From the historical review offered in these pages, I would add that the military's loss in Vietnam is also relevant here and that it is not military "victory" in civil-military conflict that is the real problem of present military policy. It is, rather, the *nature* of what the military leadership is pursuing. As noted above, military leaders now consider it their duty to prevent civilian "mishandling" of "their" services and have made a principle out of reluctance to mix service with reform.

What, then, have been the consequences of post–Cold War reforms for the professionalism of the U.S. military? With regard to the corporate identity of the force, the post–Cold War drawdown has brought to the forefront two related questions for those in military service: Are we warriors? and Are we mercenaries? The first question reflects a common problem area in professional identity after war when the military is required to shift more of its resources to peacetime activities. The second issue is a particular problem of the All Volunteer Force and its high rate of deployment in multinational operations where the benefits flow to allies at least as much as to the United States.

The mercenary issue did not become critical in American politics in the 1990s because our military avoided heavy casualties in its deployments as an All Volunteer Force. In late 2002, however, as the president threatened to send the United States back into war against Iraq, the issue was raised by Democratic Congressman Charles Rangel (NY), who proposed reinstating the draft to ensure "shared sacrifice" in the event of war.[52] Without a draft, he argued in numerous televised appearances, the president and members of Congress are tempted to use the American military as a sort of "foreign legion."[53] If those in the services ever come to share Rangel's perspective, it could warp the military's identification with civilian society.

Overall, surveys of officers in the 1990s showed a decline in morale and a lowering of expectations of the rewards of a military career. This showed up, among other places, in a decline in the proportion of military officers who reported that they would recommend military service to members of their families or to their friends. Younger officers in particular worried that civilian leaders and high-ranking military leaders did not have their best interests at heart.[54] The downsized army experienced corresponding declines in expressions of esprit de corps and concerns about the perceived rise of self-interested behavior throughout the officer corps.[55]

Two leading defense analysts in 2001 looked back at changes in the corporate identity of the post–Cold War military and welcomed what alarmed others. The soldier, they noted, was seldom called upon in the 1990s to be a "warrior." "Some more relevant identity," they wrote, "is in order." Recalling the sort of service to the nation described in this book, they go on to suggest that "in the experiences of blue jackets and blue-coated and khaki-clad soldiers of old lies an identity as servants of the nation that may convey more accurately and more completely the vital role" of today's military professionals.[56] However, they note that the issue is very much in debate, since "traditionalists" can be expected to react strongly against such recommendations.

The expertise of the military in this postwar episode was in some respects maintained well above that of previous postwar periods. There were, however, troublesome signs of a reduction in the perceived benefits of military education among officers themselves and a widespread desire among them to learn more civilian-relevant skills in order to prepare for a return to the civilian workforce.[57] Behind such changes, however, lies a bigger issue: What, exactly, should the military be expert at?

Retired Army Lieutenant Colonel Ralph Peters, a prolific contributor to debates about military policy, believes that the services are relying excessively in their planning on the anticipated benefits from America's advantage in applying information technology to warfare. Real warfare in the future, Peters believes, might well involve the United States in low-technology urban battle.[58] Other critics of the drift in military thinking toward technological frameworks similarly voiced concern at the end of the decade for the military's expertise in preventing and responding to terrorist attacks on the United States.

The responsibility of the military in the 1990s was an open question as well. With little consensus on the identity of the professional forces and their priorities in terms of expertise, it is not surprising that there was also little agreement on the extent to which U.S. forces should be responsible to global interests or "merely" to the United States' clear national interests. The Clinton Doctrine's rationale for the use of U.S. forces to respond to global crises, sometimes irrespective of U.S. national interests, left many officers and interested civilians unpersuaded.

Service

In the Cold War the military acted, not alone, but as part of a national security apparatus. That apparatus provided service to the nation in a number of indirect as well as direct ways. The Cold War provided a major impetus to the expansion of civil rights and empowered the Department of Defense to serve the nation through the Academic-Industrial Military Complex. With the Cold War at an end, it is worth asking whether these institutions and the services they provided will now erode. The first task is to examine how the Cold War built up these institutions—for example, civil rights.

In 1944 Gunnar Myrdal published his massive research compendium, *An American Dilemma: The Negro Problem and Modern Democracy.* In the foreword, written by the director of the American foundation that paid for the research, the connections were made explicit. "When the trustees of the Carnegie Corporation asked for the preparation of this report in 1937," wrote F. P. Keppel, "no one (except possibly Adolf Hitler) could have foreseen that it would be made public at a day when the place of the Negro in our American life would be the subject of a greatly heightened interest in the United States, because of the social questions which the war has brought in its train both in our military and in our industrial life. It is a day, furthermore, when the eyes of men of all races the world over are turned upon us to see how the people of the most powerful of the United Nations are dealing *at home* with a major problem of race relations."[59] Myrdal himself noted the importance of the war to civil rights. "In fighting fascism and Nazism," he wrote, "America had to stand in front of the whole world in favor of racial tolerance and cooperation and of racial equality."[60]

After the war, revelations about the Holocaust made it even more difficult than it had been during the crisis for Americans to ignore the resemblance between their own apartheid-like system of racial separation and the horrors of National Socialism. The Supreme Court, in striking down the anti-Asian land law of California in 1948, described that law as "an unhappy facsimile, a disheartening reminder, of the racial policy pursued by those forces of evil whose destruction recently necessitated a devastating war."[61]

Not only in the United States but throughout the world, the rule of whites over nonwhites collapsed during the Cold War. This created a vast new domain of nonwhite nations for whose favor the leading world powers vied. Any number of American statesmen drew the obvious conclusion. Truman's secretary of state, George Marshall, warned, "The moral influence of the United States is weakened to the extent that the civil rights proclaimed by our Constitution are not fully confirmed in actual practice."[62] Truman himself risked a white backlash in the 1948 election in reaching out to blacks by calling for civil rights as a war measure. As Truman wrote in his memoirs, "We could not endorse a color line at home and still expect to influence the immense masses that make up the Asian and African masses."[63]

Cold War pressure to expand civil rights similarly influenced President Dwight Eisenhower. Like Truman, Eisenhower acted where presidential authority permitted a strong hand: in the military, in federal agency employment, and in the District of Columbia. His administration was pressed by civil rights organizations to terminate segregation in military base schools and to work toward "the progressive elimination of segregation in the armed services."[64] The armed forces themselves became highly sensitive during this time to race relations. In the 1950s and into the 1960s, the services were desegregated and then integrated, ending discrimination in base housing, recruitment, training, and retention. Beginning in the 1970s, the leadership of the armed forces was integrated.[65]

At the commissioned level as well, opportunities for blacks expanded during the Cold War. Ironically, the Vietnam War, though highly unpopular among black civilian leaders, accelerated this trend. During Vietnam, elite, largely white universities such as Harvard terminated ROTC on their campuses. The resultant slack was picked up by the nation's historically black universities and colleges. Just after the close of the Cold War, twenty-one such institutes in the South and Border States were granting half of all black army ROTC commissions.[66] The armed forces, especially the army, grew during the Cold War into a major force for economic advancement and opportunity among African Americans.

During the Cold War, the military similarly provided "service" to the nation indirectly through its part in the Academic-Industrial-Military Complex. The AIMC was a typically American response to the demand for a constant stream of innovative technologies. The military provided almost all the money, gave some of the direction, but did little of the actual work. The basic approach was decentralized procurement. Ideology shaped this response by sharpening the interest of U.S. policymakers in distinguishing their methods from those of the adversary. In this regard, it is worth noting that the military's leadership preferred a more hierarchical approach, parallel to the War Industries Board of World War I. Civilian leadership, including Congress, the president, and industrialists, resisted such a move and prevailed, with "institutional devolution and policy constriction" following close on the heels of the Korean War.[67]

By incorporating research agendas into their contracts with the government, major defense suppliers blurred the lines between scientific research and product development and inculcated an ethos of innovation. Scientists doing pure research at IBM and Bell Labs, two of the Defense Department's major research contractors, even won Nobel Prizes for their efforts. Characteristically, their research led to advances in basic knowledge but had potential for military application.[68]

Regardless of who actually spent it, the sheer magnitude of sums spent was key. Defense spending was in fact the engine that drove the overall U.S. research and development effort from the 1950s through the 1980s. Department of Defense expenditures represented a majority of total federal support for research and development during this lengthy period.

If one includes National Aeronautics and Space Administration (NASA) funding and the approximately one-half of the Department of Energy's R&D spending that was devoted to nuclear weapons during this time, then military-related spending accounted for well over half of federal R&D spending. As Aaron Friedberg points out, there was a rough equilibrium throughout the Cold War, with about 75 percent of federal R&D dollars going to defense from 1955 to the end of the conflict.[69]

Congress also passed laws during this period creating some new bureaucratic machinery in the Department of Defense to give science greater standing within the military. Carl Vinson still worried about "Prussian" commanders and "a future man on horseback," but Eisenhower wanted "a real boss over research and engineering." A compromise was reached with the creation of a new office, the Director of Defense Research and Engineering, and a new agency, the Advanced Research Projects Agency (ARPA, or sometimes, DARPA).[70]

DARPA started out as the government's space agency, just as the president's science advisor was at first known as his "missile czar." But DARPA quickly lost out to NASA (another 1958 legislative product) and the air force in space research. So in 1959 DARPA was reconfigured as a "rapid strike force" in science and technology, able to pour critical sums of money into areas of research (materials science, for starters) that seemed to have the potential for breakthroughs.[71] The agency evolved over time into a major player in the nation's scientific and engineering community. It typically spent only a fraction (less than 10 percent) of the Defense Department's overall research and development budget, but its spending choices carried great weight in the research community. In the 1960s, for instance, at a time when the American academic base for designing computer chips was eroding, DARPA established an Information Processing Techniques Office that "spawned the first departments of computer science" at American college campuses and created the Internet. Email, computer graphics, interactive computing, and networking are among the computing techniques that can be traced directly to DARPA.[72]

American academia was an eager partner in the research and development effort spearheaded by DARPA. Academia in this country was well situated to grasp the opportunities afforded by the Cold War for several reasons. First, many of our largest and most ambitious institutes of higher education had enjoyed a research orientation since the creation of the "Research University" in the 1920s and 1930s.[73] Also, they had emerged from

World War II as even larger and more important institutions than they had been before. Ironically, while it was being fought, World War II interrupted and retarded the growth of scientific personnel. Overall, "the loss occasioned by World War II in the number of doctorates produced in science was in the neighborhood of 10,000, possibly much higher."[74] This created pent-up demand that was released in the reaction to Sputnik.

Additionally, there was the obvious significance of science to the new era of warfare and the new close relationships between government decision makers and scientists that were a product of the wartime frenzy of innovation. This new relationship was given concrete form in the procedures worked out during World War II for the awarding of research grants to scientists outside of the government. In those procedures, the government accepted responsibility for underwriting the general operating expenses of American private as well as public universities.

Peace has been difficult for all these institutions. In civil rights, "civilianization" is in evidence. The advancement of African Americans has been tied up with the imperatives of military struggle for at least the past fifty years. With the collapse of foreign threats, this particular pressure for civil rights has been all but erased. Coupled with the post–Cold War drawdown of the armed services, the result in the 1990s was a climate of open racial recriminations and widespread pessimism on the prospects for racial harmony. The fate of racial preferences in education, government, and corporate employment and contracting was an open question at the end of the decade.

It is impossible to know for sure, but had the Cold War still been ongoing in the 1990s, the nation's bipartisan establishment, including our presidents, might have done more to defend the civil rights status quo. The changes that have been made in California and Florida, for instance, might have been interpreted as an embarrassment to the nation and its international-minded elite if there were still "Third World" opinion to take into account.

The effects of civilianization on civil rights are even clearer in the declining utility of the armed forces as a *direct* instrument for racial justice in the United States. According to Andrew Billingsley in *Climbing Jacob's Ladder*, the black career soldier is a crucial link in African American culture and is a chief repository in that culture of a tradition of self-sacrifice, discipline, and pride.[75] In the broader culture, the result of black advancement in the military includes a positive cliché of the black drill sergeant or officer. In more practical terms, the results are even more significant.

Charles Moskos and John Butler have examined the record of students in the schools set up for service members' children stationed overseas or in isolated domestic posts. The difference by race in the Department of Defense schools they studied was considerably smaller than in the civilian world. While white students in base schools performed about the same as their civilian counterparts, black students did much better, as measured by their scores on the Scholastic Aptitude Test. In fact, the average score (804) attained by black students in DOD schools was higher than the score of black students in civilian schools whose parents had bachelor's degrees.[76] Furthermore, in the military environment, the difference by race in the proportion of students who plan to attend college disappears. A similar effect is seen for black veterans: "Blacks who returned to civilian life after being honorably discharged earned substantially more than blacks who had not served in the military."[77]

Because of the drawdown in the armed forces, the opportunities offered by military service are available to fewer men and women. In the 1950s and 1960s, about 65,000 black males entered the military each year. In the mid 1990s, only about 22,000 black men per year joined the armed services from a larger pool of youth. On top of this, it appeared at the close of the 1990s that African American interest in the military as a career was in decline. Each year, the armed forces survey American youth's "propensity to enlist." This figure among African Americans has declined significantly since such data was first disaggregated by race in 1984. By virtue of the timing of this trend, it is clearly not a reaction to the end of the Cold War. But with the Cold War over, there is less pressure than before to reverse this trend. (The drawdown, coupled with the fact that African American enlistment propensity started at a much higher value than that for non-African Americans, prevented this decline in propensity from having an effect, during the decade, on actual enlistment proportions.)[78]

The Academic-Industrial-Military Complex is also undergoing civilianization, though with less decidedly negative results. The military's budget came down through the 1990s more slowly than after our previous wars. Still, the drawdown led to a 40 percent reduction from 1985 to 1997, with a decline in force structure of more than one-third. The drop in the military's procurement budget was even more steep, some 67 percent over the same period.[79] By the year 2000, there were signs that the drawdown was nearing an end. Thus, as the presidential election of that year was beginning in earnest, President Clinton's national security advisor was able to observe accurately that "just about everybody believes we need a strong military" and that more, rather than less, money should be sent the Pentagon's way.[80] Indeed, President Clinton's final budget, which the new Republican president embraced upon entering office, included proposed increases in military spending unequaled since the "Second Cold War" of the early 1980s.

Still, the consequences of a decade's retrenchment have already been felt in the industrial and research base of the economy. The share of the workforce composed of federal government employees shrank considerably, to the lowest levels since the early 1930s.[81] Looking at all defense employees, both public and private, that sector of the economy employed 2.2 million workers in 1997, compared to 3.7 in the mid 1980s.[82] In terms of the number of scientists and engineers engaged in research and development in both civilian and military sectors, the trend was downward into the mid-1990s, reflecting the effect of defense-related layoffs.[83] The result, according to a professor from the National Defense University's Industrial College of the Armed Forces, is that "the rapid response capabilities of defense organizations and defense industries, as we currently know them, may never exist again."[84]

The consequences were felt in selected fields in the immediate aftermath of the Cold War. According to an expert review group, the United States in 1990 had a substantial lead over Japanese or European competitors in a number of technologies with critical military applications, including communications, computers, advanced materials, aerodynamics, and propulsion. In the first four years of the 1990s, the trend was decline in all of the mentioned fields.[85] At the same time, the flow of dollars for research and development slowed considerably, to the point where overall national R&D funding failed to keep pace with inflation for the first time since 1975.[86]

These last trends were arrested by the end of the 1990s as a consequence of that decade's record of sustained economic growth. In this new fiscal environment, R&D spending is poised to receive a substantial boost in the first decade of the twenty-first century, though of course civilian research is likely to be favored over military.[87]

Against this backdrop of declining military service through the withering of Cold War institutions, the military's direct service to the nation and the world in Missions Other Than War (MOOTW, pronounced "mootwa" in defense circles) increased considerably in the 1990s. To many military professionals, the sustained increase in peacekeeping was at best a distraction and at worst amounted to the civilianization of the military and the consequent erosion of military strength and readiness.

"The military ought to stick to its knitting," asserted the influential Colonel Summers. "The biggest consequence" of not doing so, according to Lt. Col. Charles Dunlap, "is that society might end up with a military that can't do its basic function of national defense." Moreover, deploying the military outside of its core competence of war fighting threatens to politicize the forces, warned Dunlap. If the armed forces are continually used by politicians for domestic or international non-war missions, sooner or later military leaders are going to seek influence "in the policy decisions" over such issues.[88]

In a fictionalized account of where excessive civilian involvement might lead the military, Colonel Dunlap offered a dystopian vision of the future in which the military eventually assumes command of the entire government. Remarkably, his essay shared top honors in 1991–92 in a contest for the best paper on strategy written by a student of a senior service college. The grantor of the award was chairman of the Joint Chiefs of Staff Colin Powell.[89]

Analysts debate to what extent the military had already made this alleged Faustian bargain with their civilian commanders by the end of the decade. Supporters of non-war deployments point to the high rates of reenlistment among soldiers in Bosnia, while detractors explain that personnel seeking to reenlist have a financial incentive to volunteer for peacekeeping before declaring their decision. UN peacekeeping officials as well as some U.S. military leaders agree that U.S. personnel are a mixed blessing as peacekeepers. We "don't want to have to appear before Congress every time a U.S. soldier gets a scratch," explains one UN decision maker.[90] The extreme importance that U.S. military leaders place on force protection in such deployments may simply reflect their own fear that casualties might undermine U.S. support for their work and make it difficult to complete an assignment. It may also, however, reflect a reluctance to take such jobs to heart. "I'll be damned if I'm going to lose one man in a mission we should never have been on in the first place" was the explanation for extreme force protection offered by one former commander of peace-keepers in Somalia.[91]

Still, the pressure for such missions is intense, reflecting the shift toward an "imperial" role for the United States and its military in the collapse of Cold War stability around the world.[92] President Clinton's last chairman of the Joint Chiefs of Staff, General Henry Shelton, was probably right when he issued to the incoming administration the warning noted above. The U.S. military simply can't pick and choose where it will be ordered to employ its strength.[93] It can, however, surely choose better than it has how it will combine its preparations for war with its other, more short-term tasks.

Conclusion

The results of the end of the Cold War have been difficult for the military. Institutions and practices developed during the lengthy war are now under the intense pressures of peace. The Military Industrial Complex, and even the research university, were the beneficiaries of the Cold War. The same was true for the nation-building policy of civil rights at home. In the Cold War's aftermath, the nation's research and development work can no longer count on the same level of support from the Pentagon, and the foundation is being laid for a crisis in African American integration within the armed forces. At the same time, the armed forces, weakened and demoralized, are pushed into missions abroad and social experiments at home that raise questions about the very identity of those who serve. The military has seldom "had it easy" after war. The 1990s were no exception to this rule.

Cooperation among civilian and military leaders was evident, but in this decade cooperation coexisted uncomfortably with skepticism, antagonism, and suspicion. Consensus among civilian elites on the role of the military in advancing national interests was likewise not achieved. In the absence of these important supports for civil-military relations, it is hardly surprising that the parties to the civil-military bargain were unable in the 1990s to achieve the sort of balance that has characterized the most productive postwar realignments.

CHAPTER SIX

Barriers to Balance

No matter how often it was repeated in the aftermath of September 11, 2001, that "everything changed" on that day, a great many things clearly remained the same. One item of continuity was the U.S. military's provision of large-scale support to civilian authorities in responding to a disaster. In a Total Force approach, active-duty, reserve, and National Guard forces responded. Air National Guard fighters established patrols across urban America; New Jersey and New York guardsmen and navy and marine reservists assisted local healthcare workers in Manhattan; and various military units provided logistical support, including communications and transportation to aid recovery efforts. In the rescue phase, military personnel worked alongside civilian rescue teams. Later, the Army Corps of Engineers provided critical help in debris removal. At the Pentagon, Maryland Army National Guard military police provided security. At the request of the president, finally, governors mobilized several thousand National Guard personnel to provide additional security for several months at the nation's 429 commercial airports.[1]

As surprising as it surely was to most Americans to see soldiers in uniform in the streets and at the airports, the only thing new here was the cause of the disaster. In fact, precisely because responding to disasters is something the U.S. military has excelled at historically, there is a danger in the current uncertain state of U.S. military policy that too great an emphasis might be placed on configuring the services to respond to future terrorist assaults at the expense of readiness to deter other threats and respond to other weapons of war. This would be an ironic outcome: a traditional and subsidiary non-war-fighting mission could become the template for normal military operations. We are simply too close to events to know the final resolution of the post–Cold War realignment. What is clear, however, is that even if we are not witnessing the end of the post–Cold War "world," we are at the least, and at long last, at the end of the beginning of the post–Cold War realignment.[2]

The purpose of this chapter is to assess the barriers to a balanced adjustment in military policy and in civil-military relations that still remain. First, however, it is necessary to review the steps that the new Bush administration took in 2001 and 2002 in the opening of what we are calling stage two of the post–Cold War realignment.

Stage Two

President George W. Bush moved quickly to announce a new perspective on military policy. In the second congressionally mandated Quadrennial Defense Review (QDR II), released on September 30, 2001, Bush security planners accepted many of the criticisms of the first QDR, especially those offered by the National Defense Panel. The force structure and manpower requirements of the military were for the most part accepted as providing adequate resources for current possible missions with "moderate operational risk."[3] QDR II rhetorically presented itself, however, as a restoration of the perspective that guided defense planning under the first President Bush. QDR II thus rejected "threat-based" planning in favor of a "capabilities-based" model. In a rhetorical swipe at Clinton's "Bottom Up Review," the authors of QDRII further announced that their document was "truly 'top down' in that the decisions taken on strategy, forces, capabilities, and risks resulted from months of deliberations and consultations among the most senior Defense Department leadership."[4]

Homeland Defense: From Missiles to . . . ?

Beyond rhetorically distancing itself from Clinton-era defense policy, the second QDR placed a higher priority on homeland defense. Rather than concentrating on force-on-force war planning, the military must, the new president's team asserted, accelerate planning for attacks from terrorists or rogue states. In the first year of the second Bush administration, the emphasis in this regard was on missile defense. In the last month of 2001, President Bush removed the United States from the 1972 Anti-Ballistic Missile Defense Treaty with the Soviet Union. Russia, cooperating with the United States for its own reasons in the war against terrorists in Afghanistan, accepted the unilateral withdrawal with diplomatic graciousness.[5] However, because serious technological, budgetary, and strategic questions remained regarding missile defense, the consequences of this shift for the security of the United States were unclear in 2002.

QDR II also emphasized the importance of protecting the American homeland against non-missile threats. The report was issued just after the terrorist attack of 2001, and it suggested the need for the sort of organizational and legal reform in the apparatus of national security that was, in fact, begun the next month. On October 8, 2001, President Bush created by Executive Order an "Office of Homeland Security" and the "Homeland Security Council" within the Executive Office of the President. The mission of the new office was "to develop and coordinate the implementation of a comprehensive national strategy to secure the United States from terrorist threats or attacks."[6]

On June 6, 2002, the president unveiled a proposal for a Department of Homeland Security (DHS). The next month, the president published the government's first "National Homeland Security Strategy." The plan for a DHS complemented the emphasis on homeland security proposed in the Bush administration's military planning, though its scale was so large that it is unlikely it would ever have been proposed based merely on the conceptual work of government planners. In fact, when the first proposal for a homeland security department was put forth in 2001 by a Texas Republican member of the House *before* the terrorist assault on *September* 11, it received no backing from the administration. The new department, as later envisioned by the Bush administration and backed by Congress, will be the third largest in the executive branch and will employ roughly 200,000 federal workers.[7] After months of partisan wrangling over collective bargaining and job security issues, the president's proposal was enacted shortly after the 2002 midterm congressional elections, in which Republican candidates scored notable victories by criticizing Democrats for holding up the bill's passage. The DHS is frequently compared to the famous National Security Act of 1947. There are, however, some major differences in the bills that might make the DHS's creation less significant to the functioning of government and the protection of the nation. Most plainly, there is the problem of coordinating homeland security without controlling from DHS either the nation's intelligence or its military institutions.

The military's role in homeland security, according to the "National Homeland Security Strategy," is to work with civilian agencies to collect and disseminate intelligence, secure the border and other sensitive areas and sites, and respond in the event of an attack.[8] Aside from the recapitalization of the Coast Guard, no immediate enhancements or reorientations in the military services are called for. In fact, the strategy stipulates only "three circumstances under which the Department [of Defense] would be involved in improving security at home": air patrols and maritime defense under actual attack on the territory of the United States; "during emergencies, such as responding to an attack or to forest fires, floods, tornadoes, or other catastrophes"; and in "limited scope" missions where civilian agencies have the lead, such as security at special events like the Winter Olympics in Utah in 2002.[9]

Even with such a cautious strategy as a guide, however, the sheer magnitude of possible terrorist threats, especially from weapons of mass destruction, is sufficiently alarming in the present environment that it will require aggressive military planning and training to bring traditional capabilities up to date. To coordinate the military's contribution to homeland security measures, the president therefore created in 2002 a new unified combatant command, U.S. Northern Command.

Events outpace plans to reduce high "op tempo"

While pressing for the military to devote more time to asymmetric threats and to prioritize homeland defense, the second QDR sought simultaneously to address the stresses placed on the military by its high operational and personnel "tempo" in the post–Cold War environment. As a candidate for the presidency, and in the opening months of his administration, George Walker Bush criticized the "overuse" of the military under his predecessor.[10] In office, however, the new president made no move to dismantle peace missions already underway. At the close of 2001, the United States still maintained abroad roughly the same forces it had the year before.

In the first year of the new Bush administration, out of an active duty force of slightly under 1.4 million personnel, about 260,000 served overseas or afloat, including the approximately 100,000 assigned to NATO countries. The overseas forces included more than 5,000 U.S. military personnel in Serbia, including Kosovo; 5,000 in Bosnia and Herzegovina; and 11,000 combined in Kuwait and Saudi Arabia. U.S. military active duty personnel were serving in roughly 140 of the world's approximately 189 nations.[11] As Madeleine Albright had quipped during the transition to the second Bush presidency, "It's not your father's foreign policy."[12]

QDR II did not ask whether U.S. military personnel should be in all the places to which they had been deployed. It did, however, lay out an argument that few if any military policymakers would dispute: that the pace of such deployments had led to "excessive operational demands" and that changes should be made in how the services staff such missions. New rotational policies and, most innovatively, new military specializations in peacekeeping and humanitarian roles can provide a better foundation for the continuance of such work into the future, QDR II argued.

In 2002, however, events outpaced plans, and the Bush administration accepted, at the end of that year, that an open-ended stability operation would keep thousands of U.S. soldiers in Afghanistan indefinitely. Also in that year, President Bush openly contemplated military action against Iraq. The fact that any such operation would necessarily include a lengthy constabulary phase was not lost on critics of preemptive war.[13] If the U.S. government were truly to embrace a "neo-imperialist" and militarized foreign policy, it would require a larger military force to meet the demands of continuous simultaneous deployments of peacekeepers *and* war fighters around the globe. The limitations of U.S. warfighting capacity was, in fact, highlighted at the midpoint of the Bush administration, when North Korea challenged the United States to clarify its intentions with respect to the sole Asian member of the "axis of evil."

If it's broke, fix it

Finally, QDR II represented an acknowledgment that the defense operations of the United States were, indeed, "broken" during the 1990s and were in need of fixing. In the world as envisioned by QDR II, procurement budgets were to rise, aging weapons systems to be replaced, quality of life enhanced, and service in non-war-fighting missions engaged in. All of this is to happen, moreover, while at the same time the services train for all conceivable wars and harness the revolution in military affairs to the digitization of a newly lethal and precise battlefield.

The principles behind "transformation" will be addressed later in this chapter. For now, suffice it to say that the Bush administration's plans for large-scale military reform, and the resistance that Bush's secretary of defense, Donald Rumsfeld, faced in pressing such plans on the military in 2001 and 2002, were not surprising. It is by now a familiar story: in the aftermath of war, a military-minded civilian secretary of defense struggles against the entrenched interests and mindset of a military hierarchy reluctant to change. By 2002, army officers in the Pentagon were referring to Rumsfeld privately as "the enemy," and the *Armed Forces Journal International* posed the question on its cover, "Does he [Rumsfeld] Really Hate the Army?"[14]

The remainder of this chapter examines the conceptual barriers to achieving a post–Cold War balance in military and civilian priorities, starting with myths about military force and the Cold War that exert pressure either to disarm or withdraw from potential military confrontations altogether. Some of these barriers were weakened on September 11, 2001; others, ironically, were strengthened, as we will see.[15]

Utopianism I: The Cold War Was Unnecessary

If the Cold War was unnecessary, we would be justified in casting a skeptical eye toward proposals to increase, or perhaps even sustain, the military force necessary for major war. Unfortunately, there seems to be a real possibility that, just as after World War I, at least a significant portion of the population may come to hold such a view of the late Cold War.

The first of two such potentially harmful interpretations of the Cold War might be called the Big Misunderstanding thesis. From this point of view, the Cold War resulted from the mutual fears of comparable superpowers. Unreasoning fear provoked a debilitating arms race and wasteful wars in the developing world. With better understanding of one another's cultures and histories, peace might have prevailed rather than war. This is admittedly a caricature, but caricatures draw strength from their resemblance to something familiar, and that is the case here. The Big Misunderstanding thesis is familiar because it was created long before the Cold War came to its end.

In one way, the end of the Cold War makes this thesis more difficult to sustain. The archives of the former Soviet Union are becoming open to researchers. As a consequence, we now have evidence, for instance, of the Soviet's domination of the Communist Party of the United States of

America and of Alger Hiss's status as a communist agent.[16] But in a different way, the end of the Cold War, and the way that it ended, makes the Big Misunderstanding thesis more attractive to some.

Most Americans who were not paying attention to political matters at the time will never know or care whether Hiss was rightly or wrongly accused or, for a different example, whether North Korea acted for itself or for others in invading South Korea. What everyone does know is that the Cold War simply slipped away. A natural response to such an occurrence is to wonder what all the shouting and fighting were about in the first place. If they had really meant to bury us, would they have given up so quietly? The Big Misunderstanding thesis was apparent in the 1998 Cable News Network (CNN) documentary, "The Cold War." Its moral relativism was criticized in the *New Republic* even before the series completed its initial broadcast run.[17]

A more sinister interpretation of the Cold War has also been offered on film. Where Ted Turner, the founder of CNN and the force behind the "The Cold War," is skeptical, Oliver Stone is dogmatically cynical. In *JFK*, Stone updated an old-fashioned isolationist perspective on war. In Stone's film, a peace-loving man was killed to protect the profits of war profiteers and to give reactionary politicians an excuse for suppressing domestic freedom.

There are vast differences between these two points of view. Still, they both point the way toward a military policy realignment that would reflect deep suspicions of a significant conventional role for the armed forces. If the Cold War were either a mistake or a sham, the armed forces are deserving of little support unless, perhaps, they can be thoroughly refashioned. From either of these perspectives, the usefulness of the military would be realized only through its radical transmutation.

The threat posed to a successful realignment by such utopian thinking is magnified by the partial resurgence of isolationism among the mass public. Such isolationism is most easily observed today on the Right in American politics. Newt Gingrich, Bob Dole—and, especially, Patrick Buchanan—were all accused in the 1990s of voicing isolationist sentiments. The Republican Congress of the 1990s often criticized the Clinton administration's willingness to make open-ended commitments to peace-keeping missions, urging instead a greater focus on the longer-term utility of the armed forces to fight and win wars.[18] But isolationism is not just a Republican predilection today.

On the Left in American politics, support for internationalism often does not include support for the use of force. And unarmed internationalism is as much a barrier to the making of pragmatic military policy as is armed isolationism.[19] Unarmed internationalists might support armed interventionism as a posture, but when conflict turns bloody, unarmed internationalism can easily merge with pacifism.

Among the broad public, moreover, isolationist sentiment of both the "left" and "right" varieties is potentially strong. This is so despite polls that show strong post–Cold War sentiment for American involvement in foreign affairs.[20] As Arthur Schlesinger Jr. observed, "While Americans are still ready to endorse euphonious generalities in support of internationalism, there is a marked drop-off when it comes to committing not just words but money and lives."[21] Indeed, "defending the security of American allies" was accepted by a majority of Americans as an obligation of the United States at least in theory in 1990. But by the mid-1990s only a minority agreed that it was "very important." Support for "protecting weaker nations" against aggressors similarly dropped to well below a majority before the end of the century.[22]

In addition to isolationism, skepticism, and paranoia, several other sources of utopian thought complicate the task of making good military policy in the twenty-first century. The first is the notion that war, or at least conventional force-on-force war, is simply crazy and that so long as we are sane, it need not concern us.

Utopianism II: Modern War is Insane

The insanity thesis is a looming ideological barrier to a successful post–Cold War realignment. The idea that "modern" war is unthinkable because of its terrible destructiveness has, ironically, been around through a number of terribly destructive wars. In peacetime, this thesis becomes popular when advances in technology magnify the probable costs of war. In the twentieth century, World War I stands out for the difference it made to popular attitudes about war. In the decade before that war, an absolute lust for combat inflamed European statesmen and, to a lesser degree, American leaders such as Theodore Roosevelt. In part, this was an ideological and philosophical phenomenon. Theories about race and culture, biology and history, converged in the West at the turn of the last century in ways that made war seem a noble necessity. The popularity of World War I at its inception—it was cheered in spontaneous street demonstrations in France and Britain as well as in Germany—reflected the work of the imagination.[23] But no one had imagined the brutal stalemate of trench warfare. After the war, sensitive observers tended to agree that only a madman would once again risk war in Europe. Of course, war did come again to Europe, and it came in an instructive way.

There have been crazy rulers in the history of Europe, men who barked like dogs or tore out their hair or heard voices while sleeping alone, but Adolf Hitler was not among them. The fact is that it did not take madness to start World War II. What it took was the combination of Hitler's will to power and innovations in technology and strategic thinking. Hitler, of course, had been a soldier in World War I. He loved the experience but hated the outcome. Because a large number of Germans felt similarly, Hitler rose to power at first through democratic election. After building up the military, he tested the resolve of the war's victors by taking a series of discrete steps, beginning with rearmament itself.

The seers who had thought it impossible after World War I for Europe's military powers to wage war again made a classic mistake in human relations. They seem to have believed that everyone must think the way they do. They thought, in other words, that because they could not imagine a political outcome that would justify the likely costs of employing major military means, no one else could either. They seem to have forgotten, in a curious way, that the late war had both winners and losers. The losers were more willing to take risks to change the status quo than were the winners. As the historian John Keegan puts it: "Among the victor nations the cost of winning the First World War had left the populations determined never to bear it again; in Germany the cost of losing the war seemed to be justified only if the result could be reversed."[24]

And what of events since World War II? Have those events, in particular the development of nuclear weapons, perhaps demonstrated at last the insanity of war? Unfortunately not.

First, we can never know how close to nuclear war we came during the "Long Peace." Just because the Cold War did not end in a nuclear exchange does not mean that the threat of nuclear war was an illusion. It now appears, for instance, that Premier Nikita Krushchev intended to strike back at the United States with nuclear missiles, already operational in Cuba at the time we thought they were merely in the offing, in case of an American attack on Cuba.[25] It is even possible that we escaped from Korea and Vietnam without a nuclear exchange only because Presidents Truman and Johnson carefully controlled the use of American force in those conflicts. Finally, there are grounds for suspicion that America's nuclear strategy actually called for a first strike against the Soviet Union should the United States' early-warning system detect a Soviet intention to attack.[26] The Long Peace might even have been broken through human error, either in the interpretation of intelligence or in the application of launching protocols.

For a host of reasons, then, the nonuse of nuclear weapons does not support the proposition that war is insane. In political science, there is an instructive parallel regarding the members of Congress and the "safety" of their seats. It starts with a set of observations. First: even in landmark years like 1994, when the "out" party became the "in" party, the overwhelming majority of senators and representatives who run for reelection win. Second: senators and representatives typically run scared. They act as if their seats are not safe at all, raising far more money than they seem to need and spending a great deal of time on constituency service. On first impression, it might seem that American congressmen are a paranoid lot. On reflection, though, the point comes through. The ease of reelection is the product of frenzy. Nuclear weapons and their nonuse may work the same way. To some, the worry and anxiety of the 1960s cries out for psycho-historical analysis. But maybe all that worrying about nuclear weapons explains their nonuse thus far.

The underlying problem with the insanity argument is that it ignores differences in the way people weigh costs and benefits. It is easy enough to decide war is insane when one is either sitting in a trench surrounded by human gore or sitting comfortably in an office. In the first instance, the costs are all that one can see. In the second, the potential benefits are all but invisible. But in a city of poor and hungry people, or perhaps in a prison or a terrorist-training camp, or in any number of places in which affluent Americans spend little if any time, things might look different. If war is insane, the patients may be running the asylum.

Utopianism III: Major War is Obsolete

If major war of the sort that we have fought before is not insane, is it perhaps an oxymoron? Is it, at the least, on its way out? In 2002 Secretary of State Donald Rumsfeld talked as if he thought so. "I think also what's important," the secretary stated at a press conference at the Pentagon, "is that people lift their eyes up off their shoelaces and go back to the fundamental, and the fundamental issue is that we live in a different world today. We live in the 21st century. We're not back in the 20th century, where the principal focus is conventional weapons."[27] At the time, the secretary was in the process of making a case for military intervention against a particular target, Iraq. It would be unfair to take his statement as a reflection of the policy of his administration as a whole. Still, Rumsfeld's remarks, seemingly based on hardened realism, reflect an idealistic view of the present—and future—of war. Such idealism about warfare threatens the balance of military policy and of civil-military relations.

The most extended statement of this point of view was offered in the aftermath of the Cold War by political scientist John Mueller. In the flush of excitement following the collapse of the Soviet Union but before the United States went back to war in the Persian Gulf, Mueller argued that all of the world's major powers had opted out of the "war system."[28] War, he wrote, was like slavery. For thousands of years, slavery was a taken-for-granted feature of life on earth. Now, outside of excruciatingly impoverished and isolated areas such as southern Sudan, it is a relic of the past. It is a fascinating analogy, but it is not persuasive.[29]

First, war is more basic than slavery. There were societies that did not develop slavery. But there are no peoples, kingdoms, nations, or states that have not participated in war. The exceptions, such as the Quakers, survived through accommodation with war-fighting host societies. Slavery might even be thought of as a subset of war. Slaves always had to come from somewhere. Typically, they were captives of war. The keeping of slaves extended the relationship of the parties to war into the period after systematic hostilities ceased. If, moreover, the comparison of war with slavery is broadened so as to bring into view other forms of violence and oppression, slavery's end takes on a different light. Murder, rape, pillage, and starvation are still features of life on earth. The remarkable thing may not be the continuation of war but the virtual elimination of slavery.

A variation on the theme that war is obsolete derives from the observation that most people do not like war and that, at least in democracies, what most people want rules. Since democracy is on the march, war must be in retreat. There are, of course, possible exceptions to the rule that democracies do not wage war against one another. The American Civil War is among the bloodiest of arguable exceptions. One should also recall the role of parliamentary elections in Hitler's rise to power. But by and large, it has been true that the democratic countries of the world have kept peace amongst themselves for most of this century.[30] What does this mean for the future?

If indeed democracies do not wage war against one another, the world will be peaceful to the extent that it is democratic. But the future of democracy is uncertain. Monarchy, theocracy, and despotism compete with democracy in many places. Moreover, once a nation becomes democratic, that does not mean it will stay that way forever. Democracy tends to advance in waves, and each wave hides an undertow. The undertow takes a number of states back to authoritarianism even as it brings the benefits of democratic government to others.[31]

For the sake of argument, however, let us grant that democracies have thus far not made war amongst one another and that democracy will soon sweep Asia, Africa, and the Middle East. For peace to be the natural state of the world, an additional condition would need to be met: the diverse democratic peoples of the world would have to have similar aspirations for their countries.

The democratic "database" with which we are familiar consists almost entirely of modern Western nations. These nations are welfare states, the United States included. "Welfare" has few defenders in the United States, but a welfare state is simply one in which leaders "compete for their positions by appealing to the public as benefactors of public welfare, whether by positive action, or by promising to unleash the natural forces of progress."[32] Western welfare states differ considerably in how they provide for the common good, but their populations have tended to agree in the past half-century on the importance of prosperity. "Good Times." That is what governments are supposed to bring about.

Insofar as wars promise anything but Good Times, it has been a tough sell in democracies. At times, however, even America's democratic leadership has "sold" the nation on war. Indeed, America's presidents have been prime examples of democratic leaders for whom the decision to go to war has posed enormous political challenges that they nevertheless met. School children are taught that when the United States and other democratic countries have gone to war, it has been to defend against aggression. We finish wars; we don't start them. There is something to this, but it masks an important truth.

Certainly the United States did not *have* to go to war in 1812, 1846, or 2003. And in the 1940s, in a remarkable demonstration of presidential leadership, Franklin Roosevelt adroitly maneuvered the United States into World War II. Roosevelt did not *want* war, but he did not think it was worth avoiding at all costs. He therefore adopted an aggressive goal of rolling back Japanese gains in Asia, which made the subsequent Japanese attack a surprise chiefly in its timing and location.[33] In a world in which every country is a democracy, the path to war might likewise be politically treacherous, but there is no reason to believe that it could not be taken.

It is not necessary, then, to imagine a war-loving democracy in order to foresee war in a democratic future. It is only necessary to imagine a world in which democratic leaders, like U.S. presidents throughout history, place something less than the highest value on avoiding bloodshed.

Utopianism IV: Modern War Need Not Concern the United States

Modern war is not obsolete, and its future need not depend on the rise to power of crazy rulers. Still, maybe the future of war is something that need not concern the United States. Could the future be war for them, peace for us? If so, this would be a major argument for rethinking military power in the United States and pursuing a very different type of realignment than one in which the military must balance preparation for war against the need to do other things as well.

Some analysts imagine a twenty-first century in which conflict pits the West against the "rest."[34] Western nations and the most westernized of Asian states will, in this scenario, comprise an affluent and powerful minority of the earth's population. In the rest of the world, economic, environmental, and political disasters will decimate the earth's poor. In such a future, the U.S. military, along with U.S. immigration officers, disease experts, and others, would join with security experts from other wealthy states in containing the chaos. A new policy of containment might rely on international military/police efforts to restrict the flow of migrants, microbes, and vengeful ideologies from out of the zone of chaos. Military action of some sort would frequently be called for, as in Afghanistan in 2001–2, but so long as the gap in wealth and military power between the West and the rest remains in place, major war would be highly unlikely. Western states would be reluctant to risk it for fear of loosening their grip on the torrents swirling beneath them. The chaotic states might go to war against one another, but so long as weapons of mass destruction that might imperil the West are not used, the wealthy states will have the luxury of deciding for themselves whether to intervene.

One can, of course, debate how fanciful this scenario is. But its importance lies in its presentation of war as a matter of choice for wealthy and presumably secure states like the United States. Would this not guarantee peace? Not necessarily. What if, for instance, one of the members of the West were to break ranks and take sides in one of the wars from the zone of chaos instead of merely helping to contain the conflict? If that were to happen, the United States would face a difficult choice between peace and war. By refusing to become involved ourselves, we might diminish our capacity for leadership in the world.

Moreover, even if the West remained resolute in its member nations' desire for peace, there is no guarantee of success in the containment of terror. As September 11 made clear, the difficulties of combating nonstate violence against the West might be greater than we would care to acknowledge. The basic issue that was revealed in that attack and that motivated the administration to seek military action soon afterward against Iraq is the distinction between firepower and lethality. The United States has excelled at the projection of force, understood in terms of firepower, and has come to rely in its post–Cold War missions on this advantage. Asymmetric fighters who cannot hope to match American firepower might nonetheless match the U.S. capacity to kill by relying on massively lethal, if unconventional, weapons.

If we are to continue to lead in peace, we will have to continue to lead in war. The various propositions discussed above that argue in different ways for the irrelevance of the U.S. military as a war-fighting force are myths. Their acceptance could undermine efforts to resolve satisfactorily the ongoing issues surrounding the transition from the Cold War. If these myths were to be taken as conventional wisdom, we might well find ourselves in military policy terms back in the post–World War I era, with a military that is undersized and weakly supported.

Military Doctrine

Another conceptual threat to a balanced realignment comes from the other side of the debate about the nature of war in the twenty-first century. The propositions critiqued above hold that everything changed at some point in the recent past, if not before. An equally false proposition holds that nothing except the technology of war fighting is changed.

Among those who believe future wars of at least the scale of Desert Storm are possible and will likely involve the United States, there is a general consensus on a number of scenarios that could lead the United States into military conflict. Over the longer term, there is a threat of a "peer competitor" emerging. Russia and China are the two most realistic contenders for this distinction. The *Annual Defense Review* of 2000 selected 2015 as the approximate date beyond which it is possible that either (or both) of these nations might match the United States militarily.[35] The People's Republic of China is perhaps the greater potential challenge because we know less about its military and because its economic expansion potential seems—at times—enormous. Also, the PRC's ambitions are perhaps large enough to lead it into conflict within its region, which would inevitably lead it into conflict with the United States.[36]

Two additional threat scenarios are commonly mentioned by defense strategists at the turn of the century: a reprise of the Gulf War or of the Korean War. In either or both of these "Major Regional Contingencies," the United States would seemingly find itself on familiar ground, fighting large-scale if not "all out" wars on some other country's territory. In the words of the *Annual Defense Review* 2000, "Many instances of cross-border aggression will be small scale in nature; but between now and 2015, it is entirely possible that more than one aspiring regional power will have both the motivation and the means to pose a military threat to U.S. interests."[37]

For these threats, from major war with a peer competitor to a reprisal of Desert Storm, military doctrine is meeting the challenges of the future. But what of other threat scenarios, or even missions in which the United States acts without reference to threat? Under the Clinton administration, after all, it was held that "even when important U.S. interests are not threatened, the U.S. may have a humanitarian interest in protecting the safety, well-being, and freedom of the peoples affected."[38] Humanitarian, peacekeeping, and related operations pose problems that the U.S. military may not be prepared for.

Eliot Cohen sees such frustrating missions as flowing, not from the vagaries of presidential election outcomes, but from the United States' de facto role as the imperial hegemon in the post–Cold War environment. As Cohen wrote in 1998:

The United States needs an imperial strategy. Defense planners could never admit it openly, of course, and most would feel uncomfortable with the idea, but that is, in fact, what the United States at the end of the twentieth century is—a global empire. . . . Like many past empires, the United States does not seek new commitments, or conquests. But also like other past empires, it finds itself drawn into the quarrels of other states and the anarchy of disintegrating polities. . . . U.S. planners would prefer to prepare for quick, unconstrained, knock-down fights with easily identified opponents. Instead, they will spend their years waging "savage wars of peace" in one corner of the globe while worrying about the rise of envious rivals in another.[39]

Cohen's analysis is suggestive of the need to prepare for a continuation of peacekeeping and small-scale contingency operations and of the difficulties of doing so. In Washington, D.C., in 1997, a number of generally conservative public intellectuals even established a lobbying organization and think tank dedicated to the proposition that we are entering a century of American imperialism and that this is a good thing for which we must be prepared to sacrifice ten percent of GNP per year for the military budget.[40]

The military's leadership would surely appreciate such an enormous increase in its budgets. But the imperial role is not one that U.S. officers easily embrace. Indeed, ever since the renaissance of military pride and training in the 1970s and 1980s, officers in the Pentagon have exploited weaknesses in civilian readiness to *resist* orienting military policy toward an indefinite future of small-scale peacekeeping and small-scale warfare. In doing so, they have exploited what might be called a "readiness gap" between themselves and their civilian counterparts and superiors. In the post–Cold War environment, this gap has been a recurring theme, making it tempting for officers to "call the shots" themselves.[41]

In the 1990s and into the 2000s, military resistance was permitted to flourish even in field operations, once the civilians had their way and troops were ordered into peacekeeping roles. In the field, uniformed commanders took it upon themselves to place the highest of all priorities on "force protection." Two army analysts on the faculty of West Point alleged in a recent study of the phenomenon that in doing so, officers merely followed a national policy. Even so, these professional observers worried that extreme force protection was eroding "the professional ethic."[42] Casualty aversion in non-war-fighting missions is, in fact, not simply a policy from on high, but a reflection of officers' attitudes. Casualty aversion is indeed *stronger* among military officers than among the general public, according to opinion surveys conducted at the end of the 1990s.[43]

The military, it might be said, cannot always say "no"; but when they say "yes" to new missions, they do so with their own ideas about what these operations are really worth, ideas that have undermined both military professionalism and civilian policy objectives. Among junior officers, especially, there is a pervasive sense that the result is an erosion of military skills and readiness for combat.[44]

As if these were not problems enough, additional issues of doctrinal inflexibility must be raised. First, should a non-war-fighting mission go bad, is the military prepared for the possible implications? What if, for instance, a new Kosovo-type operation turns against the United States? In such a situation, the United States might find the use of ground troops in combat unavoidable, and the casualty aversion of military (and civilian) elites might undermine the mission. An even more troubling way in which a small war could pose trouble for the U.S. military in the future is actually suggested by the rise of a peer competitor, a threat acknowledged in military planning.[45]

Because directly confronting a peer is fraught, for the United States, with danger of nuclear annihilation, a challenge will sometimes be made through a proxy. The Cold War made the Vietnam War into the disaster for the United States that it was by forcing civilian commanders to calibrate the use of force so as not to turn a proxy war into a direct war. The rise of a new Cold War competitor might well bring about the challenges of a new Vietnam.

Fortunately, the standard military critique of Vietnam is being challenged by a new generation of scholars from both the "left" and the "right." As a reviewer in the Army War College journal *Parameters* observed in 2000, two recent books on Vietnam, one entitled *American Tragedy*, the other, *Vietnam, The Necessary War*, both "challenge the conventional wisdom that U.S. forces fought well but were not adequately supported by Washington."[46]

Another war scenario that poses a serious challenge to current military policy, attack on the homeland by transnational terrorists, has now become a reality. Moreover, nuclear, biological, or chemical weapons might be used against the United States or against U.S. citizens or allies elsewhere in the world at any time. Along these lines, Fred Ikle believes it is only a matter of time before the "next Lenin" emerges with an ideology powerful enough to motivate terrorists to new heights of activity, using either the old (nuclear, biological, chemical, and explosives) or the new (cyberwar) avenues of assault. Contemporary terrorists who threaten the United States, Ikle observes, often bungle the job. Though they are deadly, they have not yet been as organized or as far-reaching in their attacks as they might be were they to find domestic U.S. recruits under the banner of some new meta-philosophy synthesizing the discontents of post-modernity.[47] Osama Bin-Laden's terrorists were not, unfortunately, bunglers. But their leader's charisma appears to have little if any resonance among American citizens. Imagine, Ikle challenges us, the danger that might result from a more Americanized version of Bin-Laden and his network of terrorists.

In a challenging look to the future, another denizen of the think tank network, Michael Vlahos, has compared the United States today with France around 1860. At that time, the French were the world's preeminent military power, confident that they held the keys to the future of war. They had invented the machine gun and the breech-loading rifle and the shell gun. Their doctrine of war, authored by Henri Jomini, was copied by other countries. But the real revolution in war turned out to be something entirely different and much more ordinary: the railroad. By transforming everyday life, the railroad spurred industrialization and the expansion of markets. This made industrial power more important than ever before in war. By offering ready transport of troops, moreover, the railroads rewarded mass armies organized along sound business lines: ready to move with all the things they would need in battle. By mastering the industrial and strategic potentialities of the railroad, the Germans, not the French, became the true revolutionaries in war.[48]

The technology that is transforming life today, according to Vlahos, is the globally networked computer. The United States, Vlahos points out, is the world's leading maker of computers, having a particular dominance in software. The good news about this is that it gives the United States more power than any other nation in mastering the true technology of future war. However, there are two items of bad news. First, precisely because it is U.S. software that dominates the world computer market and networks, it is the United States against which the losers of the future will vent their spleen. Second, nations may not, in any event, be the dominant actors in future war. Instead, it may be communities on the Internet, perhaps backed by smaller, dynamic, angry states that "act; they do things, try out new things, get aggressive—economically, mostly, but they remake the environment—while the old, great powers wait for new trends to gel before they follow" (55). The "driven communities of change" are already recognized in conventional military planning as perpetrators of terrorism, including computer sabotage, so-called hacker war. But Vlahos has something else in mind. Because of the enormous changes coming in the ways that people work and create wealth, there will be comparably great changes, he believes, in social structures and in the attempts that people always make to graft meaning onto the raw experience of life. "Industrial revolution created *anomie; anomie* demanded meaning. And meaning came: positivism, Marxism, socialism, communism, bolshevism, fascism" (55).

The onrushing world economic revolution will bring about a new round of *anomie* or something functionally similar. A new messiah of the downtrodden, those with less flashy Web sites and less chance to make a profit in the Web's global market, might ironically use the Web to mobilize a following. For the believers, "war will be essential to their becoming," writes Vlahos. "The very experience of war is realization of the new: You create yourself by destroying the stranger" (60)

A congressionally mandated commission looking into the future of warfare and the needs of the U.S. military concurred with some of these dark assessments. The panel, headed by retired Senators Gary Hart and Warren Rudman, reached the prescient conclusion in September 1999 that the greatest threat to the United States might in fact be a threat to the homeland itself. "America will become increasingly vulnerable to hostile attack on our homeland, and our military superiority will not necessarily protect us," they cautioned. Groups or nations with "resentment of American power and cultures" might pose "asymmetric" threats that the armament-heavy U.S. military might find difficult to combat.[49]

"One of the things this probably implies," noted former House Speaker Newt Gingrich, speaking about the work of the Commission in 1999, "is a capacity for homeland defense and for civil defense on a scale we have never dreamed of and which will require a significant redistribution of authority."[50] If September 11 proves to have been only the beginning, will a majority of Americans endorse such a radical redistribution of authority or the expensive defensive measures that might be needed to create a more secure homeland?

As Aaron Friedberg shows, we faced what many responsible persons thought was a very real danger of homeland attack in the early Cold War. Public figures as well as military leaders warned of the need to take drastic action. We should even, some said, relocate industrial facilities to lessen the impact of a nuclear strike and perhaps disperse the population as well. Because of the power of America's anti-statist ideology and the inability of the federal government to make dramatic changes when the nation is not convinced of their desirability, however, the nation remained unmoved.[51] It is doubtful that we will ever do as much to prepare for homeland defense as we should.

The military's planners have not yet done enough to meet the challenges of homeland wars or of "savage wars of peace."[52] The army is still enamored of its "armored warrior" culture.[53] The navy and the air force are similarly reluctant to rethink their reliance on manned aircraft and aircraft carriers, though they have reorganized themselves to better face the high operational tempo of post–Cold War deployments. Indeed, though military planners officially acknowledge that engaging in small wars and even peacekeeping operations will continue to be principal tasks and will stress the force's capacities, they were not even mentioned in the Pentagon's first statement of its "strategy for transformation."[54]

In President George W. Bush's proposed defense budget for 2003, the biggest annual increase in defense spending since the Reagan years was called for. Amidst this planned upturn in spending, however, there was little evidence of the promised transformation in thinking. The United States would continue, under Bush's plans, to build three new tactical fighter aircraft, which would make it difficult to achieve the transformation goal of relying less on expensive, manpower-intensive weapons platforms. Much less was there a call for separating peacekeeping from war fighting as separate tracks within the profession of arms or of jettisoning some capacity for missions other than war in order to focus more on readiness for major war. The Fiscal Year 2003 budget suggested that, in fact, rather than spurring it to make difficult choices, the pro-defense atmosphere of 2002 gave incentives to the administration to defer choices by giving every constituency in the military policy debate some measure of victory.[55]

The military's reluctance to engage in reforms aimed at meeting more fully the needs of peacekeeping and unconventional wars is a problem. It could easily increase civil-military tension and entail a possible further erosion of civilian leadership over military policy.

What is holding military policy back? Any number of things, perhaps, including the absence of the sort of strong civilian leadership exercised in the more successful postwar periods. Furthermore, there is the barrier of what most generously might be called military pride, or what might more simply be termed military elitism.

The idea of military elitism as a problem in civil-military relations was publicized in the 1990s by *Wall Street Journal* reporter Tom Ricks. In a series of articles and in the book *Making the Corps*, Ricks provided rich anecdotal evidence of marine contempt for the lack of discipline endemic in the civilian world. Ricks observed young marines in boot camp and wrote with approval of the influence that marine indoctrination had on young men who for the most part had been leading "part time lives." The problem, to Ricks, is that the marines are so different from civilian society that the young recruits find they no longer fit into their civilian communities after becoming marines, nor do they want to. As one of the men Ricks followed in and out of boot camp observed, "Defending my country? Well, it's not really my country. I may live in America, but the United States is so screwed up."[56]

A survey of military and civilian attitudes undertaken by the Center for Strategic and International Studies and the Triangle Institute for Strategic Studies added further evidence of a civilian-military "gap."[57] Sixteen percent of officers described themselves as either "somewhat" or "very" liberal in 1976. In 1996 there were no very liberal officers to be found, and only 3 percent of officers surveyed said they were somewhat liberal. The proportion of officers identifying with conservatism increased during the same time from 61 to 73 percent. On the civilian side, there is a parallel development: in particular, a declining awareness of, and experience with, the military.

The mere existence of a gap between military values and civilian values is not itself a problem. In a liberal society, essentially conservative military institutions will always stand apart. But the military's response to the gap *is* a problem. Today's responses within the military include an increase in partisanship and in political involvement. Among civilian elites, from 1976 to 1996, "Independent" status lost ground, while Republican Party identification picked up—from 25 percent to 34 percent of the public. Among military officers, these trends were greatly exaggerated. In 1976, 46 percent of officers were Independents and 33 percent were Republicans. Twenty years later, 67 percent were Republicans, while only 22 percent were Independent.[58] In the 1992 and 1996 presidential elections, analysts believe that President Clinton received probably less than 10 percent of the vote of officers and enlistees combined.[59] Partisanship is a counterproductive reaction to the gap between military and civilian values. The military should not have to mirror a society that is experiencing values changes of questionable worth, but the military cannot "save" a society from itself. It can only protect and defend the nation that gives it purpose and meaning.

Because the military still feels "burned" by the Vietnam experience, and because the "gap" emboldens military leaders to attempt to fill a void in civilian understanding of, and appreciation for, the military, "elite military officers believe that it is their role to *insist* and *advocate* rather than merely to *advise* on key elements of decisions regarding the use of force."[60] This, note Peter Feaver and Richard Kohn, is contrary to traditional understandings of civil-military relations.

Conclusion

It would be imprudent to plan as if conventional war is on the way out. It would be imprudent as well to plan as if the return to war means merely the return to some model war of the past. A successful realignment, one that produces a military policy that matches the real threats posed to the United States in the twenty-first century, will have to address the prospect of complex small-scale warfare, such as in Operation Enduring Freedom, where the United States defends itself against nonstate actors unleashing assaults on the U.S. civilian society; major wars, where U.S. forces battle the forces of other nations; "peace" missions such as those that characterized U.S. military operations in the first decade after the Cold War's end; and even, so long as George W. Bush is president, punitive, preemptive missions falling somewhere between a major war and a "stability operation."

This may simply be too much, in which case no amount of rethinking and planning anew will permit civilian and military leaders to achieve a successful realignment. Even assuming that the military could conceivably be organized, trained, and motivated to do all these things, the barriers to a successful realignment are considerable. They involve civilian attitudes, military doctrine, and military elitism. What they reveal is that the post–Cold War environment is closer to the environment experienced in the past during *less* successful rather than *more* successful realignments to peace. In the less successful realignments, as we saw, there was a lack of consensus on the purpose of military force. The consequence was struggle between civilian authorities and military leaders and conflict among military leaders themselves. The same lack of consensus is troubling the transition from the Cold War today.

Ultimately, the direction of twenty-first-century U.S. military policy is a matter to be decided through cooperation among senior civilian and military leaders. The mass public has its part to play as well. Only when a rough agreement is forged on the national interest of the United States in a globalizing world should we expect agreement on the proper role or roles to be played by the military in promoting that interest.

In the meantime, what qualities should a good military policy for the early twenty-first century embody? That is the question addressed in the final chapter.

CHAPTER SEVEN

Applying the Lessons of the Past

In the aftermath of war, military professionalism is put to the test of peace. The military must be flexible enough to accommodate the priority that civilians assign to the non-war-fighting capabilities of the services in peacetime. At the same time, doctrinal commitment to civilian control and political neutrality is as important after war as it always is if the military is to avoid the trap of political engagement. Unfortunately, the need to expand doctrine in peacetime runs up against the necessity felt by military professionals to prepare for the return to war, and this makes commitment to civilian control problematic.

Civilian leadership also faces challenges after war. Low-threat environments bring to the government civilian leaders inexperienced in, or ignorant of, military affairs. Their desire to enjoy a "peace dividend" or to use the services in new ways, if unleashed without respect for the military's core responsibility of preparing for war, harms morale and expertise within the armed forces.

The difficulties of civil-military relations posed by the postwar period can be resolved poorly or well. Our consideration in Chapter 1 of theories of civil-military relations led to the hypothesis that a trade-off exists between extirpation and transmutation. By accepting a measure of transmutation, military professionals can diminish the pressure for extirpation. The result, under the best of circumstances, is a peacetime military policy that balances reform of the services as they prepare for future war with more immediate service to the civilian needs of the nation. The implementation of a balanced policy of this sort was proposed as the criterion for a successful postwar transition.

From the standpoint of Huntingtonian civil-military relations theory, this criterion is paradoxical. The best postwar realignment mixes subjective with objective means of civilian control. Through subjective control, the military is integrated with civilian society through the performance of peace missions. Sometimes this means accepting civilian ways of thinking and civilian ideas about individual rights, even for soldiers, and civilian ideas about the responsibility of the military to advance the domestic interests of the nation, not just to defend it against threats. However, a core of objective control, giving the military its due to seek necessary reforms and pursue its craft, must be maintained even at such times or else the military may lose its calling and become just a "job" like any other. Because of the gradual shift of the military toward occupationalism, it is all the more important today that subjective control mechanisms not overwhelm the institutional identity at the core of military professionalism. This paradoxical outcome is possible for several reasons, including the fact that the military is not monolithic. Rigorous respect for tradition can be maintained among one subset of military personnel—Special Forces, for a prominent example—while other subsets are made more available to transmutation.

In addition, there has always been some blurring in peacetime of the line between civilian and military interests and thus between objective and subjective control orientations. The extension of frontier forts on which Secretary of War John Calhoun placed such priority after the War of 1812, for instance, was clearly in the interests of an expanding civilian population. The forts became outposts of the market economy and provided shelter against the weather and against lawless frontiersmen. However, the same forts also provided protection when necessary against hostile Native Americans and communicated the nation's belief in "manifest destiny" to other nations with an interest or a claim in North America. The use of military personnel to construct "dual use" roads and other infrastructures is another common example of the difficulty in distinguishing in peacetime between the "military" and "civilian" employment of the forces.

Ironically, in the most successful postwar realignments studied in these pages, civilian leaders played key roles in helping the armed forces maintain focus on reform while also being of immediate service to the nation.

Civilian leaders have been essential in U.S. history to the preservation of pockets of excellence and reform within the professional ranks during the transformation of the military after war. In many accounts of civil-military relations, as detailed in Chapter 1, this outcome would defy analysis. For both Samuel Huntington and Michael Desch, two prominent examples, the central issue in civil-military relations, the dependent variable in their models of good relations, is who wins when civilian and military elites come into conflict. To put it simply, that persons who come to work in suits can win a victory for those who wear the uniform of one of the services is not considered. But this is precisely what has happened, repeatedly, in American civil-military relations during the time periods studied here. At least in the postwar period, then, it is not so much a matter of *who wins*, but *to what purpose they use their power*, that must be considered in evaluating the quality of civil-military relations.

And what accounted for the difference among outcomes? Why was a fruitful balance achieved after the Revolutionary War, the War of 1812, and the Spanish-American War, but not after America's other wars? To put the issue more formally, what independent variables were associated with different outcomes in the dependent variable of achieving a balance between service and reform?

First, *cooperation between civilian and military leaders* was vital. This cooperation could be seen in military restraint from political engagement and in civilian promotion of the military profession. In the aftermath of the War of 1812 and the Spanish-American War, the role of military-minded civilian leaders was especially notable. Without the work of Secretaries John C. Calhoun and Elihu Root, these postwar periods would have been less beneficial both to the nation and to the armed forces. These civilian leaders rose above the factionalism of the most senior military professionals and made alliances with young, reform-minded service leaders. In the realignment following the Revolutionary War, a succession of civilian presidents similarly played key roles in promoting a sound but not overly ambitious military policy.

After the least successful realignments, by contrast, civilian leadership was lacking, and military cooperation was suspect. After the Civil War, the military was divided. A minority faction, led by General Otis Howard, took to the task of Military Reconstruction with enthusiasm. A majority faction, headed by General William Tecumseh Sherman, resisted the new direction in military service. After the Vietnam War, a cadre of reformers saved the armed forces from civilian hostility but developed a doctrine that elevated resistance, rather than cooperation, to a principle of military professionalism.

The other major independent variable making for a successful realignment was identified as *political consensus in support of the military and its varied uses*. After the Revolutionary War, it took years of experimentation—and failure—to bring the anti-Federalists into this consensus. The utility of military force in the expansion of the nation westward softened the opposition of the emerging Democrats to the military establishment. The utility of military force in resisting harassment of American shipping and in enforcing unpopular domestic laws also helped persuade Jeffersonians to make peace with the armed forces.

After the War of 1812 and the Spanish-American War, broad-based support for military reform and war preparations again provided a foundation for a balanced realignment. Consensus emerged quickly after the War of 1812, as the anti-war party (ironically, the pro-military Federalists) self-destructed and the formerly anti-military Democrats rushed to the aid of the armed forces. Not everyone wanted a strong military, but the nation voted with its feet and moved at a quickening pace into newly secured territories. The army had no choice but to follow, and in fact, under Calhoun's leadership, took the lead in opening the West for settlement. The western-based army was forced to become expert at more than war as soldiers built roads, surveyed canals, and farmed. But the services were permitted to uphold standards at the Military Academy and even to open new schools for the development of military expertise.

The early 1900s witnessed the functional equivalent of consensus in politics: a stable and strong majority in support of the pro-military Republican Party. The dual mission of the army and navy—to build its strength for possible war and to manage the new colonial possessions of the nation—was validated at the polls when William Jennings Bryan, in the election of 1900, suffered one of the most thorough defeats of any presidential candidate. With the Republican Party firmly in control of the government, military and civilian reformers could count on the government's support for their missions for more than a decade. When the Democratic President Woodrow Wilson took office, he confirmed the new order of things in the support he too gave to the reformed services.

On the other hand, the absence of political consensus eventually undermined the turn to the South of the army after the Civil War. Even before Reconstruction ended, the lack of consensus in Washington left army leaders in sometimes incredible situations, forced at times to decide for themselves what the government's policy might be and even to defend themselves in local courts and against a hostile president. After the Vietnam War, the military—and the nation's military and foreign policies more generally—were points of division among the political parties. In this enervating environment, military professionals eventually came to exploit civilian weakness after being forced to accommodate civilian-directed changes such as the All Volunteer Force.

The Unfinished Post Cold-War Realignment

Even some thirteen years after the fall of the Berlin Wall, the post–Cold War realignment looked more like a "loser" than a "winner." The conditions for a successful balance were not present. Civil-military cooperation was suspect. Military professionals took charge of defense planning and strategizing, and resisted civilian control at the operational level as well. On the civilian side of this equation, the executive branch, especially in the Clinton administration, was unable to provide the quality of civilian leadership associated in the past with successful realignments.

In the 1990s and into the next decade, the problems associated with a lack of political consensus emerged. There was no apparent agreement among political parties and their leadership or among intellectual and cultural leaders on either the necessity of the military for future war or for present-day nonwar missions. In fact, a key barrier to a more successful post–Cold War realignment, as identified in the previous chapter, remains a plethora of utopian ideals that cast doubt on the relevance of war, or at least "old-style" war, to America's future. The old charge that a "standing army" is a threat to liberty has not been heard in American politics for a hundred years. But these myths are the functional equivalent of that old barrier to a sound military policy. There is also no apparent consensus on the importance of peacekeeping and humanitarian missions for the services. As for the military's other, less direct service to the nation in the form of the promotion of civil rights, science, and technology, the military connection to these issues was hardly a footnote to political debate in the first decade and more of the post–Cold War peace.[1]

Overall, the first decade-plus of the post–Cold War era suggested a failure to take peace and war entirely seriously. Military resistance to peace missions was mixed with heavy-handed civilian interference in issues of military professionalism and indifference among some civilian elites to the harm that high rates of deployment were causing to the military's readiness to fight. In the remainder of this chapter, I address the question: What would it mean to take both peace and war more seriously in the making of U.S. military policy?

Taking War More Seriously

In *early* 2001, it appeared to many observers that the primary requirement that would have to be met if the United States were to prepare more adequately for future war would be to prioritize homeland defense. Asymmetric threats against the United States and against American civilian or military personnel abroad were posed by rogue states and nonstate actors. Attacks against U.S. military personnel had been recently carried out in Saudi Arabia and off the shore of Yemen by Arab extremists. The World Trade Center had been targeted in a 1993 bombing intended to topple the landmark structures. The bomb caused the deaths of six persons and more than half a billion dollars in damage.[2] As a consequence of these and other terrorist attacks in the 1990s, homeland defense was acknowledged as a part of every post–Cold War blueprint for the nation's military policy. But little in the way of concrete reforms were implemented. The nation's military strategy still emphasized force-on-force planning, and the new Bush administration prioritized missile defense in its plans for making the homeland safer.

The second terrorist assault on the World Trade Center led the Bush administration to do considerably more than it had contemplated regarding homeland defense. An organizational restructuring of elements of the civilian and military security apparatus of government was undertaken immediately, as already described. In addition to spurring organizational changes, this event led to significant increases in the budgets for the agencies (for the most part civilian) tasked with antiterrorism and terrorism response. In addition, the administration's early emphasis on missile defense gave way to a more comprehensive effort to strengthen the country's security against a full spectrum of state and nonstate threats short of, or different from, force-on-force warfare.

If September 11, 2001, marked a lasting turning point in the nation's perception of its threat environment, that could make it either easier or harder for civilian leadership, depending on how perceptions change. As we have seen, most postwar periods in the United States have been characterized by a relative absence of threats, both external and internal. But what happens when both external and internal threats emerge suddenly, which is one possible way the public might come to see the attack on the World Trade Center? Michael Desch's arguments, reviewed in Chapter 1, about the importance of the threat environment, suggest that such a change in U.S. opinion of the country's security could lead to considerable conflict between civilian and military elites. At the midway point in the George W. Bush administration, it was too early to tell whether the public perception of threats was undergoing a lasting change and, if so, whether the threats that the public newly worried about would be viewed as "internal," "external," or both. In early 2002 the government itself was sending mixed signals to the public. Homeland Security Council Director Ridge unveiled a coded warning system, focusing on the threat at home, while President Bush moved rhetorically in his State of the Union Message to focus the nation's attention on an "axis of evil" abroad.[3]

Independent of events in the war against terrorism and states allied with terrorists, the transformation of the nation's armed forces would certainly signify a step forward in the necessary reform of the armed forces. In this area, civilian leaders traditionally take the lead. Today it is Defense Secretary Donald Rumsfeld who struggles against an often-reluctant military brass. Military leaders work, meanwhile, with the defenders of the status quo in Congress and their allies in the private sector to limit the reach of transformation lest the flow of money for favored weapons systems decline or cease. In this familiar tug-of-war, who was ahead was an open question at the mid-point of the George W. Bush administration. If the post–Cold War peace is going to be marked in the first decade of the twenty-first century by salutary reforms in the services, the military's top leadership will have to demonstrate a willingness to cooperate with civilians intent on transforming the professional military.

An even greater challenge in enhancing the outcomes of military policy today and for the future relates, not to the war against terrorism, but to preparations for future wars of a kind declared out of bounds in the aftermath of Vietnam. To put it bluntly, the professional military needs at long last to accept its share of responsibility for failure in Vietnam.

Successful postwar military policy, we have seen, is characterized by civilian and military cooperation, not mistrust and resentment. Because military professionals have accepted as a matter of creedal faith a historically suspect perspective on the Vietnam War as arising from civilian mismanagement and deception, military officers today believe it is their right to evade and obstruct civilian leaders if their leadership "reminds" them of what they believe happened in Vietnam.[4] Over the long course of America's civil-military relations history, it would be tragic if, in retrospect, the post–Cold War realignment were to fail to prepare the nation for future large-scale wars because the military could not put the decades-old failure in Vietnam behind it.[5]

Taking "Peace" More Seriously

Taking peace seriously today in military policy is perhaps even more difficult because of the lack of political consensus on how the armed forces can most usefully serve the nation in the absence of major war. Certainly by preparing for war, including a war against a future peer competitor. But how else? In the nineteenth century, there was a broad consensus on the importance of national territorial expansion. In the twentieth century, a consensus slowly developed through the Spanish-American War and the world wars that the United States needed a strong military, even in peacetime, to serve the leadership interests of the nation. Over both centuries, national integrity and national unity were advanced by the armed services in peace as well as in war. At the opening of the twenty-first century, it is unclear whether the nation has the will to maintain its project of global leadership. To adapt the language of the Clinton Doctrine to our current situation, it is doubtful that there is a consensus on the need for engagement for enlargement. It is even questionable whether there is a consensus in support of engagement for its own sake, that is, for preserving American power throughout the world. There is even less support for moving beyond engagement to preemptive war as a means to enlarge the sphere of democracy.

How should military policy proceed in such an environment, when the public is uncertain, but when different influential segments of civilian society want the military to: prepare for war, "do windows," or even go away. The prudent course of action, I believe, is to pursue policies at home that keep the military integrated with civilian society and to pursue policies abroad that keep our options open so that, should consensus emerge, the military is capable of promoting what the nation comes to believe is in its core interest.

The Domestic Side of Prudence

The domestic side of prudence would involve the military in both the "dirty work" and the "good works" of peacetime and would balance the need for the military to be in contact with civilian society against the threat of military intervention in domestic police work. After the Spanish-American War and World War I, as we saw, military leaders expressed pride in the good works of the services in peacetime. Military personnel responded to crises at home such as earthquakes, floods, and fires, and helped the nation survive its worst economic catastrophe in the Great Depression. Engaging in such missions is important, but caution is needed.

At times, as in the aftermath of World War I, military professionals unfortunately also came to believe that they were responsible for uplifting the morals of civilian America. This led to political entanglement, as it did after the Civil War, with negative consequences for the military once political winds shifted.

Doing Good Works

The services today are most closely involved in good works through their reserve and National Guard components. This is as it should be. The reserves and National Guard are critical institutions in mediating the relationship between a civilian society in which fewer Americans have personal experience with the military, and a professional military establishment that requires even its part-time personnel to prepare for war.

The marine reserves provide a useful model. Because, as every marine knows, "America does not need a Marine Corps, it wants one," marines are highly attuned to the need for good public relations. The consequence is a doctrine of community service that marches right up to the line marking the trap of military elitism but usually stops short. "In addition to fighting and winning battles abroad," Major General Thomas Wilkerson, at the time marine reserves commander, wrote in the *Continental Marine* magazine, "Marine reservists also fight battles right in our own communities, in our own backyards." These are not just battles against hurricanes or floods, moreover, but "against the ravages wrought by economic deprivation in our society, battles against the human toll substance abuse takes on our citizenry, battles against the problems of illiteracy."[6] In practice, this doctrine gives support to programs such as the well-known "Toys for Tots."

In any other branch of the armed forces, such an initiative, though it reaches four million children annually, would likely be seen as mere window dressing, even for reservists. In the Marine Corps, things are different. In an edition of *Naval Institute Proceedings*, General Wilkerson and his aide-de-camp published a story on the fiftieth anniversary of the program in which they endorsed the view of a Colonel Jimmy Whitson: "The Toys for Tots program is one of the most important tasks we have in the Marine Corps. It's become part of who we are. . . . We're not just warriors; we're members of the communities we live in."

The marine model of community engagement holds out promise of a sustained civilian awareness of the military as an important institution within peacetime America. However, it does need to be approached with due consideration for the trap of moral uplift. For instance, in another article from *Continental Marine*, a couple of marine officers explained a 1996 initiative called the "Grassroots Program." The program helped reservists and their families deal with the stresses occasioned by the high operational tempo of the post–Cold War environment. But the program was also sold as part of the Marine Corp's "shift back towards community-mindedness." This is well and good, but when the authors of the report observed that the program is most valuable in ensuring that "through community Grassroot efforts . . . America is not left behind as the Marine Corps roars" into the future, they went too far.[7] Such language would not be problematic if it were not for the fact that other marines as well as members of the other services were worrying darkly in the 1990s over the possibility of America's civilian collapse.[8]

The practicality of the services' following a model of community involvement is also put at risk by the trend toward the ever-greater use of reservists and guardsmen in operations overseas, far from local communities. A turning point was perhaps reached, in fact, in January of 2000, when a guard division was put in charge of an overseas operation in Bosnia. This was the first time a guard unit has been given such responsibility since the Korean War.[9] It would be best if the guard were spared such duty and were oriented instead toward good works in peace and homeland defense. The use after September 11, 2001, of guardsmen in providing additional security at the nation's airports was also a worthwhile exercise that familiarized millions of Americans with at least the presence of uniformed military personnel.

Despite obstacles, it is clear that military engagement in civilian communities has a role in improving civil-military relations and in promoting the service side of a balanced realignment. It is also worthwhile to consider ways in which military personnel policy might best promote the integration of the services with the society they protect.

Negotiating the "Gap"

As noted already in Chapter 6, the "gap" between military and civilian America is not itself a problem, but it can lead to difficulties, principally if military leaders react to it by becoming active in political debates. The political neutrality of the military must come first from a doctrine of restraint. But it can be helped along as well by a policy that leads to a more heterogeneous military force, so that military leaders tempted to enter political battle on behalf of "the" military cannot do so without facing contradiction from within their own ranks. The relative homogeneity of professional military attitudes today reflects evidence that "the institution as a whole is increasingly attracting more conservative and Republican elements of civilian society . . . and appealing to fewer among its more liberal and Democratic segments."[10] Rather than target political partisanship or ideology directly, personnel policy might address these issues indirectly through concern with racial, regional, and class diversity.

The geographic dispersion of recruiters and the role of Congress in filling service academy positions militates against sectionalism. Nevertheless, the identification of the American South with military service goes back to before the Civil War.[11] Though there is less data on sectional "representation" than there is, for instance, on race and gender, it is well known that the Southern states are "over-represented" in military bases and retirees. Thus, in 1996, for instance, almost 32 percent of all military personnel were stationed in the South, though the southern states had only 15 percent of the nation's population. What is more, in the 1990s, the South and Southwest were the only regions of the nation that experienced increases in all three major measures of military domestic spending: contracts, payroll, and Veterans Affairs expenses.[12] Moreover, there is, at the least, a strong impression among the instructors of the National Defense University whom this author interviewed that the South is seriously over-represented in the officer corps and that the "southernness" of the officers increased in the 1980s and into the 1990s.[13]

Beginning in the mid-1980s, moreover, a significant shift began in regional accessions among enlistees. Northern representation within the services dropped, while the southern presence increased. In recent years, the South was "over-represented" by about 8 percent in enlisted accessions each year.[14] An even more pronounced southern "bias" was evident at the close of the 1990s in the Marine Corps. Fiscal Year 1999 Active Accessions from the six southern states in the Marine's 6th Recruiting District totaled 5,691; those from the ten northeastern states in District 1 numbered 4,811.[15]

Similar observations are sometimes made with respect to the "class" origins of American military officers. James Webb is the person most famously associated with the argument that in the Vietnam War the American elite stayed home while their working-class cohorts went to war.[16] Of course, in some ways this echoed a tradition: the old pattern, common for instance in the Civil War, of the affluent literally buying their way out of military service, either directly through a cash payment to the government or indirectly by hiring a substitute. But it was certainly not in keeping with American experience in the world wars.

The difference class might make is pointed out by the military sociologist Charles Moskos. In the history of American warfare, Moskos notes, the broader public's willingness to support a war "correlates with a force that drafts the children of national elites."[17] As the Spanish-American War shows, a similar boost to public support can result from voluntary enlistment of upper-class men.

The trends that are making the officer corps and the military more homogeneous may be part of a broad realignment of civilian society along a pro-military and a not-pro-military line of cleavage. This polarization raises the possibility of skepticism run riot if unified Democratic Party control of government reappears. It could also tempt the professional military into an inappropriately close association with party politics.

By addressing regional and class representation issues, along with racial diversity, the services would improve their prospects for continuing to serve as a force for national unity. What would it mean to explicitly address such issues? Neither timetables nor numerical goals would be needed. Taking such issues seriously would mean, rather, placing a higher priority than is now the case on the maintenance and deepening of institutional links outside the South and in the stomping grounds of young American "elites."

As a start, Pentagon planners might make it a goal to reintroduce ROTC instruction at the Ivy Leagues. Presently, only two of the eight Ivy League colleges (Princeton and Cornell) offer their own ROTC programs. Of course, the armed services cannot insist on being represented on a civilian campus; they must be invited there. Still, within the parameters of bureaucratic politics, military leaders and interested civilians should do what they can to encourage elite schools to extend such invitations. The services might also rethink the ROTC contract for the purpose of increasing the attractiveness of a military career to those with a more civilian orientation. Moskos has suggested, along these lines, fifteen-month enlistments for at least some ROTC graduates.[18] Such changes might help arrest the troubling trend noted by analysts of the gap toward the identification of officers with only one of the major political parties.

Some observers of the military-society relationship, including Professor Moskos, have argued for more extreme measures as well, such as a return to some type of draft or at least a much larger (and less voluntary) national service program.[19] As a matter of practical politics and historical tradition, it is difficult to imagine a return to compulsion that was not borne of military necessity.[20] Even the more modest efforts at prioritization advocated above would be difficult and would call for strong cooperation among civilian and military leaders.

With regard to other, more controversial areas of personnel policy, the absence of political consensus suggests caution. Because military professionals are reluctant to lift the ban on open homosexuals' service within the forces, it would be imprudent to force this policy on the armed forces in the absence of either military necessity or a clear political consensus in support of a change in policy. This is an instance where objective control is called for since it relates to the military's ability in the face of civilianizing pressures to maintain a measure of control over its identity. Moreover, recent research on the military, especially on the problems of retention of junior officers, suggests that dissatisfaction with the social organization of the military is driving officers out of the military and into civilian occupations. The services' leaders, under the pressures of transmutation, must be careful not to abandon the institutional identities of their branches and subunits, and should seek ways to foster bonds among officers.[21]

The contrast with integrating women more fully into the services is instructive. Women are needed in the service as a result of the shift to an All Volunteer Force. For women to serve in double digit proportions within the armed services is a simple necessity. The Department of Defense keeps close watch on trends affecting women's service and is presently concerned with data revealing that women leave the services at considerably greater rates than men. "The exodus is particularly unsettling for the army: a full 47% of its enlisted women are gone, either by choice or involuntarily, before the end of three years, despite having signed up for terms averaging four years. The comparable attrition rate for army men is 28%."[22]

By contrast to the issue of maintaining a strong female presence in the services overall, the exposure of women to ever-higher levels of risk for casualties should the nation return to war is not supported by a clear political consensus. It is doubtful, in fact, that the public is ready for the results of even its present policies, should the services have to turn from peace missions to fight a major war. At the least, the unity of the nation and the apolitical quality of military leadership do not require any further movement toward women in combat.

Foreign Service

The final factor to consider is the foreign "service" of the military in the twenty-first century, short of war fighting. Because it might be difficult to expand the use of forces overseas after a period of withdrawal, the more sensible course of action in the absence of consensus would be to reform so as to improve the military's capabilities in peace operations of the sort the services were called upon to do under the Clinton Doctrine. President George W. Bush has promised the military that he will be "sparing" in ordering such deployments himself, but it is an open question whether events will allow him to act on his wish.[23] Also, if a consensus develops against such use of the forces, they could be withdrawn more readily than they could be reoriented toward such work after a period of noninterventionism. The issue for military policy today is how best to configure the military to perform nonwar missions without detracting too greatly from the military's core responsibility to prepare for war and without propelling the military more deeply into political battles over such deployments.

The first order of business is doctrinal change. Excessive force protection, as we saw in the prior chapter, interferes with military effectiveness and challenges military professionalism. But it is not as simple a matter as instructing the military to "get with the program." Military leaders at a Naval War College conference in 1999, where arguments about force protection were aired, stated repeatedly that it was their concern with civilian reaction back home that motivated them to put so great an emphasis on force protection. Senior military leaders, in the words of another analyst of the post–Cold War situation, "may lack confidence in the reliability of civilian leaders; thus, they fear that the government will abandon the military if casualties mount." Or, as a senior officer in the office of the secretary of defense told this author, "We are in a no-win situation. We are told to deploy, deploy, deploy, and don't die."[24]

The casualty aversion thesis should not be overstated. Americans have sustained their governments, as in the Civil War and the world wars, even when their armed forces have endured high levels of casualties. It all depends on the perception of necessity and of the goals for which sacrifices are required. Still, what we know about American wars suggests that the public at the least is reluctant to accept casualties, especially when they do not seem to serve necessity or some great purpose.

In the Vietnam War, Tet was the crossover point in American public opinion. It was a catalyst for change for a number of reasons. One of them was that it gave the lie to administration and Pentagon assurances that victory was near. If those who planned and conducted the U.S. part in the war had chosen to do things differently, perhaps the public might have supported a longer war. We will never know. What we do know, though, is that American support for the war declined as U.S. casualties mounted. In fact, the Vietnam experience was remarkably similar in this respect to the Korean War.[25]

The American intolerance of U.S. casualties has been a feature of even our most major wars. World War I is instructive. When the United States entered the war, the British, Germans, and Russians had already suffered horrendous casualties, numbering in the millions, and had been fighting for three years. From April 1917 through the next year, the United States lost 116,516 military personnel in the war.[26] Yet the cost was literally too much for the U.S. commander in chief to bear. Woodrow Wilson, haunted in peacetime by American casualties, could accept those losses only if the reality of the war could be aligned with its rhetoric.

But what of recent survey data purporting to demonstrate a greater-than-expected tolerance for the loss of American lives in military missions? In answer to a hypothetical question about a presidential decision to use U.S. troops abroad, the mass public, in a 1999 survey by the Triangle Institute for Security Studies (TISS), indicated less casualty aversion than a sample of civilian elites. Military officers gave the most casualty-averse answers of all. Thus, the mass public indicated a tolerance of over 6,800 U.S. casualties in a nonwar mission "to stabilize a democratic government in Congo," while elites answered in the hundreds. To keep Iraq from gaining weapons of mass destruction, the mass public was willing to lose the lives of almost 30,000 U.S. soldiers, while civilian elites said about 19,000, and military elites about 6,000.[27]

If the American public really is willing these days to accept thousands of losses in unconventional missions, then the attention military commanders are paying to force protection is based on false premises or is, in fact, tantamount to a "work action" staged to protest civilian commands. Several notes of caution are in order, however.

First, a U.S. president would have to be highly tolerant of political risk to base a decision to intervene on answers given to hypothetical questions.[28] Second, as U.S. policymakers learned in Korea and Vietnam, public reaction to U.S. losses is dynamic; it grows over time in response to mounting casualty figures and in reaction to political events at home and abroad.[29] Third, in the TISS survey, the respondents were first told that "a President decided" to send military troops to one place or another. This wording of the question is problematic because recent opinion analysis demonstrates the importance to the mass public of leadership, from the president as well as from other public figures.[30]

James Burk, a sociologist of the military, argues, for instance, that public support for unconventional military missions in the post–Cold War era is reactive to changes in elite opinion and leadership. In Somalia at the opening of the Clinton administration, public support eroded as prior elite consensus gave way to partisan and institutional conflict over the mission's goals and potential benefits. The public's immediate response to the incident in which eighteen army Rangers were killed was actually an increase in support of the mission. For the president to have maintained support, however, he would have to have been able to provide an analysis of the benefits to be gained from such losses that was compelling enough to quell open dissent from other members of government.[31]

Other survey results in the post–Cold War era suggest that commanders are indeed wise to act with caution (though not obsession) about force protection, for the public, as we saw earlier, is in doubt over even the most basic U.S. commitments, such as "defending the security of American allies." Indeed, in surveys that move one step back from the point of presidential decision, asking in effect *when* a president should make such a decision, the uncertainty of the post–Cold War era asserts itself. This is not surprising. What it means is that, in some fundamental ways, the end of the Cold War has produced results in public opinion similar to the disillusionment with the Cold War that many Americans experienced with our failure in Vietnam. In mid-1972, for instance, opinion analysts found almost no increase in pure isolationism among the public but a strong disinclination to sacrifice to maintain American leadership. Would it be "worth going to war" if Western Europe were invaded? Only 47 percent thought so; 32 percent thought war was worthwhile to defend West Berlin. A differently worded question, Should the United States "come to the defense of its major European allies with military force" if any of them were attacked by the Soviets, elicited an affirmative answer from a bare majority of 52 percent.[32]

Given the very real problems posed by the exposure of American forces to the risk of casualties in nonvital missions then, what can be done? The issue cannot and should not be addressed by greater military resistance to civilian control. Perhaps the issue can be addressed through finesse. For nonvital deployments, it would be beneficial to all parties for the troops to be supported by a less sentimental public. For the purpose of finessing the issue of casualties in such operations, as well as for the purpose of concentrating transmutational pressures where they will do the least harm to reform, serious thought should be given to the creation of a new organizational entity for both peacekeeping and peacemaking operations.[33]

When a soldier (or sailor, airman, or marine) dies in a peace operation today, it can hardly be seen as anything but wasteful. Consensus is lacking on whether it is a soldier's job to be in a place like Somalia, Haiti, or, eventually, the Congo; and the public responds appropriately. If we had special troops for such missions, the death of "peace officers" might be perceived by the public as being akin to the loss of police officers in the line of duty. An instructive parallel might be drawn here to Foreign Service Officers. By the State Department's own reckoning—as recorded in the lobby of the State Department building—67 civilian government officials died in "heroic or other inspirational circumstances" from 1976 to 1999. Their deaths engendered no public questioning of their mission.

A peacekeeping and peacemaking force could be crafted in any number of ways. The Special Forces Command, perhaps joined with the CIA, could form the nucleus of such a group. Or the Marine Corps might more simply be tasked to fashion itself more clearly into what every marine is already taught he or she is a part of, a "global 911 force." Samuel P. Huntington has suggested something along these lines, proposing that a civil operations component be added alongside the active and reserve components, and that each of the four services be tasked to support it. Huntington offers the U.S. Coast Guard as a model of an organization with a military structure and ethos, but one *not* organized in peacetime to "fight and win the nation's wars."[34] Such an organizational innovation would have the additional benefit of permitting the war-fighting military to devote more of its resources to preparations for war.

Reorienting the reserve component toward homeland defense and service might also help, both in addressing the casualty issue—it is even less a reservist's role to sacrifice his or her life in peacekeeping than it is the role of an active-duty soldier—and in enhancing the services' abilities to meet a quiet crisis in recruitment and retention, especially among reserves.[35] Presently, plans for the reserves reflect the utopianism of military planning critiqued in the prior chapter. A report from the office of the secretary of defense in December 2000, covering the reserves, stated current policy as ensuring that reserve units and individuals will be "available throughout the entire spectrum of requirements." The report recognized the tension between this goal and the paramount duty of the reserves to train for war but offered no clues as to how to resolve this conflict.[36] Similarly, "Reserve Component Employment Study, 2005," envisions even greater reliance on "dual missioning" of reserve components, assigning particular units critical responsibilities both for force projection and homeland defense.[37]

Conclusion

Are these suggestions for military policy in the twenty-first century plausible? That is a political issue. It depends greatly on civilian leadership and on doctrinal choices made within the military's leadership.

Under the "right" circumstances, we could end up merely drifting from our present state into one of armed isolationism. We would, under such a scenario, preserve extensive defense capabilities, but we would sacrifice a large measure of foreign "service" capability as well, perhaps, as reaction capability. If that is the public's ultimate desire for the post–Cold War military, it would be perfectly possible for the military to accomplish a primarily defensive reorientation. Service to the nation in such a scenario might involve a focus on civil defense.

Or we could end up following a path toward unintended militarism. This would be an extreme outcome and is highly unlikely. Still, it is arguably where we will be headed if we resolve the issues of the present realignment through an excessive turn toward military service both at home and abroad. In this, the "Dunlap Scenario,"[38] the armed forces are called upon to do an ever-growing number of civilian tasks. Ultimately, senior military leaders decide that, if they are going to be held responsible for things such as pollution control, education, drug abuse, the stability of newly independent states, and the quality of regimes in nations with weapons of mass destruction, they should have a say in the policymaking process for such issues.

The use of military force in situations where the United States might traditionally have used diplomacy increases the plausibility of a Dunlap scenario. In the aftermath of the Civil War, "radicals" in control of Congress used the military to "make peace" in the defeated South and in the process to remake the leadership regimes in southern states. The military was hardly enthusiastic but thoroughly dutiful. The use of the services for a new type of imperial role in Iraq in 2003 will likely spur similar problems of civil-military relations. Much will depend on the lengthy "peace" that U.S. forces are struggling to maintain in post-Saddam Iraq.

Still, if we are fortunate, the post–Cold War realignment can still have a positive ending. It all depends on the nature and timing of political consensus and on the evolution of civilian and military cooperation for military policy. If a moderate consensus develops; if senior civilian leadership emerges to help reshape the military for tomorrow's challenges; if military leaders practice and teach political restraint, even in the face of controversial orders; if organizational innovations help finesse the issue of casualty avoidance; if the military represents the nation in its diversity and prepares for even its least-favorite type of war; and if civilians allow the military to prepare for wars that some civilians see as hopelessly old-fashioned—if all these things happen, the post–Cold War realignment might be one of the most successful of all. But that is a lot of "ifs."

Notes

INTRODUCTION: The Civil-Military Bargain

1. "Clinton's Quick Steps to Better Relations; After Summit Jog, General Snubbed at White House Has Warm Words for President," *Washington Post*, 6 April 1993, A7.

2. Andrea Stone, "British Female Soldiers to Undergo Battle Trials," *USA Today*, 17 July 2000, A10; Charles Moskos, "From Citizens' Army to Social Laboratory," *Wilson Quarterly* 17 (Winter 1993): 83–94.

3. See Bradley Graham, "Military Leaders Worry Privately About Impact; Some Troops Offended by Double Standard," *Washington Post*, 15 September 1998, A10. Several years later, a panel of law experts recommended the first major overhaul of the military justice system since the early 1970s, especially with regard to matters involving consensual sex. See Eric Rosenberg, "Justice Needs Overhaul, Panel Says; Law Experts Recommend Changes to Legal Code for Service Members," *Seattle Post Intelligencer*, 3 July 2001, A3.

4. Andrew J. Bacevich, "Discord Still: Clinton and the Military," *Wall Street Journal*, 3 January 1999, C1, C4.

5. Edwin Dorn and Howard D. Graves, project co-chairs, *American Military Culture in the 21st Century: A Report of the CSIS International Security Program* (Washington, D.C.: Center for Strategic and International Studies, February 2000), xvi, xix.

6. James Kitfield, "The New World Disorder," *National Journal*, 19 May 2001.

7. Mark Mazzetti, "The Thin Greenline," USN JWR, 8 April 2002, 23.

8. Maureen Dowd, "Old Guard Finds a New Landscape," *New York Times*, 23 August 2001.

9. Thomas E. Ricks, "Bush's Military Reforms Fighting for Life," *New York Times*, 7 August 2001.

10. On the historic rise in Americans' confidence in their government following the incident, see the Gallup poll release from October 12, 2001, at www.gallup.com/poll/releases.

11. Michael Barnett, "Nation Building's New Face," Foreign Policy (November/December 2002): 98–100. The United States, Barnett observes, is attempting nation building "on the cheap." He doubts that successful nation building can be done without a deeper and more costly commitment.

12. "Transformation Postponed," *The Economist*, 16 February 2002, 28–29.

See also Hans Binnendijk, "Introduction," in *Transforming America's Military*, ed. H. Binnendijk (Washington, D.C.: National Defense University Press, 2002), xvii–xxxi.

13. See Bob Woodward, *Bush at War* (New York: Simon and Schuster, 2002), esp. 242–51, and note the complete silence on the CIA's role in Secretary of Defense Donald Rumsfeld's *Annual Defense Report, 2002*, ch. 3, "Fighting the War on Terror." The need for secrecy about the CIA's capabilities is not so extreme as to justify this omission. www.defenselink.mil/execsec/adr2002.

14. In 1996 the Pentagon, against its wishes, was mandated by the Defense Against Weapons of Mass Destruction Act to provide training and advice to civilian personnel to respond to domestic attacks from weapons of mass destruction. Pentagon officials wanted the Federal Emergency Management Administration (FEMA) to do the job, but Congress and FEMA feared the task would overwhelm the civilian agency. See Richard A. Falkenrath, "Problems of Preparedness: U.S. Readiness for a Domestic Terrorist Attack," *International Security* 25, no. 4 (Spring 2001): 147–86.

15. See the White House Web site (*www.whitehouse.gov*) for the Bush National Security Strategy and the president's "axis of evil" remarks, made in his State of the Union address on January 19, 2002.

16. John Lewis Gaddis, "A Grand Strategy," *Foreign Policy* (November/December 2002): 55. See also G. John Ikenberry, "America's Imperial Ambition," *Foreign Affairs* (September/October 2002): 44–60; and in the same volume, Michael Mandelbaum's "The Inadequacy of American Power," 61–73.

17. Peter Feaver, "The Civil-Military Problematique: Huntington, Janowitz, and the Question of Civilian Control," *Armed Forces and Society* 23, no. 2 (Winter 1996): 149–78.

18. Army Assistant Secretary for Manpower and Reserve Affairs Sarah Lister, in a personal interview with the author in summer 1997, spoke of the need to "civilize" the next generation of army leaders. Lister was driven into premature departure from the Pentagon following her remarks at an academic conference. She said: "The Marines are extremists. Whenever you have extremists, you've got some risk of total disconnect from society. And that's a little dangerous." See "Wrap-up Panel Discussion on the Olin Institute's U.S. Military and Post–Cold War American Society Project," 26 October 1997, Baltimore, Maryland; "Project on U.S. Post–Cold War Civil-Military Relations," Working Paper No. 14, October 1998. Available online at www.cfia.harvard.edu/olin/pubs/n014.htm.

19. Remarks of President Bush at Argonne National Laboratory, Illinois, 22 July 2002, whitehouse.gov/news/releases/2002, accessed 10 September 2002.

20. Press conference at President's Ranch, Crawford, 21 August 2002, www.whitehouse.gov/news/releases/2002, accessed 10 September 2002.

21. "Remarks by the President to Federal Employees on Homeland Security," DAR Constitution Hall, Washington, D.C., 10 July 2002. www.whitehouse.gov/newsreleases/2002/07.

CHAPTER 1:   Postwar Realignment and the Perils of Peace

1. Eliot A. Cohen, "Making Do With Less, or Coping With Upton's Ghost" (paper presented at the U.S. Army War College, 27 April 1995), 3.

2. The quotation is from the most important work popularizing the Cycle: Major General Emory Upton, *The Military Policy of the United States*, 4th imp. (Washington, D.C.: Government Printing Office, 1917), vii.

3. Samuel P. Huntington, *The Soldier and the State: The Theory and Politics of Civil-Military Relations* (Cambridge, Mass.: Belknap Press of Harvard University Press, 1957).

4. Fareed Zakaria, *From Wealth to Power: The Unusual Origins of America's World Role* (Princeton, N.J.: Princeton University Press, 1998).

5. Aaron L. Friedberg, *In the Shadow of the Garrison State: America's Anti-Statism and Its Cold War Grand Strategy* (Princeton, N.J.: Princeton University Press, 2000).

6. Ibid., 149.

7. Peter D. Feaver and Richard H. Kohn, eds., *Soldiers and Civilians: The Civil-Military Gap and American National Security* (Cambridge: MIT Press, 2001), 2–3.

8. Morris Janowitz, The Professional Soldier: A Social and Political Portrait (Glencoe, Ill.: Free Press, 1960). Parenthetical page numbers in the text are to this work.

9. Michael Desch, *Civilian Control of the Military: The Changing Security Environment* (Baltimore: Johns Hopkins University Press, 1999). See also Desch, "Soldiers, States and Structures: The End of the Cold War and Weakening U.S. Civilian Control," *Armed Forces and Society* 24, no. 3 (Spring 1998): 389.

10. Huntington, Soldier and the State, 155.

11. Charles C. Moskos, "From Institution to Occupation: Trends in Military Organization," *Armed Forces and Society* 4 (November 1977): 41–50.

12. Huntington, *Soldier and State*, 83.

13. Peter Feaver, *Guarding the Guardians: Civilian Control of Nuclear Weapons in the United States* (Ithaca, N.Y.: Cornell University Press, 1992), 7–12; and Feaver, "Discord and Division of Labor: The Evolution of Civil-Military Conflict in the United States" (paper presented at the annual meeting of the American Political Science Association, Washington, D.C., September 2–5, 1993). See also David C. Hendrickson, *Reforming Defense: The State of American Civil-Military Relations* (Baltimore: Johns Hopkins University Press, 1988), 10–28.

14. Peter Feaver, "The Civil-Military Problematique: Huntington, Janowitz, and the Question of Civilian Control," *Armed Forces and Society* 23 (Winter 1996): 149–78.

15. Eliot A. Cohen, in *Supreme Command: Soldiers, Statesmen and Leadership in Wartime* (New York: Free Press, 2002), argues convincingly that military expertise is routinely overestimated. See especially 242–47.

16. Bruce White, "Ethnicity and Race in the Military," in *The Oxford Companion to American Military History*, ed. John Whiteclay Chambers II (New York: Oxford University Press, 1999), 252–54.

CHAPTER 2: Successful Realignments

1. The most famous incident along these lines actually occurred the year before, in December 1782, at Newburg, New York. See Richard H. Kohn, "The Inside History of the Newburg Conspiracy: America and the Coup d'Etat," in *The Military in America: From the Colonial Era to the Present*, rev. ed., ed. Peter Karsten (New York: Free Press, 1986), 79–91.

2. Emory Upton, *The Military Policy of the United States*, 4th imp. (Washington, D.C.: Government Printing Office, 1917), 74.

3. Edmund S. Morgan, *Inventing the People: The Rise of Popular Sovereignty in England and America* (New York: W. W. Norton, 1988), 170–73.

4. Upton, *Military Policy*, 78.

5. Francis B. Heitman, *Historical Register and Dictionary of The United States Army, from its Organization, September 29, 1789, to March 2, 1903* (Washington, D.C.: Government Printing Office, 1903), 1:81, 2:560–62.

6. Geoffrey Perret, *A Country Made by War: From the Revolution to Vietnam, the Story of America's Rise to Power* (New York: Vintage, 1989), 71, 77.

7. Ibid., 88–89.

8. L. D. Ingersoll, *A History of the War Department of the United States* (Washington, D.C.: Francis B. Mohun, 1879), 405.

9. Richard Kohn, *Eagle and Sword: The Federalists and the Creation of the Military Establishment in America, 1783-1802* (New York: Free Press, 1975), 229–68.

10. Samuel P. Huntington, The Soldier and the State: The Theory and Politics of Civil-Military Relations (Cambridge, Mass.: Belknap Press at Harvard University Press, 1952), 7–18.

11. Kohn, Eagle and Sword, 45–47; 55; 100.

12. Edward M. Coffman, *The Old Army: A Portrait of the American Army in Peacetime, 1784-1898* (New York: Oxford University Press, 1986), 15.

13. Washington's Seventh Annual Address to Congress, 8 December 1795, *A Compilation of the Messages and Papers of the Presidents*, James D. Richardson, comp. (New York: Bureau of National Literature, 1897), 177ff. Hereafter, *Messages and Papers*.

14. *Messages and Papers*, 7 December 1796, 193.

15. *American State Papers: Documents Legislative and Executive, of the Congress of the United States*, 12 vols., selected and edited by Walter Lowrie and Matthew St. Clair Clarke (Washington, D.C. Gales and Seaton, 1832), 1:120–21.

16. Henry Adams, *History of the United States of America During the Administrations of Thomas Jefferson* (New York: Library of America, 1986), 101.

17. Theodore J. Crackel, *Mr. Jefferson's Army: Political and Social Reform of the Military Establishment, 1801-1809* (New York: New York University Press, 1987), 38.

18. Coffman, *Old Army*, 971.

19. Colonel of Engineers, 1808, statement recorded in *American State Papers*, 1:229.

20. "In the wretched, the deplorably wretched organization of the War Department, it was impossible either to begin the war or to conduct it" (Ingersoll, History, 40). But note that even the harsh critic Emory Upton praised the action of Congress in 1812 for its attention to the needs of the Corps of Cadets, if not the organizational problems of the War Department (Upton, *Military Policy*, 144–45).

21. George Dangerfield, *The Awakening of American Nationalism, 1815-1828* (New York: Harper and Row, 1965), 8.

22. Leonard D. White, *The Jeffersonians: A Study in Administrative History, 1801-1829* (New York: Macmillan, 1951), 212.

23. Francis Paul Prucha, *The Sword of the Republic, The United States Army on the Frontier, 1783-1846* (London: Collier-Macmillan, Ltd., 1969), 322–23; and Upton, *Military Policy*, 161.

24. White, *The Jeffersonians*, 260; and John Frost, *The Book of the Navy* (New York: D. Appleton and Co., 1842), 270–71.

25. White, *The Jeffersonians*, 254.

26. Ibid., 478.

27. *American State Papers*, 2:188.

28. Ingersoll, *History of the War Department*, 102–5.

29. Upton, *Military Policy*, 144–45.

30. White, *The Jeffersonians*, 536–39.

31. Ira Katznelson misses the distinction between a truly "expansible" military service and one that is simply small one day and large the next. The difference is, so to speak, whether the professional core of the services in peacetime remains at the core of the services in wartime or is merely overwhelmed by a new mass of both enlistees *and* officers. Nevertheless, his discussion of Calhoun and antebellum military policy is highly informative. See his "Flexible Capacity: The Military and Early American State Building," in *Shaped By War and Trade: International Influences on American Political Development*, ed. Katznelson and Martin Shefter (Princeton, N.J.: Princeton University Press, 2002), 82–110, 98.

32. White, *The Jeffersonians*, 82.

33. As quoted by Ingersoll, *History of the War Department*, 89.

34. Secretary of War John C. Calhoun, to General Thomas A. Smith, 16 March 1818, in *The Papers of John C. Calhoun*, Vol. 2, 1817–1818, ed. Edwin Hemphill (Columbia: University of South Carolina Press, 1963), 194–95. For a critical appraisal, see Irving H. Bartlett, *John C. Calhoun: A Biography* (New York: W. W. Norton, 1993), 94–95.

35. Francis Paul Prucha, *Broadax and Bayonet: The Role of the United States Army in the Development of the West, 1815-1860* (Lincoln: University of Nebraska Press, 1953), 125.

36. *American State Papers*, 1:698–70.

37. *Messages and Papers*, 2:792.

38. Ibid., 925–26.

39. Prucha, *Sword of the Republic*, 170–79, 196.

40. From an open letter "To the President of the United States," *Military and Naval Magazine of the United States* 1, no. 6 (August, 1833): 333–39. The editor of this influential journal endorsed the statements quoted.

41. American State Papers, 1:779.

42. Monroe's Eighth Annual Message to Congress, 7 December 1824, *Messages and Papers*, 825.

43. Major General Edmund Pendleton Gaines, "To the Young Men of the States of the American Union, Civil and Military," Fort Jackson, La., 4 October 1838, p. 6. See also Gaines, "A Plan for the Defense of the Western Frontier," St. Louis Arsenal, 28 February 1838. Both documents are available on microfiche at the Howard Tilton Memorial Library, Tulane University.

44. Philip C. Jessup, *Elihu Root*, Vol. 1, *1845-1909* (New York: Dodd, Mead and Co., 1938), 215–17. See also the laudatory report of *The United Service: A Monthly Review of Military and Naval Affairs*, 3rd Series 2, no. 4 (October 1902).

45. Graham A. Cosmos, *An Army for Empire: The United States Army in the Spanish-American War* (Shippensburg, Pa.: White Mane, 1994), 320.

46. Ronald J. Barr, *The Progressive Army, U.S. Army Command and Administration, 1870-1914* (New York: St. Martin's Press, 1998), 195.

47. Ibid., 40–41, 60–61.

48. Report of the Commission Appointed by the President to Investigate the Conduct of the War Department in the War with Spain, 8 vols. (Washington, D.C. U.S. Government Printing Office, 1850).

49. William Jennings Bryan, *Bryan on Imperialism* (New York: Arno Press and New York Times, 1970; orig. 1900), 10, 30, 63, and 31.

50. See Stephen Skowronek, *Building a New American State: The Expansion of National Administrative Capacities, 1877-1920* (Cambridge, UK: Cambridge University Press, 1982); and Skowronek, *The Politics Presidents Make: Leadership from John Adams to Bill Clinton* (Cambridge, Mass.: Belknap Press of Harvard University Press, 1997), 228–59.

51. Barr, *The Progressive Army*, 44.

52. Skowronek, *Building a New American State*, 215, 227.

53. Barr, *The Progressive Army*, 113–14.

54. Skowronek, *Building a New American State*, 219–26.

55. Quoted in John Morton Blum, *The Progressive Presidents: Theodore Roosevelt, Woodrow Wilson, Franklin D. Roosevelt, Lyndon B. Johnson* (New York: W.W. Norton, 1980), 57.

56. Ibid., 51–58.

57. Russell F. Weigley, *History of the United States Army*, enl. ed. (Bloomington: Indiana University Press, 1984), 318.

58. Eric Fisher Wood, *Leonard Wood: Conservator of Americanism* (New York: George H. Doran, 1920).

59. James H. Hitchman, *Leonard Wood and Cuban Independence, 1898-1902* (The Hague: Martinus Nijhoff, 1971), 36, 39, 45.

60. Robert Wooster, *Nelson A. Miles and the Twilight of the Frontier Army*

(Lincoln: University of Nebraska Press, 1993), 230. See also Peter R. DeMontravel, *A Hero to His Fighting Men: Nelson A. Miles, 1839-1925* (Kent, Ohio: Kent State University Press, 1998), 340–41, 362–64.

61. Brian McAllister Linn, *Guardians of Empire: The U.S. Army and the Pacific, 1902-1940* (Chapel Hill: University of North Carolina Press, 1997), 68, 20.

62. *Ibid.*, 28.

63. Captain Cromwell Stacey, "The Philippine Scouts," *Journal of the United States Infantry Association* 4(2) (September 1907): 218–25; Major William E. Horton, Major Joseph H. Heller, Captain James A. Moss, publication committee, *Historical Sketch, Constitution and Register of the Military Order of the Carabou* (Washington, D.C.: W. F. Roberts Co., n.d.).

64. Captain John R. Taylor, "A Filipino Army," Journal of United States Infantry Association 5, no. 6 (May 1909): 893–906, argued that American officers had done *too good* a job in Americanizing the Scouts. They had imbibed not just American military procedures but American tastes and cultural expectations as well.

65. Major Carroll A. Devol, "The Army in the San Francisco Disaster," *Journal of the United States Infantry Association* 4(1) (July 1907): 59–87.

66. *Infantry Journal* 9(6) (May-June 1913): 863–65.

67. Captain I. L. Hunt, "Public Opinion and the American Army," *Journal of the United States Infantry Association* 3, no. 3 (January 1907): 64–88; Major General Charles B. Hall, "The Relation of the Military to the Civilian Authority," *Journal of the United States Infantry Association* 5, no. 2 (September 1908): 151–72.

CHAPTER 3: Poor Realignments

1. Eugene H. Roseboom, *A History of Presidential Elections* (London: Collier-Macmillan Ltd., 1970), 393–97.

2. Eugene P. Trani and David L. Wilson, *The Presidency of Warren G. Harding* (Lawrence: Regents Press of Kansas, 1977), 150.

3. Arthur A. Ekirch, *The Civilian and the Military* (New York: Oxford University Press, 1956), 205–8.

4. Allan R. Millett and Peter Maslowski, *For the Common Defense: A Military History of the United States of America*, rev. ed. (New York: Free Press, 1994), 395–96.

5. Russell F. Weigley, *Towards an American Army: Military Thought from Washington to Marshall* (New York: Columbia University Press, 1962), 227–41.

6. Typescript, n.d., Papers of John McCauley Palmer, Library of Congress.

7. Samuel P. Huntington, *The Soldier and the State: The Theory and Politics of Civil-Military Relations* (Boston: Belknap Press of Harvard University Press, 1957), 283–84.

8. William E. Leuchtenburg, *Franklin D. Roosevelt and the New Deal* (New York: Harper and Row, 1963), 14–16.

9. Michael Sherry, *In the Shadow of War: The United States Since the 1930s* (New Haven, Conn.: Yale University Press, 1995), 22–23.

10. Quoted in William E. Leuchtenburg, "The New Deal and the Analogue of War," in *Change and Continuity in Twentieth-Century America*, ed. John Braeman, Robert H. Bremner, and Everett Walters (Columbus: Ohio State University Press, 1964), 106.

11. Ibid., 101.

12. James McGregor Burns, *Roosevelt: The Lion and the Fox, 1882-1940* (New York: Harvest, 1956), 162.

13. D. Clayton James, *The Years of MacArthur*, Vol. 1, *1880–1941* (Boston: Houghton Mifflin, 1970), 382.

14. Edwin G. Hill, *In the Shadow of the Mountain: The Spirit of the CCC* (Pullman: Washington State University Press, 1990); Kenneth Holland and Frank Ernest Hill, *Youth in the CCC* (Washington, D.C.: American Council on Education, 1942).

15. Millett and Maslowski, *For the Common Defense*, 364.

16. Fred Greene, "The Military View of American National Policy, 1904–1940," *American Historical Review* 66, no. 2 (January 1961): 354–77.

17. Eliot A. Cohen, "The Strategy of Innocence? The United States, 1920–1945," in *The Making of Strategy: Rulers, States and War*, ed. Williamson Murray, McGregor Knox, and Alvin Bernstein (Cambridge, UK: Cambridge University Press, 1994), 429.

18. Robert D. Wood, "Against the Tide: The Preparedness Movement of 1923–1924," *Military Affairs* 38, no. 2 (April 1974): 59–61.

19. Huntington, *Soldier and the State*, 283–84.

20. As commanded by Chief of Staff Pershing, "Statement of General John J. Pershing, General of the Armies, Chief of Staff, relative to the new organization of the War Department General Staff," 17 August 1921, released by the War Department. Filed in Library of Congress, "Pershing, Statements, 1917–1938."

21. Greene, "Military View of American National Policy," 354–77.

22. David A. Shannon, *Between the Wars: America, 1919-1941*, 2nd ed. (Boston: Houghton Mifflin, 1979), 21. For a libertarian view stressing the war's influences, see Robert Higgs, *Crisis and Leviathan: Critical Episodes in the Growth of American Government* (New York: Oxford University Press, 1987).

23. Ann Shola Orloff, "The Political Origins of America's Belated Welfare State," in *The Politics of Social Policy in the United States*, ed. Margaret Weir, Ann Shola Orloff, and Theda Skocpol (Princeton, N.J.: Princeton University Press, 1988), 61–62.

24. "National Defense," statement given by General Pershing to *Army and Navy Journal*, 29 December 1932, in Pershing, "Statements, 1917–1938," Library of Congress.

25. G. Kurt Piehler, *Remembering War the American Way* (Washington, D.C.: Smithsonian Institute Press, 1995).

26. See letters of General James Harbord to General John Pershing, 23 March 1921, 30 March 1921, and 24 May 1921, "Papers of James Guthrie Harbord," Library of Congress.

27. Millett and Maslowski, *For the Common Defense*, 375.

28. Ellis W. Hawley, *The Great War and the Search for a Modern Order: A His-*

tory of the American People and Their Institutions, 1917-1933 (New York: St. Martin's, 1979), 51.

29. War Department Release No. 1, 17 November 1922, "Address of General Pershing Before the Meeting of the Merchant's Association at Madison Square Garden, on the Night of November 17, 1922," Pershing, Statements, 1917–1938, Library of Congress; "What the Army is Doing Today, Extracts from an Address by General Charles P. Summerall, Chief of Staff, at Chattaqua, Jamestown, New York, August 10, 1929," War Department Release, 11 August 1929, Summerall Papers, Center for Military History.

30. James, *Years of MacArthur*, 363–64.

31. Trani and Wilson, *Presidency of Warren G. Harding*, 16–17.

32. "Memo on the Military Policy of the United States," Palmer to Pershing, Palmer Papers, "1918," Library of Congress.

33. War Department Circular No. 113, War Department, 22 March 1920, "Education of the People to the New Army," Secretary of War Newton D. Baker, issued to the Army by Chief of Staff Peyton March, Palmer Papers, Library of Congress.

34. "Special Report of the Secretary of War to the President on the Conference on Training for Citizenship and National Defense," 16 November 1918 (Washington, D.C.: Government Printing Office, 1923).

35. The General Staff, during the war, had similarly judged the work of the YMCA as mixed, at best, when it came to moral uplift. Apparently, the "services" provided to soldiers by such organizations and their local volunteer hostesses sometimes went far beyond what was officially sanctioned. See Penn Borden, *Civilian Indoctrination of the Military: World War I and Future Implications for the Military-Industrial Complex* (New York: Greenwood Press, 1989).

36. "Message to the Army on Retirement," 29 August 1924, Pershing, Statements, 1917–38, Library of Congress.

37. "The United States Army as a Career," (Washington, D.C.: Government Printing Office, 1926, 1929, and 1931), 3. See also "Our Military System," (War Department, Chief of Staff, G-2, 1930). On the CMT and the Regular Army, see Clifford P. Futcher, "Manual of Citizenship Training" (War Department, Adjutant General's Office, 1927).

38. R. Alton Lee, "The Army 'Mutiny' of 1946," *Journal of American History* (December 1966): 555–71.

39. Mark Grandstaff, "Making the Military American: Advertising, Reform, and the Demise of an Anti–Standing Military Tradition, 1945–1955," *Journal of Military History* 60 (April 1996): 300.

40. Millett and Maslowski, *For the Common Defense*, 479.

41. National Security Act, 1947, Public Law 8-253.

42. Historical Division, Joint Secretariat, Joint Chiefs of Staff, *Organizational Development of the Joint Chiefs of Staff, 1942-1987* (Washington, D.C.: Joint Chiefs of Staff, 1988), 13, 27–33.

43. Charles Moskos, "From Citizen's Army to Social Laboratory," *Wilson Quarterly* (Winter 1993): 86.

44. Aaron L. Friedberg, *In the Shadow of the Garrison State: America's Anti-Statism and Its Cold War Grand Strategy* (Princeton, N.J.: Princeton University Press, 2000); Eliot A. Cohen, *Citizens and Soldiers: The Dilemmas of Military Service* (Ithaca, N.Y.: Cornell University Press, 1985).

45. Friedberg, *In the Shadow of the Garrison State*, 165.

46. Ibid., 177.

47. George Q. Flynn, *The Draft, 1940-1973* (Lexington: University Press of Kentucky, 1993), 108–9.

48. Ibid., 103–4.

49. Charles Moskos and John Sibley Butler, *All That We Can Be: Black Leadership and Racial Integration the Army Way* (New York: Basic Books, 1996), 30.

50. Geoffrey Perret, *A Country Made by War: From the Revolution to Vietnam, the Story of America's Rise to Power* (New York: Vintage, 1989), 447.

51. Ibid., 448. See also Beatrice Heuser, "NSC 68 and the Soviet Threat: A New Perspective on Western Threat Perception and Policy Making," *Review of International Studies* (1991): 17–40.

52. Dennis Ippolito, *Uncertain Legacy: Federal Budget Policy from Roosevelt Through Reagan* (Charlottesville: University Press of Virginia, 1990), 36–7, 100.

53. Lynn Eden, "Capitalist Conflict and the State: The Making of United States Military Policy in 1948," in *Strategy and Social Movements: Essays in History and Theory*, ed. Charles Bright and Susan Harding (Ann Arbor: University of Michigan Press, 1984), 253.

54. Ippolito, Uncertain Legacy, 100.

55. Lt. Col. Romie L. Brownlee and Lt. Col. William J. Mueller III, "Changing an Army: An Oral History of General William E. DePuy, USA Retired" (U.S. Military History Institute, 1986), 103.

56. Samuel P. Huntington, "Civilian Control of the Military: A Theoretical Statement," in *Political Behavior: A Reader in Theory and Research*, ed. Heinz Eulau, Samuel J. Eldersveld, and Morris Janowitz (Glencoe, Ill.: Free Press, 1956), 384.

57. Richard J. Barnet, *Rocket's Red Glare: When America Goes to War, the Presidents and the People* (New York: Simon and Schuster, 1990), 278–79; Andrew Grossman, "The Politics of Homefront Mobilization: The American Civic Garrison State, Cold War Mobilization, and Civil Defense, 1947-1953" (paper presented at the American Political Science Association annual meeting, September 1995, Chicago).

58. Theodore Cohen, *Remaking Japan: The American Occupation as New Deal*, ed. Herbert Passin (New York: Free Press, 1987).

59. Thomas U. Berger, Cultures of Anti-Militarism: National Security in Germany and Japan (Baltimore: Johns Hopkins University Press, 1998).

60. On the GI Bill, see Michael J. Bennett, *When Dreams Came True: The GI Bill and the Making of Modern America* (Washington, D.C.: Brassey's, 1996).

61. Huntington, *Soldier and State*, 357.

62. Upton, *Military Policy*, 223–24. See also Daniel J. Elazar, *Building Toward*

Civil War: Generational Rhythms in American Politics (Lanham, Md.: Madison Books, 1992).

CHAPTER 4: Two Near Disasters

1. Willie Lee Rose, *Rehearsal for Reconstruction: The Port Royal Experiment* (Indianapolis, Ind.: Bobbs-Merrill, 1964).

2. Albert Castel, *The Presidency of Andrew Johnson* (Lawrence: Regents Press of Kansas, 1979), 40.

3. Maurice Matloff, gen. ed., *American Military History* (Washington, D.C.: Center for Military History, 1985), 1:282. Contrary to the myth of America's "free defense" during the nineteenth century, the European powers were eager to exploit American weakness during the Civil War. See Dean Mahin, *One War at a Time: The International Dimensions of the American Civil War* (Dullus, Va.: Brassey's, 1999).

4. Adjutant General's Office, Memorandum, n.d., accessed online at www .carlisle.army.mil/usamhi/DL/AtoZ.html.

5. Jack D. Foner, *The United States Soldier Between the Wars: Army Life and Reforms, 1865–1898* (New York: Humanities Press, 1970), 83.

6. Russell F. Weigley, History of the United States Army (New York: Macmillan, 1967), 261.

7. Colonel R. Ernest Dupuy, *The Compact History of the United States Army* (New York: Hawthorne Books, 1961), 156.

8. Weigley, *History*, 268–9.

9. Ari Hoogenboom, *Rutherford B. Hayes: Warrior and President* (Lawrence: University Press of Kansas, 1995), 330–43.

10. Matloff, *American Military History*, 1:286.

11. Robert V. Bruce, *1877: Year of Violence* (Indianapolis, Ind.: Bobbs-Merrill, 1959), 309.

12. Mark Grandstaff, "Preserving the 'Habits and Usages of War': William Tecumseh Sherman, Professional Reform and the USA Officer Corps, 1865–1881, Revisited," *Journal of Military History* 62, no. 3 (July 1998): 521ff. See also Allen Guttmann, *The Conservative Tradition in America* (New York: Oxford University Press, 1967), 67, 115.

13. Weigley, History, 262.

14. James D. Richardson, comp., *A Compilation of the Messages and Papers of the Presidents* (New York: Bureau of National Literature, 1897), 3562, 3765.

15. Michael Les Benedict, "Reform Republicans and the Retreat from Reconstruction," in The Facts of Reconstruction: Essays in Honor of John Hope Franklin, ed. Eric Anderson and Alfred A. Moss Jr. (Baton Rouge, La.: Louisiana State University Press, 1991), 63, 67.

16. Richard Severo and Lewis Milford, *The Wages of War: When America's Soldiers Come Home from War, from Valley Forge to Vietnam* (New York: Simon and Schuster, 1989), 172–75.

17. Jack D. Foner, *The United States Soldier Between Two Wars: Army Life and Reforms, 1865-1898* (New York: Humanities Press, 1970), 6-7.

18. As quoted in ibid., 83.

19. Prepared by direction of the Adjutant General of the Army by N. Hershler, *Soldier's Handbook for the Use of the Enlisted Men of the Army* (Washington D.C.: Government Printing Office, 1884), 5.

20. Foner, United States Soldier Between Two Wars, 115.

21. Grandstaff, "Preserving the 'Habits and Usages of War.'"

22. Robert G. Atherton, *William Tecumseh Sherman and the Settlement of the West* (Norman: University of Oklahoma Press, 1956), 262.

23. "Chronological List of Indian Actions, 1866-1896."

24. George R. Bentley, *A History of the Freedmen's Bureau* (Philadelphia: University of Pennsylvania Press, 1955), 72-74.

25. Ibid., 136, 183.

26. James Sefton, *United States Army and Reconstruction* (Baton Rouge: Louisiana State University Press, 1967), 11.

27. Bentley, History of the Freedmen's Bureau, 61.

28. Ibid., 72; John A. Carpenter, *Sword and Olive Branch: Oliver Otis Howard* (Pittsburgh: University of Pittsburgh Press, 1964). In the remainder of this chapter, Carpenter is the source of information regarding Howard unless otherwise noted.

29. Formally, the "Freedmen's and Refugees Bureau," consequent to a congressional act of the same name.

30. Roberta Sue Alexander, "Presidential Reconstruction: Ideology and Change," in *The Facts of Reconstruction: Essays in Honor of John Hope Franklin*, ed. Eric Anderson and Alfred A. Moss Jr. (Baton Rouge: Louisiana State University Press, 1991), 42.

31. W. E. Burghardt DuBois, "The Freedmen's Bureau," *Atlantic Monthly* 87 (1901): 361.

32. In addition to Carpenter, see Gerald Weland, *O. O. Howard: Union General* (Jefferson, N.C.: McFarland and Company, 1995), 100.

33. Bentley, *History of the Freedmen's Bureau*, 202.

34. William Gillette, *Retreat from Reconstruction, 1869-1879* (Baton Rouge: Louisiana State University Press, 1979), 35.

35. Bentley, *History of the Freedmen's Bureau*, 50.

36. Harold Hyman, "Johnson, Stanton, and Grant: A Reconsideration of the Army's Role in the Events Leading to Impeachment," *American Historical Review* 66 (October 1960): 85-96. Joseph Green Dawson III, "The Long Ordeal: Army Generals and Reconstruction in Louisiana, 1862-1877" (Ph.D. diss., Louisiana State University, 1978).

37. William C. Harris, *William Woods Holden: Firebrand of North Carolina Politics* (Baton Rouge: Louisiana State University Press, 1987), 2, 304-9.

38. George C. Rable, *But There Was No Peace: The Role of Violence in the Politics of Reconstruction* (Athens: University of Georgia Press, 1984), 111-12.

39. Benedict, "Reform Republicans," 69.

40. William L. Richter, *The ABC–CLIO Companion to American Reconstruction: 1862-1877* (Santa Barbara, Calif.: ABC–CLIO, 1995), entries on "Sheridan," 353–56, and "Redemption of the South," 307–15. See also Rable, "But There Was No Peace: Violence and Reconstruction Politics."

41. Gillette, *Retreat from Reconstruction*, 37.

42. Emory Upton, *The Armies of Asia and Europe* (New York: D. Appleton and Company, 1878), 24.

43. Stephen Skowronek, *Building a New American State: The Expansion of National Administrative Capacities* (New York: Cambridge University Press, 1982), 98.

44. Louis Fisher, "Congress Sleeps: War Powers After Vietnam," *The Long-Term View* 5, no. 1 (Summer 2000): 118–30.

45. James Burk, "Public Support for Peacekeeping in Lebanon and Somalia: Assessing the Casualties Hypothesis," *Political Science Quarterly* 114 (Spring 1999): 57.

46. James Kittfield, *Prodigal Soldiers: How the Generation of Officers Born of Vietnam Revolutionized the American Way of War* (New York: Simon and Schuster, 1995), 149–51.

47. Burk, "Public Support."

48. Charles Moskos and John Sibley Butler, *All That We Can Be: Black Leadership and Racial Integration the Army Way* (New York: Basic Books, 1996).

49. President Bush himself provided mixed commentary on the issue in his memoirs. "Now that [Vietnam Syndrome] has been put to rest . . . ," he wrote on page 486. On the next page, though, he quotes from his diary entry of 28 February 1991: "It hasn't been a clean end—there is no battleship Missouri surrender. This is what's missing to make this akin to WWII, to separate Kuwait from Korea and Vietnam" (George Bush and Brent Scowcroft, *A World Transformed* [New York: Alfred A. Knopf, 1998], 486–87).

50. John Robert Greene, *The Presidency of George Bush* (Lawrence: University Press of Kansas, 2000), 138.

51. Ibid.

52. Fisher, "Congress Sleeps," 123.

53. Arthur Egendorf, *Healing from the War: Trauma and Transformation After Vietnam* (Boston: Houghton Mifflin, 1985), 95.

54. Dennis S. Ippolito, *Blunting the Sword: Budget Policy and the Future of Defense* (Washington, D.C.: National Defense University Press, 1994), 19.

55. Richard Crockatt, *The Fifty Years War: The United States and the Soviet Union in World Politics, 1941-1991* (London: Routledge, 1995), 306.

56. Kenneth J. Campbell makes this assertion, though he cites as evidence only a news story from the *New York Times* reporting "US Generals are Leery of Latin Intervention." See Campbell, "Once Burned, Twice Cautious: Explaining the Weinberger-Powell Doctrine," *Armed Forces and Society* 24, no. 3 (Spring 1998): 365.

57. Ibid., 365. See Caspar Weinberger, "The Uses of Military Power," *Defense* (January 1985): 2–11.

58. Peter J. Roman and David W. Tarr, "The Joint Chiefs of Staff: From Service Parochialism to Jointness," *Political Science Quarterly* 113, no. 1 (Spring 1998): 99–101.

59. William A. Owens and James R. Blaker, "Overseeing Cross-Service Trade-Offs," *Joint Force Quarterly* (Autumn 1996): 37–40.

60. Katherine Boo, "How Congress Won the War in the Gulf," *Washington Monthly* 23, no. 10 (October 1991): 31–38.

61. David C. Hendrickson, *Reforming Defense: The State of American Civil-Military Relations* (Baltimore: Johns Hopkins University Press, 1988), 57, 98–9.

62. Egendorf, *Healing from the War*, 53.

63. Eliot A. Cohen, *Citizens and Soldiers: The Dilemmas of Military Service* (Ithaca, N.Y.: Cornell University Press, 1985), 173.

64. Friedberg, *In the Shadow of the Garrison State*, 198. Friedberg notes that the libertarian who persuaded Nixon to end the draft was the same Martin Anderson who served as Ronald Reagan's first chief domestic advisor.

65. Martin Binkin, *Who Will Fight the Next War? The Changing Face of the American Military* (Washington, D.C.: Brookings Institution, 1993).

66. Campbell, "Once Burned, Twice Cautious."

67. Colin Powell's view at the time, as noted by Kittfield, *Prodigal Soldiers*, 131.

68. Cohen, *Citizens and Soldiers*, 166–67, 181.

69. Michael Lind, *Vietnam, the Necessary War: A Reinterpretation of America's Most Disastrous Military Conflict* (New York: Free Press, 1999).

70. Lt. Col. Frederic J. Brown, "The Army and Society," *Military Review* 77, no. 1 (January/February, 1997): 14; originally published in the same journal in March 1972.

71. General Fred C. Weyland and Lt. Col. Harry G. Summers Jr., "Serving the People: The Need for Military Power," *Military Review* 77, no. 1 (January/February 1997): 39; originally published in the same journal in December 1976.

72. Donald Atwell Zoll, "A Crisis in Self-Image: The Role of the American Military in American Culture," *Parameters* 12, no. 4 (December 1982): 25.

73. John Kifner, "A Case Study in Disaster for Tomorrow's Generals," *New York Times*, 28 April 2000, A1.

CHAPTER 5: Military Reform and Service in the 1990s

1. Robert L. Goldich and John C. Schaefer, "U.S. Military Operations, 1965–1994 (Not Including Vietnam): Data on Casualties, Decorations, and Personnel Involved," Congressional Research Service Report, 27 June 1994, provides somewhat lower figures for U.S. casualties. Figures used here are from Anthony H. Cordesman, "The Persian Gulf War," in *The Oxford Companion to American Military History*, John Whiteclay Chambers II, editor in chief (New York: Oxford University Press, 1999), 544–46.

2. U.S. News and World Report, *Triumph Without Victory: The Unreported History of the Persian Gulf War* (New York: Times Books, 1992), 263.

3. David Halberstam, *War in a Time of Peace: Bush, Clinton and the Generals* (New York: Scribner, 2001), 16.

4. Ibid.

5. Jean Beaudrillard, *The Gulf War Did Not Take Place*, trans. Paul Patton, (Bloomington: Indiana University Press, 1995).

6. Edwin Dorn and Howard D. Graves, project co-chairs, *American Military Culture in the Twenty-first Century* (Washington, D.C.: Center for Strategic and International Studies, February 2000), 19.

7. Ibid., xix.

8. See *Airmen* magazine, which lists major overseas air bases each year in its January edition.

9. Halberstam, *War in a Time of Peace*, 251.

10. As quoted by Andrew Bacevich, *American Empire* (Cambridge, Mass.: Harvard University Press, 2002), 143.

11. James Burk, "Public Support for Peacekeeping in Lebanon and Somalia: Assessing the Casualties Hypothesis," *Political Science Quarterly* 114 (Spring 1999): 57.

12. Halberstam, *War in a Time of Peace*, 42.

13. Larry Berman and Emily O. Goldman, "Clinton's Foreign Policy at Midterm," in *The Clinton Presidency: First Appraisals*, ed. Colin Campbell and Bert Rockman (Chatham, N.J.: Chatham House Publishers, 1996), 306.

14. Gerald Knaus and Marcus Cox, "Whither Bosnia?" *NATO Review* 48 (Winter 2000–2001): 6–11.

15. Douglas Farah, "General Calls for Pullout from Haiti," *Washington Post*, 13 March 1999, A13; see also David Broder, "Before We Send in the Troops," *Washington Post*, 17 March 1999, A27.

16. Bacevich, *American Empire*, 184.

17. Halberstam, *War in a Time of Peace*, 479.

18. General Wesley K. Clark, *Waging Modern War: Bosnia, Kosovo, and the Future of Combat* (New York: Public Affairs, 2001).

19. Bacevich, *American Empire*, 186.

20. Ibid., 194.

21. Clark, *Waging Modern War*.

22. Tom Wicker, "No End to the Threat," *New York Times*, 8 February 1990, A23; and the editorial of that day, A22.

23. Carl Conetta and Charles Knight, "Inventing Threats," *Bulletin of Atomic Scientists* (March/April 1998): 32–38.

24. David McCormick, *The Downsized Warrior: America's Army in Transition* (New York: New York University Press, 1998), 54.

25. *The National Security Strategy of Engagement and Enlargement* (White House, 1995). Available at 222.dtic.mil/doctrine/jel/research_pubs/nss.pdf.

26. McCormick, *Downsized Warrior*, 49.

27. Quadrennial Defense Review, available at www.defenselink.mil/pubs/qdr.

28. "The National Defense Panel, Assessment of the Quadrennial Defense Review," www.dtic.mil/ndp.

29. Margaret C. Harrell, Laura L. Miller, *New Opportunities for Military Women: Effects on Readiness, Cohesion and Morale* (Santa Monica, Calif.: Rand, 1998).

30. "Women in Defense," *Defense Issues* 11, no. 31 (March 1996): 1–2. "Rand Report: New Opportunities for Military Women," News Release No. 556–97, Office of Assistant Secretary of Defense, Public Affairs, 21 October 1997.

31. Eric Schmitt, "Pentagon Chief Warns Clinton on Gay Policy," *New York Times*, 25 November 1993, A1.

32. See the Service Members' Legal Defense Network's reports tabulated from data provided by the Department of Defense. Available at www.smldn.org.

33. Richard H. Kohn, "Out of Control: The Crisis in Civil-Military Relations," *National Interest* 35 (Spring 1994): 3–18, and "An exchange on civil-military relations," including a reply by Chairman Powell, *National Interest* 36 (Summer 1994): 23–32. Lorna Jaffee, *The Development of the Base Force, 1989-1992* (Washington, D.C.: Joint History Office, 1993), and Personal interview, Lorna Jaffee, Office of the Joint Staff, 9 April 1992. See also Sharon K. Weiner, "The Politics of Resource Allocation in the Post Cold-War Pentagon," *Security Studies* 5, no. 4 (Summer 1996): 125–42.

34. Berman and Goldman, "Clinton's Foreign Policy at Midterm," and "Engaging the World: First Impressions of the Clinton Foreign Policy," in *The Clinton Legacy*, ed. Colin Campbell and Bert A. Rockman (Chatham, N.J.: Chatham House Publishers, 2000), 235.

35. Charles A. Stevenson, "The Evolving Clinton Doctrine on the Use of Force," *Armed Forces and Society* 22, no. 4 (Summer 1996): 511–35.

36. Office of the Secretary of Defense, Staff, Chairman, Joint Chiefs of Staff, *Joint Publication 3-0*, Doctrine for Joint Operations.

37. www.dtic.mil/jv2020/history/jv2010.pdf. *Joint Vision 2010* has been supplanted by *Joint Vision 2020*, issued in June 2000 by Chairman, Joint Chiefs of Staff General Henry Shelton, available at www.dtic.mil/jv2020.

38. Charles Dunlap Jr., "Joint Vision 2010: A Red Team Assessment," *Joint Force Quarterly* (Autumn/Winter, 1997–98): 47.

39. Huba Wass De Caege and Antulio J. Echeveria II, "Landwar and Future Strategy, Insights from the Army After Next," *Joint Force Quarterly* (Spring 1999): 64; Steven Metz, "Which Army After Next? The Strategic Implications of Alternative Futures," *Parameters* (Autumn 1997): 15–26.

40. In 1997 the Air Combat Command sharply curtailed training exercises and competitions and proclaimed "reducing operations tempo" "a top priority." ACC Commander (1996–99) General Richard Hawley was an outspoken critic of the high op tempo of the time and its effect on his service. See Philip Shenon, "Air Force Acts to Cut Stress Among Pilots," *New York Times*, 20 August 1997, A20. General Ryan's announcement the next year signaled a more positive organizational response. See "Air Force to Shed Cold War Structure and Reorganize," *New York Times*, 5 August 1998, A16.

41. Robert Burns, "General Speaks His Piece on Peace, Military Not Just War Machine, General Says," *New Orleans Times Picayune*, 17 November 2000, A17.

42. Personal interviews, National Defense University faculty, summer 1996; Personal interviews and observations at the USNWC intersession seminar, Fall 1999; and confidential conversations with officers of the USMC and USAF, seminar on The Military in American Politics, Tulane University, Spring 1998, Fall 2000.

43. McCormick, *Downsized Warrior*, 54.

44. Ibid., 29.

45. Ibid., 208.

46. The Quadrennial Defense Review, Committee on National Security, United States House of Representatives, 105th Congress, 1st Session, Hearings held April 16, May 21 and 22, 1997 (Washington, D.C.: United States Government Printing Office, 1997).

47. Col. Harry G. Summers Jr., "Operations, Procurement, and Industrial Base," *Orbis* 41, no. 2 (Spring 1997): 199–208.

48. QDR hearings, as cited in n. 45 above.

49. See *New World Coming: American Security in the 21st Century, The Phase I Report on the Emerging Global Security Environment for the First Quarter of the Twenty-first Century* (The United States Commission on National Security/21st Century, 15 September 1999), available online at www.nssg.gov/; and National Defense Panel, "Assessment of the May 1997 Quadrennial Review," available online at www.dtic.mil/ndp/.

50. Michael Desch, *Civilian Control of the Military: The Changing Security Environment* (Baltimore: Johns Hopkins University Press, 1999), Appendix, "Major U.S. Civil-Military Conflicts, 1938–1997," 135–39.

51. Peter Feaver, "Crisis as Shirking, An Agency Theory Explanation of the Souring of Civil-Military Relations," *Armed Forces and Society* 24(3) (Spring 1998): 407–34.

52. "Cong. Charles Rangel Plans move to reinstate the draft for war with Iraq." Press release, 30 December, 2002. www.house.gov/apps/list/press/ny15_rangel/draftrelease.html.

53. Congressman Charles Rangel, interviewed on Lou Dobbs' Moneyline, CNN TV, 8 January 2003.

54. McCormick, *Downsized Warrior*, 126–29.

55. Ibid., 138–46, 161.

56. Eliot Abrams and Andrew J. Bacevich, "A Symposium on Citizenship and Military Service," *Parameters* 31 (Summer 2001): 20.

57. McCormick, *Downsized Warrior*, 161–62.

58. Ralph Peters, interview by the author, summer 1996.

59. Gunnar Myrdal, with the assistance of Richard Sterner and Arnold Rose, *An American Dilemma: The Negro Problem and Modern Democracy* (New York: Harper and Row, 1962; orig. 1944), L; see also p. 2.

60. Ibid., 1004–5.

61. Michael Lind, *The Next American Nation: The New Nationalism and the Fourth American Revolution* (New York: Free Press, 1995), 104.

62. Ibid., 106. See also Mary L. Dudziak, "Desegregation as a Cold War Imperative," *Stanford Law Review* 41 (November 1988): 61–120.

63. Harry S. Truman, *Memoirs* (New York: Doubleday, 1955–56), 2:183.

64. Russell L. Riley, *The President and the Politics of Racial Inequality: Nation Keeping from 1831 to 1965* (New York: Columbia University Press, 1999), 171, 176–77.

65. Charles C. Moskos and John Sibley Butler, *All That We Can Be: Black Leadership and Racial Integration the Army Way* (New York: Basic Books, 1996).

66. Ibid., 48.

67. Aaron L. Friedberg, *In the Shadow of the Garrison State: America's Anti-Statism and Its Cold War Grand Strategy* (Princeton, N.J.: Princeton University Press, 2000), 222–26.

68. Ibid., 118.

69. Ibid., 320–21, 336.

70. Aaron L. Friedberg, "Review Essay: Science, the Cold War, and the American States," *Diplomatic History* 20, no. 1 (Winter 1996): 107–18.

71. Stuart W. Leslie, *The Cold War and American Science: The Military-Industrial-Academic Complex at MIT and Stanford* (New York: Columbia University Press, 1993), 205.

72. Robert Mullan Cook-Deegan, "Does NIH Need a DARPA?" *Issues in Science and Technology* (Winter 1996–1997): 25–28.

73. Alexander J. Morin, *Science Policy and Politics* (Englewood Cliffs, N.J.: Prentice-Hall, 1993), 93–95.

74. Douglas E. Scates, Bernard C. Murdoch, and Alice V. Yeomans, *The Production of Doctorates in the Sciences: 1936-1948* (Washington, D.C.: American Council on Education, 1951), 37.

75. As cited by Moskos and Butler, *All That We Can Be*, 99.

76. Ibid., 101.

77. Ibid., 103.

78. Benjamin O. Fordham, "The Civil-Military Gap and Peacetime Military Policy" (paper prepared for the Triangle Institute for Security Studies Project on the Gap Between the Military and Civilian Society, Draft of Oct. 1, 1999), 42. Also, all is not well among the officer corps; see Remo Butler, "Why Black Officers Fail," *Parameters* 24. no. 3 (Autumn 1999): 54–69.

79. Statement of Defense Secretary William Cohen before the Committee on National Security of the House of Representatives, Hearings held May 21, 1997, *The Quadrennial Defense Review* (Washington, D.C.: United States Government Printing Office, 1997), 60.

80. Samuel Berger, "American Leadership in the 21st Century," Remarks to the National Press Club, 7 January 2000 (White House: Office of the Press Secretary).

81. *Economic Report of the President* (Washington, D.C.: United States Government Printing Office, 1997), charts 1–4.

82. From the Secretary's Message, *Quadrennial Defense Review*, iii, iv.

83. Ibid., 3–25.

84. Lynn M. Scott, "Strategic Human Capital: Preserving a Vital National Asset," *Strategic Forum* 116 (June 1997): 1–2.

85. National Science Board, *Science and Engineering Indicators, 1996* (Washington: U.S. Government Printing Office, 1996), 6–5.

86. "National Patterns," a report of the National Science Foundation, available at www.nsf.gov. *Science and Engineering Indicators*, 4–4.

87. Though not enough, asserts the journalist William Greider, in *Fortress America: The American Military and the Consequences of Peace* (New York: Public Affairs, 1998).

88. Center for Defense Information, "New Civilian Tasks for the Military," TV program, transcript from the CDI, 1993, 7.

89. Charles J. Dunlap Jr., "The Origins of the American Military Coup of 2012," *Parameters* (Winter 1992–93): 3–20.

90. Confidential interview with a UN official involved in East African peacekeeping missions, Spring 2000.

91. Confidential interview with a U.S. Navy admiral, Fall 1999.

92. Eliot Cohen, "Calling Mr. X: The Pentagon's Brain Dead Two War Strategy," *New Republic*, 19 January 1998, 19.

93. Elain Monahan, "Albright Issues Thinly Veiled Challenge to Bush," CNN All Politics, www.cnn.com, posted 21 November 2000.

CHAPTER 6: Barriers to Balance

1. Office of Homeland Security, *The National Strategy for Homeland Security* (Washington, D.C.: U.S. Government Printing Office, 2002), 44.

2. President Bush said the nation had awakened to a "new world" the day after the attack. Address to a Joint Session of Congress, 20 September 2001, accessed at www.whitehouse.gov/news/releases/2001/09/20010920-8.html.

3. Quadrennial Defense Review Report (Department of Defense, September 30, 2001). Available at www.defenselink.mil/pubs/qdr2001.pdf. Because it was the second such review, it is cited hereafter as QDR II.

4. QDR II, Foreword.

5. See "Remarks by the President on National Missile Defense," 13 December 2001, issued by the White House as a press release, available at www.whitehouse.gov/news/releases/2001.

6. Executive Order Establishing the Office of Homeland Security, text available in a White House press release, 8 October 2001, available at www.whitehouse.gov/news/releases.

7. See David B. Cohen and Alethia H. Cook, "Institutional Redesign: Terrorism, Punctuated Equilibrium, and the Evolution of Homeland Security in the United States," paper presented at the Annual Meeting of the American Political Science Association, Boston, September 2002.

8. Office of Homeland Security, *National Homeland Security Strategy*, July 2002.

9. Ibid., 13.

10. David E. Sanger, "A New View of Where America Fits in the World," *New York Times*, 18 February 2001, sec. 4, p. 1. See also Kathleen T. Rhem, "Bush: U.S. will be 'Sparing' on Overseas Commitments," American Forces Information Services, 13 February 2001.

11. *Defense Almanac*, 2000. Available at www.defenselink.mil/pubs/almanac/almanac/people/serve.html. As of the year 2000, there were 189 member states in the United Nations (www.un.org/Overview/growth.htm).

12. Elain Monaghan, "Albright Issues Thinly Veiled Challenge to Bush," cnn.com/2000/AllPolitics/stories/11/21/president.Albright.reut/index.html.

13. G. John Ikenberry, "America's Imperial Ambition," *Foreign Affairs* (September/October 2002): 44–60.

14. Peter J. Boyer, "A Reporter at Large: A Different War, Is the Army Becoming Irrelevant?" *New Yorker*, 1 July 2002, 54–67.

15. One of the first journalistic accounts of the influence of *September 11, 2001,* and the war that followed, on the Department of Defense's "transformation," was pessimistic. *See* "Transformation Postponed," *The Economist*, 16 February 2002, 28–29, commenting on the Bush administration's proposed FY 2003 budget.

16. Harvey Klehr, John Earl Haynes, and Kyrill M. Anderson, *The Soviet World of American Communism* (New Haven, Conn.: Yale University Press, 1998).

17. Jacob Heilbrun, "Viewer Discretion Advised," *New Republic*, 9 November 1998, 21; Charles Krauthammer, "CNN's Cold War, Twenty-four Hours of Moral Equivalence," *Washington Post*, 30 October 1998, A27.

18. Arthur M. Schlesinger Jr., "Back to the Womb? Isolationism's Renewed Threat," *Foreign Affairs* (July/August, 1995): 2–8; and idem, "America and the World: Isolationism Resurgent?" *Ethics and International Affairs* 10 (1996): 149–63. Also Bradley Graham, "Military Forces are Near 'Breaking Point,' GOP Report Charges," *Washington Post*, 9 April 1997, A1.

19. See Eugene R. Wittkopf, *Faces of Internationalism: Public Opinion and American Foreign Policy* (Durham, N.C.: Duke University Press, 1990), on "accommodationism."

20. See Introduction to Randall B. Ripley and James M. Lindsey, eds., *United States Foreign Policy after the Cold War* (Pittsburgh, Pa.: University of Pittsburgh Press, 1997), 7.

21. Schlesinger, "Back to the Womb?" 7.

22. *Ibid.*

23. Modris Ekstein, *Rites of Spring: The Great War and the Birth of the Modern Age* (Boston: Houghton Mifflin, 1989).

24. John Keegan, *A History of Warfare* (New York: Alfred A. Knopf, 1993), 368.

25. Aleksandr Fursenko and Timothy Naftali, *One Hell of a Gamble: The Secret History of the Cuban Missile Crisis* (New York: W. W. Norton, 1998).

26. Geoffrey Perret, *A Country Made by War: From the Revolution to*

Vietnam—the Story of America's Rise to Power (New York: Vintage, 1989), 482–83, 550–51.

27. Secretary of Defense Donald Rumsfeld, press briefing, 3 September 2002, at the Pentagon. Accessed at http://www.defenselink.mil/news/Sep2002/t09032002_t0903sd.html.

28. John Mueller, *Retreat from Doomsday: The Obsolescence of Major War* (New York: Basic Books, 1989).

29. Carl Kaysen provides an excellent commentary on Mueller's work in "Is War Obsolete? A Review Essay," *International Security* 14 (1990): 42–64. See also Barry Buzan, "The Present as a Historic Turning Point," *Journal of Peace Research* 30(4) (1995): 385–98.

30. Spencer R. Weart, *Never at War: Why Democracies Will Not Fight One Another* (New Haven, Conn.: Yale University Press, 2000).

31. Samuel P. Huntington, "The Errors of Endism," in *Conflict After the Cold War: Argument on Causes of War and Peace,* ed. Richard K. Betts (New York: Macmillan, 1994), 38.

32. Kaysen, "Is War Obsolete?" 58.

33. Marc Trachtenberg, "The Future of War," *Diplomatic History* 15 (1991): 287–90.

34. Kishore Mahbubani, "The West and the Rest," *National Interest* (Summer 1992): 3–13.

35. *Annual Defense Review (ADR)* 2000, ch. 1, p. 3.

36. James D. Ellis and Todd M. Koca, "China Rising: New Challenges to the U.S. Security Posture," *Strategic Forum* no. 175 (October 2000): 1–4. See also "Global Fears of Another Cold War," *World Press Review* (June 1997): 6–11.

37. *ADR* 2000, ch. 1, p. 2.

38. *Ibid.*

39. Eliot Cohen, "Calling Mr. X," *New Republic,* 19 January 1998, 17–19.

40. See the Web site of The Project for the New American Century, www.newamericancentury.org. See also Donald Kagan and Frederick W. Kagan, *While America Sleeps: Self-Delusion, Military Weakness, and the Threat to Peace Today* (New York: St. Martin's, 2000).

41. This issue came up repeatedly in the author's interviews with civilian policymakers, in particular at the Pentagon in the summer of 1996 and among faculty and students of the Naval War College in the fall of 1999.

42. Don M. Snider and Gayle L. Watkins, "The Future of Army Professionalism: A Need for Renewal and Redefinition," *Parameters* 30, no. 3 (Autumn 2000): 9.

43. Peter Feaver and Christopher Gelpi, "The Civil-Military Gap and Casualty Aversion" (paper prepared for the Study of the Gap Between the Military and Civilian Society, a Project of the Triangle Institute for Strategic Studies, Durham, N.C., October 1999). See the discussion of the same data in Ole R. Holsti, "Of Chasms and Convergences: Attitudes and Beliefs of Civilian and Military Elites at the Start of a New Millennium," in *Soldiers and Civilians: The Civil-Military Gap and American National Security,*

ed. Peter D. Feaver and Richard H. Kohn (Cambridge: MIT Press, 2001), esp. 36–47.

44. Edwin Dorn and Howard D. Graves, project co-chairs, *American Military Culture in the Twenty-first Century* (Washington, D.C.: Center for Strategic and International Studies, February 2000), xxii–xxiii.

45. Michael Lind, *Vietnam, The Necessary War* (New York: Free Press, 1999).

46. Col. Vince Goughding, "Three Looks Back at Vietnam," *Parameters* 30, no. 3 (Autumn 2000): 147. And Michael C. Desch, "Wounded Warriors and the Lessons of Vietnam," *Orbis* (Summer 1998): 473–80.

47. Fred Ikle, "The Next Lenin: On the Cusp of Truly Revolutionary Warfare," *National Interest* (Spring 1997): 9–19.

48. Michael Vlahos, "The War After Byte City," *Washington Quarterly* 20 (Spring 1997): 41–72. Page numbers in the text are to this source.

49. *New World Coming: American Security in the 21st Century, The Phase I Report on the Emerging Global Security Environment for the First Quarter of the Twenty First Century* (United States Commission on National Security/21st Century, September 15, 1999), available online at www.nssg.gov/.

50. *Air Force: Journal of the Air Force Association* 82, no. 12 (December 1999): 7.

51. Aaron L. Friedberg, *In the Shadow of the Garrison State: America's Anti-Statism and Its Cold War Grand Strategy* (Princeton, N.J.: Princeton University Press, 2000).

52. See the book by *Wall Street Journal* reporter Max Boot, *The Savage Wars of Peace: Small Wars and the Rise of American Power* (New York: Basic Books, 2002).

53. Andrew Krepenevich, quoted in "The Shape of the Battle Ahead," *Economist* 18 (November 2000): 33. See also Ralph Peters, "The Future of Armored Warfare," *Parameters* (Autumn 1997): 54–59.

54. *ADR* 2000, ch. 11.

55. "Transformation Postponed," *The Economist*, 16 February 2002, 28–29.

56. Thomas Ricks, *Making the Corps* (New York: Scribner, 1997), 236.

57. See Peter Feaver, Richard Kohn, and Lindsay P. Cohn, "Introduction: The Gap Between Military and Civilian in the United States in Perspective," and Feaver and Kohn, "Conclusion: The Gap and What It Means for American National Security," in Feaver and Kohn, eds. Soldiers and Civilians, 1–12, 459–74. See also Lindsay Cohn, "The Evolution of the Civil-Military 'Gap' Debate" (paper prepared for the Triangle Institute for Strategic Studies Project on the Gap Between the Military and Civilian Society, 1999).

58. Ole R. Holsti, "A Widening Gap Between the U.S. Military and Civilian Society? Some Evidence, 1976–1996," *International Security* 23, no. 3 (Winter 1998/99): 5–42.

59. George H. Quester, "Defense Policy," in *The Clinton Presidency: The First Term, 1992-1996*, ed. Paul S. Herrnson and Dilys M. Hill (New York: St. Martin's Press, 1999), 144.

60. Feaver and Kohn, "Digest," 7. See also Feaver and Kohn, "Conclusion:

The Gap and What It Means for American National Security," ch. 13 in Feaver and Kohn, eds., *Soldiers and Civilians*, 464–65.

CHAPTER 7: Applying the Lessons of the Past

1. But see Stan Crock, "Commentary: Reveille for Government Arsenals," *Business Week*, 10 January 2000, 50.

2. David B. Cohen and Alethia H. Cook, "Institutional Redesign: Terrorism, Punctuated Equilibrium, and the Evolution of Homeland Security in the United States" (paper presented at the Annual Meeting of the American Political Science Association, Boston, September 2002).

3. March 11, 2002, Homeland Security Presidential Directive-3, creating the Advisory System, White House press release, 12 March 2002. President George W. Bush's State of the Union Address, January 29, 2002.

4. Peter D. Feaver and Richard H. Kohn, "Conclusion," ch. 13 in *Soldiers and Civilians: The Civil-Military Gap and American National Security*, ed. Feaver and Kohn (Cambridge: MIT Press, 464–65.

5. Michael Lind, *Vietnam: The Necessary War* (New York: Free Press, 1999).

6. Major General Thomas L. Wilkerson, "Marine Force Reserve: MARFOR-RES," *Continental Marine* Almanac Issue [1996]: 6.

7. Major Carl Lammers and Captain Mike Snyder, "Making 'Grassroots' a Reality: The Commandant's Readiness Support Program," *Continental Marine* 20 (March/April 1996): 13.

8. See especially, William Lind, Major John Schmitt, and Colonel Gary Wilson, "Fourth Generation Warfare: Another Look," *Marine Corps Gazette* (December 1994): 34–37.

9. Guard officers in Bosnia, in fact, command regular army combat troops. This is remarkable but appears less so in light of the fact that today guard and reserve soldiers outnumber regulars in the army. See Steven Lee Myers, "Reservists' New Role Transforms Military," *New York Times*, 24 January 2000, A1.

10. Benjamin O. Fordham, "Military Interests and Civilian Politics: The Influence of the Civil-Military 'Gap' on Peacetime Military Policy," ch. 9 in *Soldiers and Civilians*, ed. Feaver and Kohn, 352–60.

11. Samuel P. Huntington, *The Soldier and the State: The Theory and Politics of Civil-Military Relations* (Cambridge, Mass.: Belknap Press of Harvard University Press, 1957).

12. James Burk, "The Military's Presence in American Society" (paper prepared for the Triangle Institute for Strategic Study's project on the Gap Between the Military and Civilian Society, 1999), 11.

13. Personal interviews with National Defense University faculty members, summer 1996.

14. Fordham, "The Civil-Military Gap" (paper prepared for the Triangle Institute for Security Studies Project on the Gap Between the Military and Civilian Society, Draft of October 1, 1999), 42.

15. Numbers courtesy of Lt. Col. John Carey, Headquarters, USMC.

16. For a recent statement of this thesis, see James Webb, "Heroes of the Vietnam Generation," *American Enterprise* 11, no. 6 (Summer 2000): 22–24.

17. Charles C. Moskos, letter in *Parameters* (Winter 1996–97): 139.

18. Charles C. Moskos, "What Ails the All Volunteer Force: An Institutional Perspective," *Parameters: The US Army War College Quarterly* 31(2) (Summer 2001): 29–47.

19. Charles C. Moskos, *A Call to Civic Service: National Service for Country and Community* (New York : Free Press, 1988). See also Eliot A. Cohen, *Citizens and Soldiers : The Dilemmas of Military Service* (Ithaca, N.Y. : Cornell University Press, 1985).

20. James Burk explores the difficulties of running a draft in an increasingly rights-oriented society, in "Debating the Draft in America," *Armed Forces and Society* 15(3) (Spring 1989): 431–48. In Europe, meanwhile, even in states such as France, with a "hard state" tradition quite unlike that of the United States, the general movement is away from compulsory service regimes. Nevertheless, see Gary Hart, *The Minuteman: Restoring an Army of the People* (New York: Free Press, 1998), and Paul Richter, "With Recruitment Down, Draft is Gaining Support," *Los Angeles Times*, 28 July 1999, A12.

21. Leonard Wang, *Generations Apart: Xers and Boomers in the Officer Corps* (Carlisle, Pa: U.S. Army War College, Strategic Studies Institute, 2000).

22. Paul Richter, "Exodus of Female Recruits Signals Trouble for Military," *LA Times* 29 November 1999; accessed online at www.latimes.com/news/nation/updates/lat_milwomen991129.htm.

23. Kathleen T. Rhem, "Bush: U.S. Will be 'Sparing' on Overseas Commitments," *American Forces Information Service*, reporting on a speech the president made at Fort Stewart, Georgia, 13 February 2001.

24. Confidential interview with the author. A similar statement is made by Stephen S. Rosenfeld, "A Strange Path for a Global Power," *Washington Post*, 8 September 1995, A25.

25. John Mueller, *War, Presidents, and Public Opinion* (New York: Wiley, 1973).

26. Department of Defense, "Principal Wars . . . U.S. Military Personnel Serving and Casualties," available at http://web1.whs.osd.mil/mmid/m01/SMS223R.htm.

27. Peter D. Feaver and Christopher Gelpi, "A Look at Casualty Aversion, How Many Deaths are Acceptable? A Surprising Answer," *Washington Post*, 7 November 1999, B3. See also Ole R. Holsti, "Of Chasms and Convergences: Attitudes and Beliefs of Civilian and Military Elites at the Start of a New Millennium," in *Soldiers and Civilians*, ed. Feaver and Kohn, 36–47.

28. Of course, some presidents are tolerant of such risks. President Clinton saw himself as a "delegate" doing the bidding of public opinion in foreign affairs. Other modern presidents have considered themselves more the "guardians" of the people, therefore doing their best to ignore short-term pressures from the public's moods. On the complexities of the relationship between presidential behavior and public opinion on foreign policy, see Douglas C.

Foyle, *Counting the Public In: Presidents, Public Opinion and Foreign Policy* (New York: Columbia University Press, 1999).

29. This was a thesis of John Mueller's classic book, *War, Presidents, and Public Opinion* (New York: Wiley, 1973). See also the results to hypothetical casualty scenarios from the Gulf War and the Bosnian deployment, as reported in Miroslav Nincic et al., "Social Foundations of Strategic Adjustment," in *The Politics of Strategic Adjustment*, ed. Peter Trubowitz, Emily O. Goldman, and Edward Rhodes (New York: Columbia University Press, 1999), 176–212.

30. Richard A. Brody, *Assessing the President: The Media, Elite Opinion and Public Support* (Palo Alto, Calif.: Stanford University Press, 1992).

31. James Burk, "Public Support for Peacekeeping in Lebanon and Somalia: Assessing the Casualties Hypothesis," *Political Science Quarterly* 114(1) (1999): 53–78. See also Eric V. Larson, *Casualties and Consensus* (Santa Monica, Calif.: Rand, 1996).

32. See the misnamed work: H. Schuyler Foster, *Activism Replaces Isolationism: U.S. Public Attitudes, 1940-1975* (Washington, D.C.: Foxhall Press, 1983), 324–25, 332–33, 345. See also Robert W. Tucker, *A New Isolationism: Threat or Promise?* (New York: Universe Books, 1972).

33. See Olara A. Otunnu and Michael W. Doyle, eds., *Peacemaking and Peacekeeping for the New Century* (Lanham, Md.: Rowman and Littlefield, 1998), and the summer 1995 edition of the *Cornell International Law Journal*, which was devoted to peacekeeping and peacemaking as practiced by the United Nations.

34. Samuel P. Huntington, comments recorded in Michael C. Desch and Sharon Weiner, eds., "A Growing Civil-Military Gap? Wrap-up Panel Discussion of the Olin Institute's U.S. Military and Post Cold-War American Society Project," Working Paper #14 (Cambridge, Mass.: Olin Institute, 1998), available at http://hdc-www.harvard.edu/cfia/olin/pubs/no14.htm, accessed 25 July 2000.

35. The active duty components met their recruiting goals for 2000 for the first time since 1997, but the reserves, aside from the marines, fell well short. See Steven Lee Meyers, "Military Reserves Are Falling Short in Finding Recruits," *New York Times*, 28 August 2000, A1. The air force has declared the adoption of a "wartime mentality" to meet recruitment objectives. See Report of the Secretary of the Air Force, 2000, available as Part VI, Statutory Reports, *ADR 2000*, 268.

36. *A Guide for Effective Peacetime Employment of Reserve Component Units and Individuals* (Washington, D.C.: Office of the Assistant Secretary of Defense, Reserve Affairs, December 2000), 5.

37. *Reserve Component Employment Study 2005, Vol. 1, Study Report*, 4, available online at www.defenselink.mil/pubs/rces2005_072299.html, accessed 21 February 2001.

38. Charles J. Dunlap Jr., "The Origins of the American Military Coup of 2012," *Parameters* (Winter 1992-93): 3–20.

Index

3-23-r4